Charles J. Caes

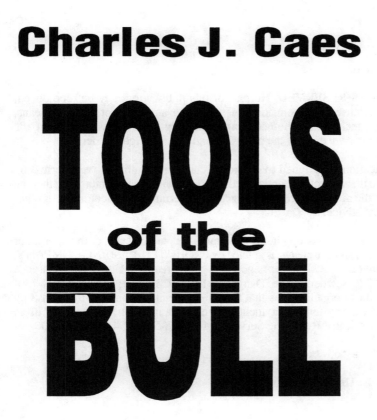

TOOLS
of the
BULL

How to Make
Big Money
in Bull Markets

PROBUS PUBLISHING COMPANY
Chicago, Illinois
Cambridge, England

ISBN 1-55738-563-7

Printed in the United States of America

BB

1   2   3   4   5   6   7   8   9   0

TAQ/BJS

TABLE OF CONTENTS

INTRODUCTION

This book is for independent stock investors who want to add a new level of sophistication to their adventures in making money. It is for those bulls who want to do more than just buy stocks, who want to utilize additional tools such as put options and other options.

You will find that this book looks at the topics at hand from an investor's rather than a broker's point of view. For instance, in the discussion of margin trading, you will find an emphasis on the possibility of losing more than 100 percent whereas from a broker's or tax accountant's point of view you are only losing 50 percent because that is how much the stock decreased. Such changes in perspective such as this are just as necessary as the change in perspectives between the pitcher and batter in a baseball game.

Additionally, you will find that in many instances even the most basic ideas are clarified with examples in order to accelerate your understanding of the material.

Investing Is Not Easy

It is never easy to make a lot of money; it always takes a great deal of knowledge, equity, the kind of sophistication that comes with experience, and practice. This book cannot make you rich or even promise that you will be a winner in the market, but it will add to your knowledge base. And knowledge is power. It is, however, up to you to employ that power to your own best interests. Independent investors have enough strikes against them, not the least of which are poor liquidity, stale information, little negotiating power on commissions, and encyclopedias of information designed for the Big Money. Unfortunately, those with the Little Money cannot employ the same strategies as those with the Big Money. For example, consider the tried and true advice about spreading one's risk. That's a great idea when you've got $100,000 to play with; but what if you've only got $5,000?

Investors have to learn to go for the money or stay out of the stock market altogether. This does not mean being careless or overly speculative; it means having a big tool shed so you can store the tools you need to build or fix your portfolio.

Questions of Understanding

The stock market is a tough game. The independent investor is bombarded with contradictory advice and strategies that are not always appropriate to his or her financial situation or particular goals. So while introducing you to tools of the bull, this book attempts to captain you through and around the general misconceptions that plague new and intermediate investors alike.

When asked the following questions in classrooms or general discussions about stock and options markets, even the more experienced investors are often unable to answer correctly:

- Is options trading really riskier for the independent investor than stock trading?

- Are puts and calls the only types of stock options available to investors?

- When puts go up in price, do calls go down in price?

- Should the small investor really be investing in stocks?

- Can the independent stock investor really make a killing in the stock market?

- Which is the better philosophy: "The right stock at any price" or "Any stock at the right price."

- Are discretionary accounts (wherein the broker is given the right to trade an account as frequently as he or she wants without asking permission) the smartest bets for new investors until they learn the ropes?

The answer to these questions will surprise most readers. No, options trading is not necessarily riskier than stock trading and is probably the smarter ball game for the independent investor who has liquidity problems. No, puts and calls are not the only types of stock options. Puts and calls may or may not move in opposite directions; they both may very well depreciate in price, for instance. The small investor should probably not be trading in stocks, particularly when one considers some of the outstanding returns mutual funds are reeling in. The chances of making a killing in the stock market are almost nil for investors unless they are dealing in puts or calls, and even then their chances are slim. The best philosophy is "Any stock at the right price." And discretionary accounts are dangerous to your financial life.

These questions are only a sampling of the questions this book is designed to answer. Keep in mind that some of the perspectives this book gives will catch many by surprise. I am not a financial advisor or a broker. I have nothing to gain by selling one idea or another, one tool or another, a mutual fund or a stock. I am an independent investor like yourself. I have only something to gain if this book makes you smarter, helps you make money, and interests you in other books I have written or will write.

What This Book Is About

This book is about a few of the tools every investor should have in his or her tool shed. It is about buying stocks long, cash and margin, writing put contracts, buying calls, buying warrants, and buying stock rights. The majority of investors will find these topics brand new, despite the fact that the Smart Money has been well versed in them from the start.

To simplify your grasp of these topics, this book is divided into five major parts, each consisting of four to seven chapters.

Part 1 is designed to give you the history of experience with terminology you will need to understand concepts in tools of the bull. Other chapters relate the tools to the things that are specifically important to every investor: leverage, money management, and informed trading. This last is concerned with types of orders and their benefit to the bull.

Part 2 looks at the first tool of the bull, buying stocks long. Understanding the necessity of buying low and selling high, however, is only a minute part of understanding what buying long is all about. Investors need to understand how to select those stocks or options to buy short or long, know some basic strategies and rid themselves of prevailing misconceptions. The chapters in this section are designed to provide this type of guidance.

Part 3 is about buying calls. It is about speculating in a stock without owning the stock. It is about staying liquid, saving money, and making money. Buying calls is no easy subject to learn, so every care has been taken to simplify the material for quick understanding.

Part 4 is about writing put contracts, a game few bulls ever play, but a game which affords very quick income. There are risk factors associated with put buying and this chapter explains them, as well as explaining basic strategies and guidelines for limiting risk and increasing profits.

Part 5 is about two types of options most investors do not even think of as being options, and in which they rarely ever deal: stock warrants and stock rights. Warrants afford the little guy the kind of leverage that brings him into the market in the first place, and rights are icing on the investment cake.

In fact, what this book is really about is this thing called leverage. You'll learn how to get it with margin as well as with options. Leverage is what you need to make lots of money. Keep in mind, however, that where there are opportunities for lots of money, there are opportunities for lots of losses.

Limitations and Capabilities

The most successful investors usually have one thing in common: They are very aware of their limitations and capabilities, and they act accordingly. Do you know how much you can afford to invest? Have you developed the patience and nerves of steel that will keep you from trading too heavily? Do you have the discipline to study the market and pay attention to your portfolio? Can you tell good advice from bad? The answer to all of these questions must be yes.

Most successful people also know what they can expect from a book or college course. A recent MBA graduate is not ready to take over a corporation. A recent accounting graduate is not ready to assume the duties of a controller. A reader who has just finished a book on how to play golf is not ready for the U.S. Open. And when you finish the last page of this book, you will not be ready to make a million, or even be a winner in the stock market.

On these pages, however, you will find some of the tools you will need to build capital and increase income.

PART ONE

THE BASICS

CONTENTS

1

MACRO VIEWS

The stock market is the place where people invest or gamble their money to get a better return on their investment than they can hope to get from fixed-income markets, such as those for bonds or real estate mortgages. It is true that the returns from investments in common stocks can sometimes be substantial, but in reality the frequency of above-average returns is somewhat slim. This means that the odds of getting rich by playing the stock market are not stacked in the investor's favor. Yet, people like to play the stock market (as indicated in Table 1–1).

Even if you are lucky enough to double a $10,000 investment in a one-year period, what are you going to do for an encore? Will the next one you pick perform as well? And the next one? History tells us no. And if you do select a stock that doubles in price, it could take 8, 10, even 15 years.

Money makes money. If you have $10 million in the stock market, maybe you can make a million or more a year. But you don't have any such sum to play with. For you to make $1 million, you've got to pick a lot of winners, leverage yourself to the hilt, and diversify your portfolio with stock options.

If you go into the stock market with dreams of big killings one after another, you are misleading yourself. It can happen—but it is not easy to make money in the stock market. So many things can affect the performance of a stock. You can tie up your money, sometimes for years, wasting other opportunities that could have been more profitable.

If you go into the stock market with the hope of possibly doing better than you can from, say, the money markets (certificates of deposit, banker's acceptances, mortgage-backed government securities, etc.) but understanding that "getting rich" takes lots of money, lots of risk, and lots of luck, then you've got your wits about you and will probably do well—or at least not as badly as everyone else.

Winning Perspectives

The more than 100 stock exchanges around the world, as well as the over-the-counter securities network, that we refer to as the stock market, are places to invest and to speculate. They are arenas where many financial games can be played. And it is necessary to know the different ways in which stocks can be played, directly and indirectly, in order to turn a profit.

Table 1–1
Major U.S. Stock Markets

REGISTERED EXCHANGES

American Stock Exchange
Boston Stock Exchange
Chicago Board of Options
Cincinnati Stock Exchange
Intermountain Stock Exchange
Midwest Stock Exchange
New York Stock Exchange
Pacific Stock Exchange
Philadelphia Stock Exchange
Spokane Stock Exchange

OTHER MAJOR MARKETS

Over-the-Counter (OTC)
National Securities Market

These are registered exchanges on which the public generally trades common and prefered corporate stocks or options. The National Market System links most of the major exchanges with the National Association of Securities Dealers Automatic Quotation System.

After all,

- You do not have to own a stock to profit by it. Instead of spending $10,000 on the stock, you can spend $1,000 on an option contract. If the underlying stock goes up 10 percent, the option may go up 20 percent, 30 percent, 100 percent or more. You can profit from the stock's movement (or lose from it) without ever owning it.

- You do not have to put up money on every stock that you purchase. You can buy stock "on margin." For instance, if you have in your margin account $10,000 worth of stock you have paid cash for, and suddenly another opportunity presents itself, well, you can use this stock as collateral to buy up to $10,000 of another stock with the broker's money instead of your own. If the stock goes up in price and you sell in good time, the only cost to you is the interest on the borrowed money. This means that if the stock goes up 10 percent, say, in the next month, and you sell, your profit is $1,000 on a meager investment of about $50 in interest charges and $200 in brokerage commissions. You turned $250 into $1,000 in one month!

- You can earn income from stocks you do not own. If you expect AT&T not to drop below a certain dollar amount, you can sell a put contract on the stock, and receive immediate income. If the stock does not drop below the agreed-upon price by the end of the contract period, you come out a winner.

These are only some of the games that bulls play, and there is much more to these games than meets the eye. They will be explained more fully in coming chapters, but you know from life's experiences that where there is profit, there is always risk. This is especially true in the stock market. The greater the opportunity for profit, the greater the possibility for loss. Money does not come easily—all the more reason why you must understand the many different ways there are to profit from stocks!

Still, knowing all the games to play and how to play them does not guarantee success. You need also to understand the player. That's you.

- *You must be sure your expectations are realistic.* If you need an extra $5,000 for a closing on a house next month, don't try to make it in the stock market. Such great things rarely happen in so short a time. And, actually, a stock usually goes down after you buy it, not up. It's rare for anyone to buy at the low (or sell at the high).

- *You must understand the risks involved.* What happens if the stock you buy goes south for a few months? What will it do to your liquidity? Don't make the mistake of making a long-term investment with short-term funds.

- *You must fully evaluate your current cash position.* If you have purchased a stock on margin and borrowed from your credit card to put up your down payment, you have borrowed money on top of borrowed money invested for the term. Chances are good that you are going to lose a bit more than just your shirt if your stock goes south in price.

The astute investor knows instinctively that the stock market is a risky place. There are no guarantees. Many things impact the price performance of a stock. Among them are interest rates, inflationary trends, debt financing, and liquidity levels. Interest rates are a major driver of stock prices. It's true that they affect mainly preferred stocks, but it's also true that even the common stock market is highly sensitive to changes in interest rates. Inflation is also a major driver. As it eats away at the purchasing power of the dollar, it drives up interest rates, which in turn put the downside pressure on stock prices. Debt-to-equity ratios add to market dilemmas particularly when corporations depend upon the lending communities to finance their operations, thereby creating corporate economies with a soft or cracking equity base. And liquidity levels? Well, when a pressed-for-cash seller of a stock cannot find a buyer, he quickly lowers the price, thereby inciting a bear campaign.

These are not the only problems with which an investor must deal. There are many even further beyond her control. A storm in New York City can crash volume on New York and American stock exchanges. The lower volume, in turn, may bring down stock prices and start a major downslide. Wars, major political events, and major bankruptcies can also cause stocks to plummet.

As you can see, all the painstaking research an investor may go through, and all the analyses he may do, can be to no avail. International events, the weather, elections—all can override the most painstaking fundamental and technical analyses. So why does anyone take a chance on the stock market? They take a chance completely out of ignorance, or they are gamesmen. They are men and women who enjoy the challenge and excitement that the stock market offers, who are excited by the chance to be able to do more with their money than others can. In short, they like to manage their own money. Whether or not they will be successful depends upon so many, many factors.

Many investors today would be much smarter to put their money in any of the high-performance mutual funds. Some of these funds are showing 35 percent to 40 percent returns in a one-year period and average returns in the high teens over the past five years. That is an incredible performance.

Now, if you are wondering why a book on the stock market is advising that you buy mutual funds, bear the following in mind: This is a book on strategy for investors who expect the market to go up. It is designed for investors who want to invest and speculate in the stock market, or who are already in the market trying to turn a profit. It is not designed to convince anyone to invest on his own, or select equity investments over fixed-income investments, although the stock market will probably do very well under the Clinton administration, allowing for occasional pull-backs. The Dow Jones Industrials can possibly reach 4,400 by 1997.

This may not mean very much because you will not be invested in all of the Dow Jones Industrials. The market may very well go up, but the stocks you pick may very well go down. But when the DJ Industrials are going up, most of the market is going up also, which means your chances of success are much better.

Markets

The most flexible approach to investing in the stock market entails buying and selling securities which are optionable. This means you want to purchase stocks on which puts and calls are readily available. Just because a stock is listed on the New York Stock Exchange, however, does not mean that its options are listed on the same exchange. For instance, Citicorp and Dow Jones are stocks listed on the New York Stock Exchange, but the option contracts for Citicorp are traded on the Chicago Board Options Exchange, and those for Dow Jones are traded on the Philadelphia Exchange.

However, you should feel little need to limit yourself to optionable stocks in your search for worthwhile opportunities. There are many markets in the United States (Table 1–2) that offer great buying opportunities; additionally there are the over-the-counter market, the Canadian stock exchanges, and more than 100 other foreign markets.

The largest market for stocks, to almost everyone's surprise, is really the over-the-counter market. The total value of securities traded in this market is over $1 trillion. The OTC, as it is called, trades thousands of stocks that have too small a trading volume to be considered by the major exchanges or have limited assets, capital, or shareholders. However, the OTC also trades those stocks and other equity issues that are available on the major exchanges.

Table 1–2
25 Actively Traded Stocks

American Express	Johnson & Johnson
American Telephone and Telegraph	Limited, Inc.
Blockbuster Entertainment	McDonald's Corporation
Bristol-Myers Squibb	PepsiCo
Chase Manhattan	Philip Morris
Citicorp	Pfizer
Coca-Cola	Royal Dutch Petroleum
Exxon	Shering Plough
Eli Lily	Syntex
Ford Motor Company	Telefonos de Mexico
General Electric	Upjohn Company
General Motors	Westinghouse Electric
Hewlett Packard	

Another market for stocks is the National Securities Market, which is networked through NASDAQ (National Association of Securities Dealers Automated Quotation System). It functions a bit differently from the major U.S. exchanges in that it is not a true auction market, for the prices of stocks are negotiated rather than auctioned. But the market is extensive and sophisticated enough to sometimes handle over 2 million transactions a day. Like the New York Stock Exchange, and others, NASDAQ requires stocks traded in its automated system to meet certain criteria. These criteria include $2 million in total assets, 100,000 outstanding shares, and at least two market makers.

Investors and Speculators

Probably the best strategy is to consider yourself a long-term investor with occasional speculative forays when opportunities present themselves.

The investor is the long-term player. He takes a position in a well-recommended stock with proven management and strong fundamentals; he is prepared to wait for the payoff. Meanwhile, he is satisfied with the additional income he may be receiving from dividends and from the sale of covered calls. His goal is to double his money in five or six years. He looks for the stocks that can be great performers—stocks of corporations with the opportunity and know-how to take advantage of growing markets in the 1990s or that can win greater shares of current markets. He looks at stocks like AT&T, Coca-Cola, McDonald's, PepsiCo, Procter & Gamble, and stocks such as those listed in Table 1–3. He wants stocks of companies with strong management, a good track record, a strong financial base, and a good future. He wants minimal risk. He is usually slow to go in, perhaps using dollar cost averaging, but quick to come out of his holdings when he reaches his profit or stop-loss point.

The stock speculator is after quick and many dollars; she is willing to take a great deal of risk. She will sometimes trade a stock in seconds, particularly when playing a stock that is priced differently on two separate exchanges. She will take a chance

Table 1–3
Stock Ownership in Public Corporations

Description	1980	1985	1990	1995	1998
Individuals	30 million	47 million	51 million	55 million	59 million
Adult Females	14 million	17 million	18 million	21 million	23 million
Adult Males	14 million	27 million	30 million	32 million	34 million
Median Age	46	44	43	42	41

Figures are approximate and based on New York Stock Exchange statistics. Figures for 1995 and 1998 are author's projections, and take into account the following: the increasing number of women and minorities in the work force and in the higher income ranks and the increasing awareness of all young adults about the stock market and its opportunities.

on stocks that have strong upside potential despite the fact that their performance has been weak—she wants turnaround opportunities like RJR-Nabisco, which has been overly leveraged and attacked by bears, yet has strong possibilities for a bull run. She likes stock options because they can increase her investment a thousand-fold; so she is willing to chance that the underlying stock will move within the time frame of the option contract. She is also quick to go in and quick to get out.

You want to be both an investor and a speculator—or you would not have purchased this book. Actually, the terms *speculator* and *investor* are defined differently by various agencies, publications, and analysts. These definitions are affected by what may be considered long-term and short-term strategies.

Long-term investors are usually those who hold a security for at least a year, and speculators are the short-term traders who hold a security for less than one year. Some analysts, however, define long term to be four or five years or even a lifetime (as in the case of some trusts.) Anything less is considered short term.

The Securities and Exchange Commission actually has three general investment periods: *Long term*, for securities held at least a year; *short term*, for securities sold within a year; and *trading*, for securities sold within 30 days.

For our purposes, we will consider the investor to be an individual who purchases a stock with the intention of selling only when it is absolutely necessary and generally expects to hold a stock for at least a year but probably five or more. He will trade only when opportunity cost dictates the necessity.

We will consider the speculator as the trader looking for stocks that will give her a total yield of 10 percent or more per month and seeking to buy them as they are taking off, to short sell them when they are falling, and to close out as soon as profits begin to diminish. The speculator and the investor always establish different criteria for the stocks they intend to play.

You need, therefore, to set some guidelines for yourself. Following are some recommendations. Pay special heed to them, for they may be very different from what has been recommended to you in the past.

1. *Start out as an investor.* Look for stocks with strong fundamentals and that are optionable (that is, options contracts are available on them). Go into them slowly, possibly dollar-cost averaging. When you have accumulated a few hundred shares, consider selling covered calls when you understand them.[1]

2. *Evolve into an occasional speculator.* Begin to speculate only after you have studied the market for awhile. Try your best to only speculate in optionable stocks so that you can hedge your positions with calls or puts and thereby reduce your risk (as well as profit) if you so desire. As you gain experience, try limited participation in puts and uncovered calls.[2]

3. *Limit your diversification.* No more than two stocks for up to $10,000 of investment money, and one for each additional $10,000. (Stock options do not count.) If you are going to diversify more than this, get out of the market and into mutual funds. The law of diminishing returns takes effect very quickly for the small investor as he increases the number of stocks in his portfolio. You cannot successfully track a half-dozen stocks; and how many winners can you pick? Besides, the safety that diversification affords can be obtained by stock and option combinations.[3]

4. *Don't be afraid to take a loss.* If the prospects for a particular security turn sour, don't hold on and pray. You can lose even more money and better opportunities. If you are dollar-cost averaging, however, your stop-loss target can be lower than if you are buying in large blocks. In the latter case, always cover your initial position with low-cost puts or high income (but not in-the-money or at-the-money) covered calls. This is because stocks usually depreciate or maintain their price level for the period immediately after purchase. Again, assume that you will rarely buy at the annual low.

5. *Stay on top of your investments.* Once you become an investor/speculator, you have to plug yourself into the marketplace and the world. Stay on top of the news and how it affects the prices of your holdings.

These and other topics will be covered in further detail. For now, however, realize that the most effective investors have one thing in common: They know the ways to play the game, and they keep on their toes. Winning at anything never comes easily.

Bulls, Bears, and Possums

There are three types of investors: possums, bears, and bulls. The possum is the middle-of-the-roader, the bear is the nihilist, and the bull is the optimist. However, they are equally optimistic about their ability to make money in the marketplace.

The possum[4] does not expect the market to move much in either direction; he plays a waiting game, trying to squeeze as much income from his portfolio as he possibly can. He looks for stocks that are good income (dividend) candidates and that are also ideal covered-call candidates. The more daring possums may try to draw additional income into their portfolios by selling uncovered calls or puts. The possum can usually benefit from market upswings, but the mix of his option and stock holdings usually limit his profits.

The bear believes that the stock market is about to decline drastically in price. He makes his money primarily by selling short or buying puts. No one is a bear on the entire market; this would be careless. Even in recessions, there are stocks with strong upside potential (either because of market or takeover possibilities), and the bear may very well be bullish on these stocks while being bearish on the market in general.

The bull believes that the stock market is about to increase drastically in price. He makes his money primarily by buying stocks or calls long and selling puts short. Like the bear, he may have one perspective on the market in general and another on certain segments of the market. He has other effective tools, also, and these include buying and selling stock warrants and stock rights. These tools are reviewed in the next chapter and discussed in detail in those that follow.

Business Cycles

Possum, bear, or bull, an investor must understand that the stock market follows the same cyclical movements as the economy in general. In the classical sense, this means that stock prices will increase, settle, contract, and recover. This is basically the way the economy moves. Every investor must expect that the value of her portfolio will fluctuate, sometimes drastically.

This means that you have to expect that the stock you buy will not soar in one direction only, but will fluctuate even on a daily basis as long as there is any substantial interest in it.

There are actually more than four phases to the business cycle, which writers and economists number and define differently. For our purposes, we interpret each phase as consisting of at least three cycles. For example, even during increases (or expansion), the price movement of a stock will show short periods of settlement, brief periods of contraction, and then a recovery period that brings its price to even newer highs.

Individual stocks follow the same cycles. They have their own bear and bull phases, their own periods of expansion, settlement, contraction, and recovery. In its own bull market, a stock's recovery after each contraction will excite periods of expansion that bring its price per share to new ground. In its own bear market, a stock's recovery will only be short term before contraction resumes.

While economists identify anywhere from four to 12 phases in business or stock cycles, you must keep in mind that all phases need not occur in succession or with equal severity or intensity. Advances can follow declines or settlement periods and can be longer than contraction periods or shorter. There are no hard rules, no dependable formulas that work in every case. There are no sure bets in the stock market except perhaps for the income to be received from selling covered calls.

But using the right tools will help any investor increase profits or limit losses.

Notes

1. For a detailed study on how to employ covered calls, see Charles J. Caes, *Covered Calls: The Safest Game in the Options Market* (Blue Ridge Summit, PA: Liberty Hall, 1990), Chapters 7, 9, and 10.

2. For ways to use puts and uncovered calls, see Charles J. Caes, *Tools of the Bear* (Chicago, IL: Probus, 1993), Chapters 11 and 16.

3. This recommendation stems from the fact that in addition to not being able to pick winner after winner, the independent investor generally has too little money to spread over many stocks and still make investing in the market worthwhile. Contrary to current popular advice, it is better to limit diversification and not tie up a large amount of funds, and to hedge by going long on stocks and puts, long on stocks and short on calls, or short on stocks and long on puts. Even long-term investors will want to periodically cover themselves with puts or covered calls.

4. Caes, *Covered Calls*, Chapter 10. Possum is a term suggested by the author to represent those who are neither bears nor bulls but expect the market to remain within a narrow range.

2

THE FIVE TOOLS

You now have the basic perspectives to help you understand the approaches described in this book for investors who are bullish on the market:

- There are no guarantees in the stock market except premiums from covered-call writing, but covered-call writing is primarily an income play and not for those who are truly bullish on the market.

- To succeed as a bull, you must be both an investor and a speculator, expecting that the odds are against buying at the low (or selling at the high), that stock prices will swing, that leverage is important, and that hedging will shield you on downswings.

- You must understand the more widely used tools of the bull: buying stock long, selling (writing) puts, and buying calls; and some not very well known tools, such as warrants and rights.

The major tools will be discussed briefly in this chapter, to provide you with background, and then discussed in detail after Chapter 5.

Buying Stocks

Those bullish on the market will buy stocks first and then sell them, hopefully at a higher price. This differs from the strategy of those who are bearish on the market. They will sell the stocks first and then buy them, hopefully at a lower price.

The bull buys long; the bear sells short. (See Table 2–1 for a summary of important definitions.)

EXAMPLE #1. Buying Long

You purchase 100 shares of Citicorp at $18 per share because your research has made you bullish on the stock. Two years later, the stock reaches a market price of $35 per share and proves you were right. You sell the 100 shares. Your profit before commissions and other fees is $17 per share, or $1,700.

Table 2–1
Important Terms

Term	Definition
Bear	Investor who expects a stock or the market in general to go down. A bear generally shorts stock and calls, and buys puts.
Bull	Investor who expects a stock or the market to go up. A bull generally shorts puts but goes long on stocks, calls, warrants, and rights.
Buy Long	Traditional trade. Stock is purchased first, then sold later for a profit or to cut losses.
Hedger	Investor/speculator who uses a combination of investment tools to limit risk or, possibly, to assure profit if the market moves substantially in either direction.
Investor	Generally buys long and for the long term. Rarely shorts stock but may write covered calls.
Primary Movement	Long-term price direction for a stock or the market in general.
Secondary Movement	Temporary price movement for a stock or the market in general.
Sell Short	Stock is sold first, then purchased later for profit or to cut losses. Profit and loss is still determined by the difference between purchase and selling prices.
Speculator	Trades often. Buys long or short in stocks or options— uses any tool and plays any game that can mean short-term or big profits.

Profit is determined by simple arithmetic. Subtract the cost of the stock from the selling price.

EXAMPLE #2. Selling Short

You sell short 100 shares of Citicorp at $35 per share because your research has made you bearish on the stock. (Note that you do not already own this stock you have just sold.) Over a period of about a year, the stock falls back to $20 per share and proves you were right. You buy the 100 shares with instructions to your broker that you are "covering your short position." Your profit before commissions is $15 per share, or $1,500.

In this example, profit is determined the very same way. Subtract the cost of the stock from the selling price. In the first example, the stock must go up in price for you to profit because you "bought long." In the second example, the stock must go down in price for you to profit because you sold short.

You can be both a short seller and long buyer at the same time, playing some stocks to go down and others to go up. However, in this book the emphasis is on buying long, so the strategies are designed for stocks expected to go north in price.

Notice the word *expected*. Stocks do not always go the way you would like them to go. And if they do, it is rarely in the time frame you expect. It often happens that they go down in price when you own them, and go up in price after you sell them.

Stocks generally have primary and secondary movements. The primary movement indicates the major trend of the stock. If the primary trend is bullish, then despite occasional dips in price, the stock will continue to reach for new high ground. If the primary trend is bearish, then despite occasional climbs in price, the stock will continue to fall to new lows. The secondary movements are the occasional changes in price direction because of profit taking, bear raids, or rallies.

Understanding Put and Call Terminology

Before we move on to the basics of dealing in stock options, it is necessary to have a firm grasp of options terminology.

Puts and calls are types of stock options. They are ideal for investors who do not like to tie up a great deal of cash. Puts and calls can be traded just as stocks are. They can be bought long or sold short. In put and call trading, however, a short seller is usually referred to as a "writer." This is because when he sells an option he actually "writes the contract" for it.

In reality, there are no contracts changing hands. Option contracts are standardized, so the only transaction records that are necessary are the statements from your broker. It is a perfectly legal way of doing business and one that helps to keep the options markets quick and efficient.

When you buy and sell puts and calls, it is almost always through the secondary markets provided by the exchanges dealing in these options (Table 2–2).

As investors become more aware of the different ways to invest directly and indirectly in the stock market, they are becoming more and more interested in dealing with stock options. They especially like puts and calls for a number of reasons:

- The leverage available from low-priced puts and calls gives investors opportunities to double, triple, and even quadruple their money in short time. These types of returns are very rarely possible from stocks.

- The low price of the options encourages portfolio diversification. A couple of thousand dollars can have an investor playing six or seven different options on underlying stocks that would ordinarily be out of the small investor's reach.

This does not mean, however, that options are not risky business. Writers of options stand the risk of losing a great deal of money. Writers are short sellers, and there is no ceiling on the losses short sellers can incur—not in the stock market, and

---

Table 2–2
Major Stock Option Markets

New York:	American Stock Exchange
	New York Stock Exchange
Chicago:	Chicago Board Options Exchange
District of Columbia:	National Association of Securities Dealers
San Francisco:	Pacific Stock Exchange
Philadelphia:	Philadelphia Stock Exchange

These exchanges/markets are all owner-members of the Options Clearing Corporation, which functions as the guarantor of all listed option contracts in the United States. Through its associate members, the OCC is also the guarantor of options traded on major European exchanges. Its function is to assure that there are writers and buyers for all listed options.

---

not in the options market. In the options market, these losses can be incredibly large because of the percents of increase and decrease that options experience.

There are basically two types of transactions in options trading, an opening transaction and a closing transaction. The first position, whether long or short, is called the opening transaction. The second position, whether long or short, is called the closing transaction.

Often there is only an opening transaction. Why? First of all, many options quickly lose so much of their value that if the owner sells, she will not make enough to cover the cost of the sell commission. Second, many stocks do not reach the striking price, so writers never have to cover their positions. Third, often a buyer exercises her option to deal in the underlying stock, in which case the writer does not have a chance to cover her position and must instead—and unfortunately—trade the underlying stock to meet her obligations.

Not all options listings take the same format, and sometimes the same financial source will list them differently. For instance, Mondays through Saturdays, the *New York Times* lists all calls then all puts for each underlying stock but then on Sundays lists them still by underlying stock but also by order of striking price.

Options listings only represent a scoreboard of the previous day's activities. They are not meant to be the basis for any decision making on what option to write or buy. Only a thorough analysis of the underlying stock and a thorough understanding of the time and intrinsic value of the related options will help you avoid a bad decision. (See Table 2–3.)

In the list provided in Table 2–3, note that the underlying stock is identified by the alpha characters in the left column under the heading "Option and NY Close," and the closing market price of the stock is listed directly under it, once for reference purposes on each line associated with a striking price. Following are other definitions and explanations of the column headings.

Table 2–3
Put and Call Terminology

Term	Definition
Expiration Date	The date on which an option expires. Puts and calls expire on the Saturday after the third Friday of the month.
NY Close	Price at which the underlying stock closed on the previous day. It is not the price at which the last option was traded.
Option Buyer	Long buyer of a put or call. Trades the options as she would trade stock.
Option Writer	Short seller of a put or call. Trades for income from the premiums she will receive.
Premium	The market price of the option. The listed premium is almost always $1/100$ of the cost of the option. If the premium is listed at $2½, the price of the option is $250 before commissions. (Each put or call represents 100 shares of stock.)
Strike Price	Price at which a buyer of an option can exercise her rights.
Underlying Stock	The corporate stock on which a stock option is written.

Strike Price

Also referred to as the expiration price, this is the price at which an option is "at-the-money" and may be exercised. When you write a put, you will generally want the striking price to be relatively lower than the market price of the stock so that the option remains out-of-the-money. When you buy a call, you will generally want that striking price to be lower than the market price of the stock so that you are in-the-money.

As the underlying stock changes in price, new contracts at adjusted striking prices will be introduced. New options on higher priced stocks are not usually introduced unless there has been a price movement of 10 points in either direction. New options on lower priced stocks may be introduced on price movements in either direction of 2½ to 5 points.

Calls Last, Puts Last

The numbers under these columns are the premiums for the calls and puts or, more specifically, the market price of the listed puts and calls. As these are the prices at the close of the bell on the last day's trading, you will have to call your broker to find out what the current bid and ask prices are for each of these options.

The prices that appear in these columns are based on the assumption that the puts and calls represent 100 shares of stock. So, multiply any of the listed values by 100 to determine what is the true value of the related put or call.

Option premiums are generally quoted in bid-ask spreads of anywhere from ⅛ of a point to ½ of a point. When bidding on an option, generally start with an offer to buy or sell at the mid-point between the buy and ask prices, unless you are expecting a significant decrease or increase in the price of that option.

These premiums are what drive the options markets. Options traders are no different than stock traders; they want to buy low and sell high. This is true even if an option buyer is not interested in trading the option but, rather, is interested in later acquiring the underlying stock. In the latter case, as soon as there is enough of a difference between the stock's market price and the related option's striking price to impress the trader, he will exercise his option.

Whether or not the stock price must be below or above the striking price for the related option depends upon whether the trader is dealing in puts or calls. (See Table 2–4.) If he is the buyer of a call, he will want the stock's price to be above the striking price. This is because call buyers are bulls, and look to profit from upswings in a stock's price. If he is the buyer of a put, he will want the stock's price to be below the striking price. This is because put buyers are bears, and look to profit from downswings in a stock's price.

Option writers, on the other hand, are mainly interested in the premiums. These premiums represent added income to portfolios. Speculators short their options when they feel the premiums are worth the gamble. This means they feel the underlying stock will not move enough to make it beneficial to the buyer of the option to ever exercise her rights and force the writers to cover their positions by taking a loss on the resulting stock trade.

Months

The months listed represent the expiration dates of the contracts. The specific date is not given because it is expected that all options made available on the U.S. options exchanges expire on the first Saturday after the third Friday of the month. Sometimes this is the third Saturday of the month; sometimes it is the fourth.

Expiration cycles differ for individual stocks. Not all are on the same monthly or quarterly cycles. As one expiration date expires, another is usually listed unless the options for a given stock will be terminated.

All equity options traded on the major exchanges mature according to a series of monthly cycles.

> 1st cycle: January sequential
> 2nd cycle: February sequential
> 3rd cycle: March sequential

These cycles have been initiated in response to demand for short-term trading opportunities. But as the cycles are structured so that expirations can actually occur as late as eight months away, they also offer the type of environment in which longer-term traders will be interested. This last means that if in December, you are interested in IBM options with later expirations, you can write or buy long July puts and calls.

Table 2–4
Money Positions

I. Calls

In-the-money if the striking price is below the market price of the underlying stock.

Out-of-the-money if the striking price is above the current price of the underlying stock.

At-the-money if the striking price is the same as the current market price.

Examples

Stock	Market Price	Strike Price	Money Position
AT&T	$60	$55	In-the-Money
AT&T	60	65	Out-of-the-Money
AT&T	60	60	At-the-Money

II. Puts

In-the-money if the striking price is above the market price of the underlying stock.

Out-of-the-money of the striking price is below the current price of the underlying stock.

At-the-money if the striking price is the same as the current market price.

Examples

Stock	Market Price	Strike Price	Money Position
AT&T	$60	$65	In-the-Money
AT&T	60	55	Out-of-the-Money
AT&T	60	60	At-the-Money

If an option is in-the-money, this means it has intrinsic value and generally commands a high premium. If it is out-of-the-money, this means it has no intrinsic value. If it is at-the-money, it can be in-the-money with any decent increase in the price of the underlying stock.

For example, if you own the in-the-money call on AT&T, you can exercise your option and buy the stock at $55 per share and immediately sell it for a profit at $60 per share, because the call gives you the right to "buy" at the striking price. But if the call is out-of-the-money or at-the-money, there is no profit potential.

In the case of puts, if you own the in-the-money put on AT&T, you can exercise your option and buy the stock for $60 and immediately sell at the striking price. But if the put is out-of-the-money or at-the-money, there is no profit potential in exercising your option.

You will notice that there is a relationship between the value of premiums and the time to expiration date. This is because the prices of options decay with time. As expiration dates approach, option prices generally fall in value, sometimes even when the underlying stock is increasing in price. Time decay is not the same for all options; many factors influence the rate of decay. Nonetheless, some mathematicians and market experts continually attempt to formularize the decay rate. The rate of decay generally accelerates considerably during the few days before expiration date, but is often close to zero during the first few days after an option is made available. Movement in price of the underlying stock inhibits, reverses, or accelerates time decay of an option, depending upon when (in relation to the expiration date) the price change takes place.

Writing Put Contracts

A put option is a contract on an underlying stock. A put almost always represents 100 shares of the underlying stock. If there is any price movement in a put contract, it is usually in the opposite direction that the stock price is moving.

A little while ago, you were given an example of selling short. You sold a stock in the hopes of buying it back later at a lower price. You were using a tool of the bear: short selling. Another tool of the bear is buying a put. It is a way of profiting when a stock goes down in price without actually having to buy the stock. Why buy the put option instead of the stock? Because the put option may cost dollars per share, whereas the stock may cost tens of dollars per share. The put gives an investor the kind of leverage that comes from owning something that may double in price with just a change in price of two bits or more—or even an eighth of a dollar.

Now, the bull always does the opposite of a bear. He wants to sell puts because he does not expect the underlying stock to go down in price. The bear, however, expects the underlying stock to go down, so he buys the put.

But the writer of a put will not see his profits increase as the underlying stock moves in price. Writing puts is an income play for the bull, and the writer will never receive more than the premium (selling price) he gets when the put is written.

Let's look at the mathematics of profiting and losing by writing puts. These examples are very basic and not as detailed as they will be when we revisit puts in Part 3. They are meant only to give you a general idea of the how and why of puts.

EXAMPLE #3. Profiting by Writing a Put

You write one put contract for 100 shares of IBM stock. Assume the price of the shares at this time is 48.

You do not already own the put, but you can sell it just as you can sell a stock you do not already own.

The buyer of this contract you have just written now has the right to sell IBM stock at, say, $45 per share. You, in turn, will have received a premium (price at which you sold the put) of, say, $250. The put contract expires January 21.

The stock never drops below $45 per share before January 21. The contract, therefore, expires worthless. You make $250.

You have not sold the stock. Nor have you bought it. You have only written a contract that has given someone else the opportunity to profit if the stock declines in price, for as the stock declines in price, the put usually increases in price. ("Usually," because there are many factors that influence the price of a put, and these will be discussed in Part 3.)

Writing a put contract is easy money in a bull market for the underlying stock. But there is a very serious downside to this game.

EXAMPLE #4. Losing by Writing a Put

You write one put contract for 100 shares of IBM, giving the owner the right to sell the stock at $45 per share by January 21. The put is listed for $2.50. As each put represents 100 shares of stock, the true value of the put is $250, which is what you receive when you sell it. Assume that the price of IBM is $48 per share at the time you write the put.

The stock begins to fall in price, to $45, then to $40. Meanwhile, the price of the put has increased in value. It is now listed for $5. The owner of the contract now has the right to exercise her option. This means she can buy 100 shares of IBM stock at $40 and immediately sell them at $45 for a $500 profit. If she does, you will have to buy the stock at $45 so you can sell it to her. This means that while you made $250 on the put, you will have lost $500 on the stock transaction.

Your other option is to buy back your put before the owner exercises her option or the put generates any more losses. In this case, you are covering a short position that is showing a loss.

Writing puts is risky business. If IBM dropped to $30 per share, you might have to buy back that contract for $2,000. In this case, your loss would be $1,750 ($2,000 buy-back less the $250 sale price). At no time could you have made more than $250, but at any time you could have lost thousands . . . and more thousands.

Put writers generally try to limit their risk by selecting underlying stocks that have little or no downside risk, or else writing puts with striking prices that seem to go well beyond probability. (A striking price is the contract price; it is the price at which the buyer of a put can exercise his rights.)

In the previous example, you could have played the game with less risk by writing a put on IBM that had a striking price of $40 or $35 instead of $45. But the further from the market price that the striking price is, the less money you will receive for writing the put contract. In fact, the premium for puts with lower striking prices may be so low that it is hardly advantageous for you to even consider them. In fact, you may want to bear in mind that the greater the premium on a put contract, the greater the risk.

But remember, you are not locked into your contract. You can always close out your position while it is still profitable, if it is ever profitable.

EXAMPLE #5. Early Profit-Taking on a Shorted Put

You have written a put on IBM stock, currently selling at $48 per share. The striking price is $45, and the expiration date is two months away. The premium you receive for writing the contract is $250.

Before the expiration date, the stock increases in price to $52 per share, and the put decreases in value to $.50 (or $50). You now learn that there is a good chance IBM will decline in price. Therefore, you call your broker and tell him to close out your position by purchasing the put back. Your order is executed, and you buy the put for $50. Your profit (excluding commissions, of course) is $200 ($250 premium for writing, less $50 for closing out the position).

In each of the above examples, you were dealing in one put. Because of their low price, speculators generally deal in many puts at one time. On the buy side, this is a worthwhile risk; but on the write side, it is too great a risk. The rule of thumb is this: when writing puts, write one or two at most, unless you are going to hedge your positions in some way.

It is important to remember, however, that it is not always possible to buy a put contract back at the same price or less than you sold it for. Such luck depends on the current market price of the stock, the striking price for the put option, and the time remaining until contract expiration.

Will a bull ever want to buy a put? Most assuredly; but he will be interested in using the put as a hedge.

Consider that a well-selected put usually goes up in price if the underlying stock goes down in price. Buying the put assures the bull that if his stock plummets, the put will reduce his losses and possibly even bring him into the black (profit zone). You may wonder how this can be, because the usual logic says that the losses on the stock and the gain on the put will just cancel each other out. This is not usually true. The way a put moves in price is very complicated. Many factors influence the rate at which it will increase or decrease. (See "A Buy Play" in Chapter 21.) It may move on a 1-to-1 ratio opposite the underlying stock; it may move on a 2- or 3-to-1 ratio—or even better—opposite the underlying stock. A put gives the buyer a great deal of leverage because of its low price.

"Even so," you may argue, "the put will be a liability if the stock goes up in price; for as the stock goes up, the put goes down."

The trick answer to this question is that you can never lose more than you pay for a put (plus commissions). If you purchase $500 worth of puts to hedge on a long position, and if the underlying stock goes up $1,000 and the puts decrease to zero, you manage a $500 profit.

"Then," you will observe, "the stock must move high enough up in price to cover the cost of the puts before I can profit."

You are absolutely correct. And you will see how this all works in Chapters 12 through 14.

Buying Calls

A call is just the opposite of a put. But never for one moment believe that puts and calls always move in opposite directions. It is important to fix this fact in your mind as quickly as possible so you are extremely careful about buying puts and calls with the same expiration dates and striking prices on the same stock.

The put, as you have learned, is a contract giving the buyer the right to "sell" the underlying stock. The put contract specifies the striking price and the period of time during which the put can be traded or executed. Neither the buyer nor the writer of puts are ever dealing directly in the underlying stock but only in the put options on the stock. They may or may not own the underlying stock. Anyone may be both a writer and a buyer of puts.

The call, on the other hand, is a contract giving the buyer the right to "buy" the underlying stock. The call contract specifies the striking price and the period of time during which the call can be traded or executed. Neither the buyer nor the writer of calls are ever dealing directly in the underlying stock but only in the call options on the stock. Anyone may be both a writer and a buyer of calls.

One safety feature that puts and calls have in common is that, providing they have a value exceeding the cost of commissions, often you can bail out of your short positions by buying the options back, or bail out of your long positions by selling your contracts— just as you can do with stocks.

Bears write calls, but bulls buy them. Bulls buy them because well-selected calls will increase in price as the underlying stocks increase in price. Why buy the calls instead of the stock? Because the calls cost less. Why buy the stock instead of the calls? Because the calls have time constraints, just like puts. And there are other contract limitations including the striking price and delivery requirements when a buyer exercises her rights.

EXAMPLE #6. Profiting by Buying and Selling a Call

You have purchased one call on Merck stock for $300. The value of the stock when you purchased the call was $30. Before the expiration date of the contract, Merck advances to $35 per share. The call, meanwhile, has increased in value to $600. You decide to take your profits and sell the option. Your profit is $300 ($600 – $300).

You never at any time owned the stock. But you profited as though you owned 100 shares. How much would 100 shares of Merck have cost? Why, $3,000. How much did the one call cost? $300. (Remember that each put or call is the equivalent of 100 shares of the underlying stock.)

It looks easy, doesn't it? But it isn't easy. There are a lot of things working against your chances of success. The stock can go down in price. The option will decay in price as the expiration date nears. The option may increase in price but then decrease below its original price before you sell. If something can go wrong, there is a good chance it will.

EXAMPLE #7. Losing on a Call Because of Time Decay

You have purchased one call on Merck stock for $300. The value of the stock when you purchased the call was $30. The stock remains in a very narrow trading range and does not increase the value of the call. It goes to $30⅛, back to $30, up to $30¼. Meanwhile, the expiration date approaches, and the call begins to lose its value. It depreciates to $250, to $200, to $150. Finally, you decide to sell before the contract expires at $150, at which time the option becomes completely worthless. Your loss is $150 ($300 − $150).

If the stock moved up enough to counter the time decay in the related option, you might have broken even or made a profit. But when an underlying stock moves very negligibly in price, expect that the related option will decay, and decay rather rapidly during the two to three weeks before expiration.

EXAMPLE #8. Losing on a Call Because of Expiration

You have purchased one call on Merck for $300. The value of the stock when you purchased the call was $30. Great things happen! The stock skyrockets to $40 per share and the call increases in value to $1,100. You lose track of the expiration date. Trading on the third Friday of the month ends. It is too late for you to sell your call. You lose $300, actually, and also lose the opportunity to have made $800.

The lesson is that you must pay attention to that expiration date. It means a lot to an option trader. Once a contract expires, it is worthless. The expiration date works for writers of puts and calls, but works against buyers.

Buying Warrants

Warrants are also a type of stock option, as well as a fixed-income option. They are tradeable instruments that confer on the buyer the right to purchase the underlying security or the right to sell the underlying security.

There are two types of stock warrants available to investors. These are subscription warrants and stock-purchase warrants. Warrants, just like puts and calls, have exercise (striking) prices and exercise dates (unless they are perpetual warrants). Unlike those assigned to put and call contracts, the exercise periods for stock warrants are usually long term.

The stock-purchase warrant confers to the owner the legal right to purchase shares of an underlying stock. Stock-purchase warrants are often privileges attached not only to common stocks but also to preferred stocks, bonds, and debentures. But they do not necessarily have to be made available only to holders of certain corporate securities. They may also be issued separately for purchase by the public.

Subscription warrants are tied in with incentives for the purchase of newly issued stocks or bonds. They are rights to a stockholder to subscribe to a new issue in some proportion to their current ownership of the issuing corporation's common stock.

Just as with puts and calls, there are exercise prices and expiration dates to be taken into account when trading in these options. In any case, the great advantage to owners of stock warrants is their low price. As they move in relationship to the demand on the underlying stock, a one-point movement in the stock may represent only a 10 percent gain for the stockholder but a 100 percent or more gain for the warrant holder.

The exercise price of a stock warrant is the price that must be paid to take ownership of the underlying security. This exercise price will almost always exceed the current market price of the underlying security. For instance, if Karen Rigg, Inc. shares are selling for $20, the exercise price for the newly issued warrants will generally be above $20. If you should misjudge the potential of the underlying stock and purchase the warrants at a striking price that the stock will never reach, then you stand to lose everything you paid for the warrant. If you should judge the stock correctly and it advances passed the striking price, you can buy the stock at the striking price and then immediately sell it at the higher market price. Or you can just deal in the warrants, which will have increased in value as the stock climbed in price.

The warrant only gives you the right to purchase the underlying stock. You do not own the stock unless you exercise your option, just as in the case of call options.

Stock Rights

Stock rights are the privileges a corporation attaches to each share of common stock, allowing the owner of that stock to purchase full or fractional shares.

There are two major differences between stock rights and stock warrants. The first is that stock rights are usually offered free to current stockholders. The second is that stock rights usually carry an exercise price that is below the current market value of the related stock.

Rights work like this: Suppose that AT&T decides to issue an additional 10 million shares of stock. It has the opportunity to offer them on the open market, to negotiate with investment bankers to buy the shares at or close to the market value of current stock, or to raise whatever capital is needed from existing shareholders. In this last case, the corporation offers rights to stockholders who wish to participate. These rights will usually allow a discount to participants on the purchase of additional shares, the number of which are specified by the rights. If the stock is selling at $60 per share, the rights may allow purchase of the shares at $55.

Greater detail on warrants, rights, puts, and calls will be forthcoming. But now that you understand the fundamentals, we can toss these terms around as we look at the concerns, issues, and opportunities for the independent investor like yourself. Then, as you begin to understand how these tools fit in with investment strategies, we can go deeper into the tool box.

See Table 2–5 for a summary evaluation of bullish strategies.

Table 2–5
Advantages and Disadvantages of Bull Strategies

Strategy	Major Advantages	Major Disadvantages
Buying Stocks Long	Stocks can theoretically climb forever; you own a piece of the corporation, share in dividends. You can play for income and/or capital gains.	Stocks are generally slow climbers; need great patience, solid strategy, great picks. You will tie up a lot of money.
Writing Puts	You can greatly increase your investment income. Time decay works to your advantage.	Picking the wrong underlying stock can result in tremendous losses. The initial amount received for selling the put is the maximum amount of money you can earn.
Buying Calls	Return on investment can be substantial; you cannot lose more than your original investment. Big wins possible.	Time decay works against you; too many variables affect call movement; must keep an eye on expiration date, after which option becomes worthless.
Buying Stock Warrants	Low price in relation to underlying stock offers great leverage. Big wins possible.	Striking prices and expiration dates can work very forcefully against you.
Buying Stock Rights	Below market striking prices put you in the money quickly; low price affords great leverage.	Incentives may bring you into additional stock during market downturns.

3

THE IMPORTANCE OF LEVERAGE

Leverage, for our purposes, is a way of making a little money do the work of a lot of money. This is important for the independent investor who is primarily interested in building his capital.

In favorable markets, leverage can skyrocket your profits. In unfavorable markets, however, it can multiply your losses. The higher your leverage, the greater your risk. The greater your leverage, the greater your potential for getting richer.

Buying calls, warrants, and rights automatically leverages your money, as does buying stocks on margin.

The Math of Big Profits

A quick example of the advantages of leverage is the difference between buying low- and high-priced stocks.

EXAMPLE #9. Rate of Return on High-Priced Stock

You purchase 100 shares of Merck at $20 per share. Your investment in the stock is $2,000 (100 shares × $20). The stock increases $2 per share. You sell at the new price of $22 per share. Your rate of return is 10 percent ($2 ÷ $20).

You purchase 400 shares of RJR-Nabisco at $5 per share. Your investment in the stock is $2,000 (400 shares × $20). The stock increases $2 per share. You sell at the new price of $7 per share. Your rate of return is 40 percent ($2 ÷ $5).

Each ⅛ of a point that the lower-priced stock moves represents a higher return on your money than each ⅛ of a point the higher stock moves. A simple understanding of percentages tells you this. The guiding rule in bull markets, then, is to find good, low-priced stocks. Each point they move brings you a higher return on your investment.

But never go for a stock just because it is low priced. Think percent! If a higher-priced stock has a better chance of moving within a given time frame than a lower-priced stock, go for the higher-priced stock.

EXAMPLE #10. Going for a Higher-Priced Stock with Potential

You have $4,000 to invest. There are many low-priced stocks, but you cannot measure their potential. The lowest-priced stock that you feel will move on the intermediate term is Citicorp. You buy 100 shares of common at $40. The stock climbs to $60 per share within two years. You sell for a profit of $20 per share ($2,000.) That is 50 percent on your money.

I have $4,000 to invest. I want to gamble on a low-priced stock. I like Citicorp, but it's too expensive for me. I want to buy a lot of shares with my $4,000. So, I purchase 500 shares of RJR-Nabisco common at $8 per share. The stock moves to $10 per share after two years, at which time I sell. My profit is $2 per share ($1,000). That is 25 percent on my money.

Clearly the lower-priced stock was not the best buy. Citicorp proved the higher rate of return. The lesson here is that every stock investor must think in percent, not in number of shares. It is not the price of the stock that should be your main interest but, rather, the rate at which it will gain market value.

Look for the lowest price stock that has great potential for a high rate of return. But do not buy a stock just because it is low priced.

Leverage with Margin

Margin has many different meanings, like quite a few terms used by the financial community. You will find that its meaning in stock trading is very different from its meaning in options trading.

In stock trading, it refers to the amount of money you are required to put up when you purchase stock. Put another way, it indicates how much you can borrow from your broker to buy stock. For instance, if you purchase $4,000 worth of Citicorp common stock for $2,000, your margin is 50 percent.

How much can you borrow from your broker to purchase stock? It varies and depends upon Federal Reserve requirements, stock exchange regulations, and broker guidelines.

There are actually two types of margin requirements, initial and maintenance. The Federal Reserve sets initial margin rates. It uses these rates as one of its economic controls. Since 1974, the initial margin requirement for buying long and selling short has been 50 percent. From October 16, 1958, until July 27, 1960, it was at its second highest rate, 90 percent It was at 100 percent from January 21, 1946, until January 31, 1947. (See Table 3–1 for a history of initial margin rates and Table 3–2 for margin regulations.)

This means that, given the current rate of 50 percent, to make your first margin purchase on 200 shares of the *New York Times*, traded on the American Stock Exchange at $28 per share, you would have to put up $2,800. Your broker would put

Table 3–1
History of Federal Reserve Equity (Initial) Margin
Requirements for Short and Long Positions

Effective Date	Long Positions	Short Positions
October 1, 1934	25–55%, depending on present price to lowest price ratio for each security	Determined by broker
April 1, 1936	55%	Determined by broker
November 1, 1937	40	50%
February 5, 1945	50	50
July 5, 1945	75	75
January 21, 1946	100	100
February 1, 1947	75	75
March 30, 1949	50	50
January 17, 1951	75	75
February 20, 1953	50	50
January 4, 1955	50	60
April 23, 1955	70	70
January 16, 1958	50	50
August 5, 1958	50	50
October 16, 1958	90	90
July 28, 1960	70	70
July 10, 1962	50	50
November 6, 1963	70	70
March 11, 1968	70	70
June 8, 1968	80	80
May 6, 1970	65	65
December 6, 1971	55	55
November 24, 1972	65	65
January 3, 1974	50	50

up the rest. Your margin need not be in cash. The Federal Reserve allows you to use other securities as collateral.

The other type of margin—maintenance margin—is set by stock exchanges and brokers, and is not necessarily uniform. But in every case, the stock exchanges in the United States require that you deposit $2,000 in cash or collateral with the broker to cover your first margin purchase. This means that even though the Federal Reserve only requires 50 percent initial margin, if you buy, for example, $2,500 worth of Novell (NASDAQ), you must deposit $2,000. (Many foreign exchanges do not allow margin purchases.)

Table 3–2
Federal Reserve Margin Requirements

Regulation	Summary
G	Regulates margin credit to be offered by anyone other than brokers, dealers, and bankers who must register with the Federal Reserve Board of Governors.
T	Regulates credit extentions made by securities brokers and dealers. Designed to guard against preferred treatment of brokers and dealers to establish margin requirements, and governs cash transactions among brokers, dealers, and customers.
U	Regulates credit extended by banks. Designed to limit any credit that is secured by stock.
X	Extends the provisions of Regulations G and T to borrowers of the other nations. Assures adherence to applicable margin requirements governing any credit agreement within the U.S.

Each exchange and brokerage firm also sets additional maintenance margin requirements for their own protection. For many stocks with a market value of under $5, the requirement is 100 percent. On stocks with a market value of $5 or more, it is usually 25 percent to 50 percent, with the lower margin allowed for accounts having two or more stocks in street name. The term "street name" refers to securities held in the name of the broker instead of the customer. The majority of margin accounts are in street name; this facilitates record keeping and provides additional efficiency to back-room operations.

Margin provides very heavy leverage. It gives each dollar invested a chance to do the work of many more dollars.

EXAMPLE #11. Profiting with 50 Percent Margin

You have $6,000 to invest. You are bullish about an American Stock Exchange stock called Echo Bay, selling at $15 per share. You expect it to move $5 to $10 per share in the next six months. If you make a cash purchase, you can purchase 400 shares ($6000 ÷ $15). But if you buy on 50 percent margin, which you finally do, you can purchase 800 shares. As expected, the stock goes up $7.50 per share, and you sell your holdings. Your profit on the stock is $6,000—twice as much as you would have earned if you'd traded on a cash basis.

With $6,000, you earned $6,000. You started with $6,000 and now have $12,000. That's almost a 100 percent profit in six months—much, much better than you could ever do with a CD. Why "almost?" Because the broker will charge you interest on the money you borrowed for the trade, and you will have to pay commissions.

EXAMPLE #12. Losing with 50 Percent Margin

You have $6,000 you want to invest in Echo Bay stock. Using 50 percent margin, you actually purchase $12,000 worth of the stock and acquire 800 shares (at $15.). Your target is $20 per share. The stock goes up a couple of points, then falls in price; eventually it drops to $7.50 per share. Your broker calls you to put additional money in your account or sell the stock. You have no additional money to invest or feel the stock is a lost cause. You sell the 800 shares and receive $6,000. But you owe the broker $6,000 plus interest on the borrowed money. You, therefore, receive absolutely nothing. And you still owe the broker some bucks.

In this last example, the stock depreciated 50 percent, but you lost 100 percent of your money. The lesson: Be sure you are in a bull market for the underlying stock before you trade it, and be especially sure you are in a bull market if you're even thinking of trading on margin.

The amount of margin you use depends upon your objectives. You can trade on full or partial margin. If you are a gambler with a record of success and you have a stock that is fundamentally and technically strong, you might want to margin yourself to high profits. Most brokers, being highly conservative in nature, will recommend using margin only to round out your lots. (A round lot is 100 shares.) That is, if you are dealing in a stock that is too expensive for you to purchase a full 100 shares (or 200, whatever the next round lot is), they might recommend using margin for the extra shares you need.

The "call" from your broker mentioned in the above example is what is technically referred to as a "margin" call. It does not always come by phone, but always comes by mail. The call is always for the extra money or additional securities needed to cover some of the losses that put your account in harm's way. Technically, the money is due immediately or the broker has the right to sell off part or all of your portfolio to cover your position in accordance with margin requirements.

The margin call can be devastating. Consider a situation in which you have been building your portfolio by investing in three or four stocks, in which case you only need to maintain 25 percent margin. Suppose on July 1 the value of your holdings is $20,000. Your equity, given 25 percent margin, is $5,000. On July 7, while you are on vacation, all the stocks take serious hits and depreciate considerably in price—some 25 percent, or $5,000. That brings your equity down to zero. You are totally wiped out. Your broker tries to get in touch with you, but cannot. He also mails out a margin call. Meanwhile, the value of the portfolio keeps dropping, and the broker sells off the remaining shares. You come back from vacation, find the margin call, check your account—and find out you not only no longer own any stocks, but you owe your broker money. And all this happened on a mere 25 percent drop in the value of your portfolio.

On the other hand, a 25 percent gain in the portfolio would mean a 100 percent gain for you. Consider that a 25 percent gain means a $5,000 profit for you ($20,000 × 25%). Your equity in the account has now climbed from $5,000 to $10,000. Your $5,000 made $5,000.

Consider, now, what would happen if the portfolio were to double in price from $20,000 to $40,000. In this case, your $5,000 in equity has now climbed to $25,000. Your $5,000 has made $20,000. This is a 400 percent return.

That's the advantage of using margin. And it is one way the little guy, like you and me, can make big money . . . or, of course, lose big money.

Leverage from Long Positions on Calls

Margin, as indicated earlier, has a very different meaning in put and call trading. Actually, puts and calls cannot be traded long on margin; all trades must be cash transactions. They can be traded short on margin—but here margin means not a fraction of the total price of the trade but the full price of the trade plus additional money so the broker can sleep well at night. (See Table 3–3.) Unlike stocks, you do not have five business days on which to deposit money after you buy a put or call. The money must be in your account before you trade, either in the form of cash or marketable securities to be used as collateral.

This is one of the added features of a margin account. Suppose you own 100 shares of Dow Jones at $30 per share, which you have on deposit in street name in your margin account. The equity in your account is, therefore, $3,000. Because you are only required to have 50 percent of the value of the stock in the margin account, that means the balance can be used to purchase other stock or options. If you buy 10 calls on Dow Jones at $1.50, you can use the excess equity in your margin account to buy the call (or put). In other words, the options must be purchased in cash, but you can borrow money from the broker against stock on deposit to make the purchase.

Table 3–3
Margin Requirements for Stock and Stock Options

Margin has a very different meaning in options trading than it does in stock trading. Here margin is cost plus. The broker is asking for more money than is required by the purchase so he or she has insurance if there are extraordinary percentage losses.

Strategy	Requirement
1. Buy Puts or Calls	Cash transactions only; but securities in a cash or margin account may serve as collateral.
2. Write Uncovered Calls or Puts	Payment must equal the market value of the option, plus the commission, plus from 5–15 percent of the stock.
3. Write Covered Calls	Margin requirements are immediately satisfied because the buyer owns the underlying stock, which must be on deposit with the broker.

For put or call *writing*, the margin requirements are much more strict. The writer must have in his account the amount required to cover the premium for the option plus 5 percent to 15 percent of the underlying stock's value. Additionally, brokers usually require initial margin before any trading will be allowed. This is because writing options is extremely risky.

Buying options, however, though risky, is not quite as risky as writing them; and despite the fear many investors have about them, they offer distinct advantages over stock trading. Options contracts offer the potential for:

- Relatively high returns on minimal investments.

- Liquidity.

- For long positions, a ceiling on the amount of losses that can be incurred. (You cannot lose more than you have paid for the option plus commissions.)

The liquidity advantage comes from not having to tie up great deals of money in stock. Five hundred shares of AT&T can cost $30,000. Five in-the-money calls (representing 500 shares of the underlying stock) can be purchased for as low as $1,000. Out-of-the-monies can be purchased for as low as a few hundred dollars.

It is true that put and call buyers are faced with the prospect of time decay on their holdings, as well as the fact that calls may expire worthless. But at the same time, contract expirations are often a better alternative to holding on to stock for too long a time. Consider the $30,000 investment in AT&T. Suppose the investment is in the red for five years, and when you finally do profit, it is a mere 5 percent on your money. The opportunity cost is substantial. Not only could that money have been used for other investments, but it would have possibly prevented the investor from hitting his credit cards or borrowing in other ways to stay liquid. Dealing in puts and calls keeps the small investor much more liquid.

As a market bull, your primary interest is in buying calls, not writing them. You may buy the very high-priced far in-the-money calls or the very low-priced far out-of-the-money calls. Or you may stay in the middle of the range with at-the-monies.

Example #13, which follows, shows what might happen if you purchased calls on a stock that moved in price from $30 to $35. While to invest in the stock would require tying up $3,000, investing in any of the options would require a maximum of $750. (These prices do not take into account broker commissions.)

Notice that the in-the-money calls will move roughly point-for-point with the stock, but the out-of-the-monies do not have any significant movement until they are at- or in-the-money. The in-the-monies are always your safest bet because they generally have value right up until expiration time. But it is the out-of-the-monies, when purchased in quantity, that can bring the high rates of return.

Suppose that when the stock was at $30, you purchased the October 25 calls for $5. When the stock moved to $35, these calls were now worth $10½. A mere ⅙ of a movement in the price of the stock resulted in a doubling of the value of the call.

If you purchased the October 30s in September, you would have seen your money increase 2½ times.

If you purchased the October 35s, your money would have tripled.

EXAMPLE #13. Examples of Call Prices as Influenced by Strike Price and Expiration Dates

A. Stock price: $30 per share. Date: Late September

Call Premiums

Strike Price	October	November	February	Money Position
25	5	6	7½	In-the-Money
30	2	3	3½	At-the-Money
35	½	s	1½	Out-of-the-Money
40	s	r	r	Out-of-the-Money

B. Stock price: $35 per share. Date: Early October

Call Premiums

Strike Price	October	November	February	Money Position
25	10½	10¾	12⅛	In-the-Money
30	5	5½	6	In-the-Money
35	1½	2⅛	3¾	At-the-Money
40	⅛	½	1½	Out-of-the-Money

In the above listings, r = no trade, s = no option available. Additionally, the relationship between premiums and stock prices has been devised to simplify the arithmetic and, therefore, the instruction. Bear in mind that all option prices do not move in the same ratios to the price movement in the underlying stock, and prices of options for different stocks will differ despite the fact that they may be in the same relationship to the striking price or expiration date.

You can see how the calls provide a special kind of leverage to investors. They move in some relationship to the underlying stock; but each ⅛ of a movement in the stock is a mere percentage of what a ⅛ movement in the related option may be.

You can also see how important the underlying stock is. Gains in the calls are highly dependent upon the movement of the underlying stock. Thus, when you are buying calls, you must not only pick the right stock, you must pick the call with the best potential; that is, the call with the right money position, striking price, and expiration date to offer you a worthwhile return.

Calls are fun. There are so many to pick from and so many ways to play them in combination. And you are not limited to buying one call on any given stock. In the listings in Example #13, you could choose to speculate in every call available.

Calls are not only fun, but can result in incredible rates of return. There is, of course, one big caveat: Not too many investors are able to make money on calls. Excellent timing, as well as selection, is necessary to stay in the black, to make the good money. It can be done, but do not for one moment believe that it is easy.

In Example #13, if the market price of the stock never passed the striking price by expiration date, all of the out-of-the-monies and at-the-monies would have expired worthless. If the stock depreciated in value, even the in-the-monies could have expired worthless.

Calls are a gamble, but a low-priced and sometimes worthwhile gamble.

Option Price Movement

There are a number of factors which influence the price of an option, so thinking of premiums simply in terms of intrinsic and time values does not put the market in proper perspective. These factors are:

a. Price movement in the underlying stock

b. Volatility of the underlying stock

c. Time remaining until expiration

d. Striking price

e. Dividends

f. Interest rates

The price movement in the underlying stock naturally affects the permiums for the related options. This relationship has already been discussed. But it is important to realize that very often a stock can move up in price but the options do not respond. A lot depends upon how far out of the money an option happens to be and how close the expiration date may be. You will find examples in coming sections on buying puts and writing calls that show the price movement of options over a given period. In some cases you will see fractional or full-point changes, at other times you will see none—depending on the striking price and the expiration date for the option. These examples will reinforce in your mind the fact that options will move very differently depending upon their instrinsic and time values. Hidden influences on time value include such things as interest rates, volatility of the underlying stock, and dividend periods.

Volatility of the underlying stock must be considered in addition to "price movement" as it is discussed in the above paragraph. This is because if the market defines the underlying stock as being highly volatile and interprets it as being in a bull phase, premiums for the underlying calls will be higher than normal; if it is interpreted as being in a bear phase, then the puts will be commanding a higher premium.

The time remaining until expiration is a very important factor. You would be much less willing to buy an option with a very close expiration date than one which has an expiration date allowing plenty of time for the underlying stock to increase or decrease in value (depending upon whether you are a writer or a buyer of puts or calls). Time is a precious commodity in options trading, and traders are willing to pay for it.

Above the striking price means intrinsic value for calls; and below the striking price means intrinsic value for puts. Thus, where the price of the underlying stock is in relation to that striking price will also affect the related options, generally placing upside pressure on calls and downside pressure on puts. At ex-dividend date, the calls usually follow the decline that also occurs in the underlying stock unless they are far out of the money, and the puts usually increase in value unless they are far out-of-the-money.

Interest rates represent a big impact on the price of options. Usually, the higher the interest rates, the higher the call premiums. This is because the writers of options are going to lose interest in playing equity options for income if there are better opportunities with less risk. This is one example where opportunity costs influence market activity.

Leverage from Stock Purchase Warrants

The low price of stock purchase warrants gives these equity privileges the same type of built-in leverage that puts and calls offer. This is what makes them very popular with speculators looking for faster-paced trading activity than they will find with stocks. For just hundreds of dollars, speculators have the advantage here of being able to maintain a position equivalent to what would ordinarily require thousands of dollars in the underlying stock.

Warrants also have their money positions. If a warrant has an exercise price above the current market value of the stock, then it is out-of-the-money and has no intrinsic value. Usually when a warrant is first offered, it has no intrinsic value; but it will have time value, nonetheless.

If a warrant has an exercise price below the current market value of the stock, then it is in-the-money and has intrinsic value as well as time value. (See Table 3–4.)

Usually a stock-purchase warrant is out-of-the-money when first offered. There is also a period after issue, usually about one year, before the warrant can be used.

EXAMPLE #14. Making Money with Stock Purchase Warrants

You purchase newly issued warrants for Albert Construction stock, each of which entitles you to purchase two shares of the underlying stock for $10. The stock is currently selling at $8 per share, which means that the warrants are out-of-the-money, because currently you cannot exercise your option. This may be expressed by the following formula:

$$\frac{\text{Stock Price}}{10} \text{ Less } \frac{\text{Warrant Exercise Price}}{12} \times \frac{\text{Shares per Warrant}}{2} = \frac{\text{Intrinsic Value (Each Warrant)}}{-4 \text{ (or zero)}}$$

You have paid $2 per share for the warrants nonetheless, because you feel the stock will go up in time, and you equate that time value to be worth $2 per warrant. For once you are right, and the stock does indeed go up. The value of your warrant now increases accordingly:

$$\frac{\text{Stock Price}}{15} \text{ Less } \frac{\text{Warrant Exercise Price}}{12} \times \frac{\text{Shares per Warrant}}{2} = \frac{\text{Intrinsic Value (Each Warrant)}}{6}$$

> The value of each warrant has tripled (to at least $6 each) with just a 50 percent movement in the underlying stock.

How much each stock-purchase warrant will actually appreciate as the underlying stock increases in value actually depends upon a number of factors, including not only its intrinsic value but also the time value the marketplace is willing to place on it. If the market is highly bullish on the underlying stock, this will put upward pressure on the price of the related warrants.

Owners of warrants can always exercise their rights when the warrants are in-the-money, or they can just trade the warrants as they would stock.

You will not find separate listings for individual warrants as you will for stocks or puts and calls. When they are listed, you can usually find them in the very same stock tables showing trading activity in the underlying stock. Your broker will be of special help in targeting other available warrants. (And Chapter 25 will provide additional information.)

Table 3-4
Money Position for Stock Warrants

Stock Price	Less	Exercise Price	Multiplied by	Shares per Unit	Equals	Intrinsic Value
$20	–	$25	×	$2	=	$ 0
21	–	25	×	2	=	0
22	–	25	×	2	=	0
23	–	25	×	2	=	0
24	–	25	×	2	=	0
25	–	25	×	2	=	0
26	–	25	×	2	=	2
27	–	25	×	2	=	4
28	–	25	×	2	=	6
29	–	25	×	2	=	8
30	–	25	×	2	=	10

Despite the fact that a stock warrant may not have intrinsic value (the exercise price is less than the market price), it may have market value, due to the expectation of traders that the underlying stock will increase in price, thereby bringing future intrinsic value to the stock warrant. Additionally, the market value of stock warrants that are in-the-money (have intrinsic value) will usually be worth more than their intrinsic value.

Leverage with Stock Rights

Subscription warrants represent the legal right to subscription privileges. As is the case with stock warrants, these subscription privileges are assignable. As with other options, their low price and ratio of movement to the underlying stock make them highly attractive to traders who like this kind of leverage.

Stock rights are, specifically, subscription privileges to current stockholders to purchase additional shares of the underlying stock. Their purpose is to give the current stockholders a chance to maintain their same proportional interest in the corporation when additional stock is to be issued. Unlike stock warrants, stock rights are usually issued with an exercise price that is below the current market price of the stock. That is, they are issued with intrinsic value.

Prior to issuance, the underlying stock is considered "rights-on." After the date of issuance of the privileges, old stock is considered to be "ex-rights." Once the stock is ex-rights, its value must necessarily be depreciated because it no longer provides any subscription privileges. The new value of each share of stock may be determined by finding out the market value of each right, and then subtracting this value from the price of each share. Using the formula given in Example #15, we can guess at what may be the market value of rights to be offered and, therefore, the new value of the old stock after at ex-rights.

EXAMPLE #15. Determining the Value of Rights-On Privileges and Ex-Rights Stock

You own shares in National Education, selling at $10 per share. Rights are offered to shareholders to purchase new stock at $8 per share. Each right entitles the holder to one share of stock. The value of each right may be determined as follows:

$$\frac{A\ (\$10)\ less\ B\ (\$8)}{C\ (1) + D\ (1)} = \$1$$

where:
A = market price of old stock
B = subscription price of new stock
C = qualifier to indicate rights add market value to stock
D = rights required for each new share
E = number of rights to be issued

Now that we know the value of each right, we may subtract this value from the rights-on price of the old stock:

Old Stock Price ($10) less Value of Rights ($1) = $9

Knowing the new value of the stock allows us to compute the value of the rights beginning with the ex-rights date. This is important because the market value of the rights will now move in relationship to the underlying stock, and the bullish or bearish perspectives on the underlying stock will drive the value of the rights up or down.

EXAMPLE #16. Making Money with Stock Rights

Your rights are worth $1 each at issuance, but the underlying stock is now substantially less (10 percent less). Nonetheless, the rights you own are highly marketable securities and can bring you relatively high profits. Using the following formula, we can guess at what might be their market value after issuance as the underlying (old) stock goes up or down.

$$\frac{A\ (\$10)\ less\ B\ (\$8)}{D\ (1)} = \$2$$

If the underlying stock increases in price, the value of the rights will increase in greater proportion. If the value of the stock moves 20 percent, the value of the rights double.

$$\frac{A\ (\$12)\ less\ B\ (\$8)}{D\ (1)} = \$4$$

You can see the financial muscle that rights can give you. If, for any reason, you do not wish to exercise your rights, you can trade them. But trading rights is not quite as easy as trading warrants because of high commissions and the quantity of rights generally needed to effect low break-even points.

The life of preemptive rights is usually very short term, perhaps 30 to 60 days. On expiration date, the rights become worthless.

(See Table 3–5 for further examples of determining the intrinsic value of stock rights and Chapter 26 and related tables for additional information.)

Table 3–5
Money Positions for Stock Rights

Market Price (Old Stock)	Less	Subscription Price (New Stock)	+	(Rights Available [Each Share]	+	1)	=	Intrinsic Value
$10	–	$8	+	(1	+	1)	=	0 At-the-Money
11	–	8	+	(2	+	1)	=	1 In-the-Money
12	–	8	+	(1	+	1)	=	2 In-the-Money
14	–	8	+	(2	+	1)	=	2 In-the-Money
9	–	8	+	(1	+	1)	=	0 Out-of-the-Money
8	–	8	+	(1	+	1)	=	0 Out-of-the-Money
7	–	8	+	(1	+	1)	=	0 Out-of-the-Money
6	–	8	+	(1	+	1)	=	0 Out-of-the-Money

Time value may add to the market value of stock rights as it does to stock warrants. Stock rights differ from warrants in these two major ways: Rights are offered free to holders of record; they are offered with exercise prices below the market price of the underlying stock. In the above example, any result less than zero is expressed as 0 (zero) intrinsic value.

4

THE IMPORTANCE OF HEDGING

Hedging means covering yourself in case your primary plans go afoul. Speculators and investors use hedging to protect themselves when securities move in the opposite direction from what they had hoped. Hedging is a form of insurance in investment games. In some cases, hedges are designed simply to limit losses; but in others, they are designed to also multiply gains if an investment goes backwards. In stock and options investing, most hedges include long and short positions in stock and option combinations, or in option combinations.

Investment Risk

Inherent risks in any type of investment make hedging a necessity. Regardless of your sophistication in stock and options investing, there are too many variables that are beyond your control, that you cannot possibly predict, and that will happen every time you have everything going for you.

Munn lists these risks as interest rate risk, market risk, inflation risk, business risk, financial risk, and liquidity risk.[1] Interest rate risk is probably the least of these major investment concerns because interest rates are generally predictable and the astute investor keeps her wary eye on the prime rate and reacts to developments quickly. Falling rates are generally a plus for the market, and rising rates are generally a negative. Inflationary trends, too, are relatively predictable but business, financial, and liquidity strength of corporations can change very, very quickly. New competition, drying markets, changes in the executive suite, scandal, wars, even the weather can send income into a nose dive and corporate stock into the cellar. Just think of past investment disasters (unless you were a short seller): asbestos and Johns Manville, IBM and its changing marketplace, Digital Equipment and its marketing management, and Union Carbide and Bhopal.

There are also other risks associated with investing that can destroy any portfolio, no matter how solid the fundamentals of the securities it contains. These include governmental and political risk, war, defaults, and foreign exchange and expropriation risks.[2]

Buying Puts

Bullish investors sometimes like to hedge their long positions in stock with long positions in puts. In Chapter 2, you were introduced to puts from the perspective of the writer. Now, let's look at them from the perspective of the buyer, and then from the perspective of the hedging bull.

Bears buy puts because puts generally go up in value when the underlying stock goes down in price. It is a way for bears to profit very handsomely when the stock market tumbles.

In the next part of this book, we begin looking at tools of the bull in detail. The first subject is buying stocks long, then buying calls long. Stock and options traders need to know how to hedge with puts. While the real detail on puts does not come until later in this book, you have had at least an introduction to them in Chapter 2 and know something about the leverage they can provide from Chapter 3. Now you will see they can be used to hedge positions. By the time you reach Part 4 of this book, which covers puts in detail, you will already be acquainted with them, and will be able to breeze through an otherwise complicated subject.

EXAMPLE #17. Profiting by Buying a Put

You have purchased one put on Merck stock for $300. The value of the stock when you purchased the put was $30. Before the expiration date of the contract, Merck slides to $25 per share. The put, meanwhile, has increased in value to $800. You decide to take your profits and, therefore, sell the put. Your profit is $500 ($800 − 300).

You never at any time were required to maintain any position in the underlying stock, but you profited as though you sold short 100 shares, for each put represents 100 shares of stock. How much would you have had to put up if you sold short 100 shares of stock? Given 50 percent margin, $1,500. How much did the put cost? $300.

The risks are somewhat more limited for put buyers than they are for short sellers of stock. This is because the stock can double or triple in price and losses can mount significantly. But the put buyer can only lose the amount he pays for the put plus commissions.

But why would the bull want to buy puts when this is the bear's game?

Consider that the put usually goes up when the stock goes down (and down in price when the stock goes up). This means if you are long on the underlying stock, and the market goes against you, the put will cover part or all of your losses and possibly even let you come out a winner altogether. As puts can be expensive, generally investors hedge with very low-priced puts, hoping to make the profit on the stock. As indicated in Table 4–1, the lower-priced puts with the same expiration date and striking price are almost always the out-of-the-monies.

The best rule of thumb for buying puts is that if you are going to hedge, hedge with low-priced puts; if you are going naked, buy the higher-priced puts. As a bull, however, you will be much more interested in *writing* puts for additional income and in selling (writing) them as a hedge.

Table 4–1
Put Premiums

Option/Strike		Exp.	—Call— Vol.	Last	—Put— Vol.	Last
ADT	10	Mar	95	$11/16$	. . .	. . .
AFLAC	30	May	47	2	. . .	. . .
ALC Cm	35	Apr	50	$2 1/16$	501	$15/16$
A M R	60	Mar	100	$2 5/8$	105	$1/8$
63	65	Mar	3	$1/8$	65	$2 1/2$
63	65	Apr	48	1	15	$3 3/4$
A S A	45	Mar	146	$1/4$	8	$3/8$
$44 3/4$	45	Apr	95	$1 3/4$	71	$1 3/4$
$44 3/4$	50	Apr	100	$7/16$	50	$5 1/2$
AST Rs	20	Apr	45	4	. . .	. . .
$23 3/4$	25	May	58	$1 5/8$	. . .	. . .
$23 3/4$	30	May	37	$9/16$	. . .	. . .
Abbt L	30	May	222	$9/16$	11	$2 7/16$
$28 3/8$	30	Aug	171	$1 1/8$	. . .	. . .

Note that for each of the puts in the above listings, as well as for the calls, the premiums at each striking price are higher for later contract expiration months. Additionally, premiums for the puts increase as the stock prices retreat from the striking price.

Straddles

Hedging a long position in stock with a long position in a put is called a straddle. The straddle is a valuable strategy when dealing with volatile situations; these may be stocks that are targeted for takeover, that may be affected by some political or natural catastrophe, or that stand to gain by some new product. You take positions in these stocks expecting them to soar. As the insiders will already be taking positions in these stocks, the stock prices will already have begun to move. When you jump in, then, you need a parachute—for what if you guess wrong or the stock has already had its run?

This is where the put comes in.

EXAMPLE #18. Breaking Even on a Straddle

You purchase 200 shares of Golden Nugget stock, anticipating that it will be taken over by Mirage, Inc. You pay $3,000 for the stock. Fearing that the takeover may fall apart, you also purchase some low-priced far-out-of-the-money puts—perhaps 10 at $.25 each (for a total of $250).

As luck would have it, the takeover does not occur (but does later on). The stock falls to $15 per share, and you lose $1,000. However, the puts increase in value to $1.25, while the stock declines in price. (Remember that each put represents 100 shares of stock.) That means their total value is now $1,250. As you only paid $250 for them, your profit is $1,000. The straddle has allowed you to break even despite the heavy loss on the stock.

The cost of the puts and of the shares of stock influence your break-even point on the straddle. This means the stock or the options have to move much more for you to make a profit than they would if you were long on only the stock or only the puts. However, it is worth the higher break-even point to reduce the downside risk.

The straddle is not a particularly good strategy on stocks that have a narrow trading range, such as utilities, which are rarely, if ever, volatile. The cost of constantly opening new positions on the options after the old positions expire will mount up and cancel out your dividends as well as, possibly, your capital gains.

On the more volatile—or potentially more volatile—issues, the straddle can be played for top dollars, with either long or short positions on either the stock or the puts.

For example, suppose that, in the above example, you hedged with 20 puts instead of 10. In this case, the profits from the puts would double to $2,000. Subtract from this the $1,000 you lost on the stock, and you come out ahead by $1,000. The takeover never occurred, but you still made money.

But if something can go wrong, it often will. Suppose in either instance, the stock just stayed where it was, or retreated too slightly and too close to the expiration date of the puts to affect any upward movement in the options. In this case, you might lose all the money you paid for the puts, plus commissions. You would also lose additional money on the closing stock transaction and/or commissions.

There is another type of straddle, and this involves two options—a put and a call. In this case, you are long on the put and long on the call. The position is based on the premise that if the underlying stock moves sufficiently, the put and the call will move in opposite directions, and one or the other will assure profit.

The catch here, of course, is that often a stock does not move enough before the puts and calls expire and the straddle is ineffective. Puts and calls do not necessarily move in the opposite direction. Remember, these are decaying assets. As expiration dates approach, if the underlying stock does not make a substantial move in price, both the related puts and the calls will depreciate in value. Straddles, whether made of stock and options or just options, can only be successful under the following circumstance: The underlying stock must move substantially enough to offset any time decay in the options and allow either the put or the call to advance far enough to offset the cost of the straddle. (See Table 4–2 for further clarification.)

Spreads

Spreads are designed to take advantage of the price relationship between two or more options. Bullish speculators use primarily what are called "bull spreads" to reduce their risk. In the bull spread, the speculator buys and sells calls having the same (but not always) expiration date. The striking price on the calls, however, will

Table 4-2
The Option Straddle

Option /	Strike	Exp.	Call Volume	Call Last	Put Volume	Put Last
Comcst	20	Mar	187	15/16	—	—
21⅛	20	Apr	130	1¾	—	—
Cmc sp o	20	Mar	70	3/8	—	—
Cmdr In	5	Aug	40	¼	—	—
Comp USA	20	Mar	612	1⅜	—	—
21½	20	Apr	40	2¼	10	7/16
21½	20	May	44	22¹¹/16	—	—
21½	22½	Apr	290	11/16	68	1⅝
21½	22½	May	51	1½	—	—
21½	25	Aug	41	1⁹/16	—	—
21½	30	May	45	⅛	—	—
Compaq	85	Apr	13	19¼	68	¼
104¼	85	Jul	200	22	30	1⅝
104¼	90	Mar	38	14⅛	5	1/16
104¼	90	Apr	275	15	245	9/16
104¼	95	Mar	176	9¼	5	1/16
104¼	95	Apr	287	10¼	69	⅞
104¼	100	Mar	2079	4⅛	498	1/16
104¼	100	Apr	1286	6¼	583	1⅞
104¼	100	Jul	55	10½	10	5
104¼	105	Mar	6924	¼	973	1¹/16
104¼	105	Apr	1301	3¼	92	3⅝
104¼	105	Jul	65	7¾	189	7½
104¼	110	Apr	787	1⅜	3	6¾
104¼	110	Jul	96	5¾	9	9½
CmprsL	12½	Mar	40	5/16	—	—
Cmptrx	5	Mar	45	3/8	—	—
CmpAsc	35	Mar	104	4⅝	—	—

Option straddles work only if each option has the same expiration date and the same striking price. In the above listing, some put and call combinations representing straddles are circled. Any put and call combination above, however, would be a straddle as long as expiration and striking prices are the same.

be different. In a bull spread, the call written will always have a higher striking price than the call purchased. (See Table 4–3.)

Another type of spread that may be attractive to the bullish investor is the calendar spread, wherein the speculator buys and sells calls with different expiration

Table 4–3
The Bull Spread

Stock: IBM

Stock Price	Strike Price	Expiration	Call Price	
55	45	Jul	10	
55	50	Mar	6¾	
55	50	Apr	7¾	Sell
55	50	Jul	8⅞	
55	55	Apr	3¼	Buy
55	55	Jul	5¾	
55	55	Oct	6½	

The bull spread is a strategy designed for those who have a very positive outlook for the underlying stock but want to hedge just in case. They buy and sell calls at the same time. The call bought will have a lower striking price than the call sold but have the same maturity. The easiest way to do a bull spread is to purchase an at-the-money call and sell an out-of-the-money call on the same stock. The objective is to be long on the option that will have a greater price increase if the market rises. The short position, which produces income, reduces the cost of the long position.

dates, hoping that when she makes her closing transactions the credits to her account will exceed whatever the costs of the spread were. The buy and sell transactions required to close out the calendar spread must be made simultaneously.

There are other types of spreads, but these are either combinations of bull and bear strategies or require so many positions at one time that they represent too much of a hedge to make being in the market worthwhile except when some very special price movements occur.

Spreads of the above type, which are especially designed to hedge the speculator's bet, are very different from the types of spreads that speculators, such as arbitragers, may use as part of their aggressive speculative programs. In arbitrage, profits are realized from the spread between stock prices in different markets.

Arbitrage, however, is no game for the little guy. It is a game for only the highly skilled, the highly experienced, and the well-placed. By well-placed I mean that the investor is able to take advantage of immediate developments, which the average investor, listening to cable reports or occasionally checking his computer's stock quote program, cannot do.

Covered Calls

Covered calls are by nature a hedging tool. With the covered call, you are immediately long on the underlying stock and short on the option.

With a covered call strategy, you can bring in extra income even when the underlying stock is relatively stagnant. This is because once you sell the call, you receive the premium (less commissions). The premium is yours to keep. If the underlying stock never reaches the striking price before expiration time, you get to keep the stock as well as the premium.

On the other hand, if the stock is called, you get to:

- Keep the premium.

- Profit on the underlying stock.

But you can only be sure of profit on the underlying stock if you have written covered calls that are sufficiently out-of-the-money, as Table 4-4 indicates.

Do you have to give up your stock if the related calls go in the money? No, absolutely not. If the underlying security reaches the striking price or passes it, you may buy back your covered call and then if you wish to reduce the loss on the option, may sell another one that is out-of-the-money. The premium from the second call will offset some or all of the loss from buying back the first, while you continue to profit from the surge of the underlying stock. (For further clarification, see Table 4-5.) You may continue to buy back and write new covered calls as long as it appears to be to your advantage.

The rule remains, however, that the safest bet is in writing out-of-the-money calls. The underlying stock is less likely to be called out from under you; the value of the call will depreciate quickly as the expiration date nears (which, as a writer, you want to happen; that is, time decay is on your side); and you will almost always sell the underlying stock at a higher price if it is called.

There are advantages, also, to writing at-the-monies and in-the-monies, but the disadvantages outweigh the advantages. For instance, with in-the-monies, the stock may be called at any time, and the chances of participating in a bull market for the underlying stock are rare; and with at-the-monies, a small upward movement in the price of the underlying stock puts your position in jeopardy. Premiums are also higher for at-the-monies and in-the-monies, which means higher commissions.

There is a serious mistake that even the pros managing trust accounts often make. This involves the selection of the underlying security for any covered call trades. Brokers like to set up discretionary covered call programs for their customers. On the surface, these are great income producers for the portfolio as well as for the broker. The broker stands to earn much more in commissions from a covered call account because he can legitimately buy and write options on the same underlying stock many times throughout the year.

Less sophisticated portfolio managers will often select underlying stocks that have calls commanding typically high premiums. These are generally higher-priced stocks which the marketplace feels have great upside potential. The broker gets to write calls and to buy them back as the underlying stock approaches the striking price. Or he just lets the stock be called. His argument is that the portfolio gains in the long run because of the high income received from the call writing. But the truth is, the portfolio often does better when the call writing program is balanced so that the portfolio can not only be buffeted by call premiums but also by the underlying stock's participation in any bull market.

Table 4-4
Profiting on the Underlying Stock in a Covered Call Strategy

Stock: ADMIN ASSOCIATES, INC.
500 shares purchased at $30 per share on 12/21/92

Call Trade Dates	Buy (B) or Sell (S)	# of Calls and Expiration	Stock Price	Call Price	Net after Commissions	Dividends Received	Date
12/22/92	S	5 Apr 30	29½	1¾	$ 800	175	3/15/93
8/2/93	S	5 Jan 30	25⅜	7/16	180	175	7/5/93
1/21/94	S	5 Apr 30	27½	⅜	140	200	9/17/93
5/6/94	S	5 Jul 30	27⅛	⅜	140	200	12/14/93
8/1/94	S	5 Oct 30	29½	¾	325	200	3/15/94
10/21/94	S	5 Jan 30	26⅛	⅛	15	200	6/14/94
1/17/95	B	5 Jan 30	30⅝	⅝	(315)	200	9/16/94
1/17/95	S	5 Apr 30	30⅝	1½	680	200	12/16/94
				Totals	$2,280	$1,150	

500 shares sold at $32 on 1/20/95

Here we have an example of a $2 per share profit on 500 shares held for 25 months. However, a relatively successful call writing program brought in another $2,280 in profits bringing the total profit to $3,280 on an original investment of $15,000. This is better than a 20 percent total return for the period. When dividends are included, the profit is $4,530 for the period or roughly 30 percent for the period. (Note that on 1/17/95 the calls sold on 10/21/94 had to be covered and there was a loss of $300. This sometimes occurs during a covered writing program.)

Table 4-5
Churning Covered Calls

Stock: SHERMAN PRINTING, INC.
500 shares purchased at $30 per share on 12/21/92

Call Trade Date	Buy (B) or Sell (S)	# of Calls and Expiration	Stock Price	Call Price	Net after Commissions	Dividends Received	Date
12/22/92	S	5 Apr 30	29½	1¾	800	175	3/15/93
8/2/93	S	5 Jan 30	25⅜	7/16	180	175	7/5/93
1/21/94	S	5 Apr 30	27½	⅜	140	175	9/17/93
3/15/94	B	5 Apr 30	26	¼	(75)	175	12/14/93
3/15/94	S	5 Apr 25	26	1¼	675	175	3/15/94
5/6/94	S	5 Jul 25	26	1½	700	175	6/14/94
7/8/94	B	5 Jul 25	24	¼	75	175	9/16/94
7/8/94	S	5 Oct 20	23	3¼	1,550	175	12/16/94
9/21/94	B	5 Oct 20	20	¾	(325)		
				Totals	$4,120	$1,400	

500 shares sold at $18 on 10/21/94

Here we see a lot of income generated from both call writing and dividends. But losses on the stock are $6,000. If activity such as this is a recurring situation in a discretionary account, it may be the result of deliberate churning and should be seriously investigated, for the effort appears to be mainly for commissions on options transactions and not on total return or at least the preservation of capital.

Covered call writing is a balancing act. The portfolio manager must always be calculating the comparative advantages of a straight call writing program against one that also squeezes additional profits from capital gains in the underlying stock.

Shorting against the Box

Shorting against the box is another type of hedge, but one which is used for very different reasons. It is basically the shorting of an equal amount of the same stock in which you are currently maintaining a long position. It is generally used as a delaying tactic—either for tax or delivery purposes. It puts your positions on hold. For example, if the long position goes up 10 points, the short position goes down 10 points.

EXAMPLE #19. Shorting against the Box

Karen Rigg owns 1,000 shares of Citicorp common, which she purchased at $15 per share. The stock is now at $40 per share, and her taxable gain if she were to sell the shares is $25,000. However, it is to her advantage to take these profits next year when she expects to be in a lower tax bracket. But if she tries to hold onto the shares until next year, they may go down in price. Thus, by trying to save tax dollars, she may lose three times as much through price depreciation. She, therefore, informs her broker to sell 1,000 shares "short against the box," and holds onto her short and long positions until after the first of the year. If the stock goes down in price, she gains on the short position while losing on the long. If the stock goes up in price, she gains on the long position while losing on the short. In other words, any price movement in the stock cannot affect her. She locks in her $25 per share profit less the additional commissions the short position will necessitate. However, she also prevents herself from being able to participate in any bullish surge by the stock. But that's the trade-off necessary in shorting against the box.

There are other reasons for shorting against the box. Sometimes an investor is not in a position to deliver securities in time to her broker, and she opts for also shorting an equal number of shares in the stock in which she is long. In doing so, she locks in her profits until she returns from her European vacation and can access her safe deposit box for the shares to be delivered.

An equally good reason to sell short against the box is the one that follows.

Suppose that someone gives you shares of stock as a gift. These shares have been in their portfolio for years. And suppose that these shares are at a price four times or more above their original purchase price. If you sell the stock, the cost basis for tax purposes is the original purchase price. Thus, you decide to hang on to the stock, for the capital gains are far too much at this time—meaning, for someone in your tax bracket.

Good idea! But now assume that the stock is Merck or some other pharmaceutical under tremendous downside pressure because of the Clinton Administration's policies. This puts you between the devil and the deep blue sea. If you sell the stock, the tax impact is enormous. If you keep the stock, you will lose drastically when it plummets. Either way, it seems, you will lose—either to the IRS or to the market-place.

What to do? You guessed it. Sell short against the box until it is advantageous to take your profits or maintain only a long position in the stock.

Perspectives

Hedging is expensive because it requires positions in two or more securities. It is not always ideal for the heavily bullish investor who wants to make a killing in the market. But few independent investors ever make a killing in the market, so playing it safe is always the best way to go.

It seems a contradiction to consider that speculators should hedge, for hedging by its very nature takes the speculation out of investing. Yet there are speculative investments, such as options, which remain speculative even when spreads or straddles are being employed. There are many types of hedges, some designed for futures trading, others for options, some for bears, some for bulls, and so on. Those discussed in this chapter are, however, among the most practical for the small, independent investor.[3]

The Smart Money often hedges. Being naked (meaning unhedged or uncovered) in the market often tries one's mettle and often results in quick turnarounds or closing positions (in the case of options). Investors usually sleep better when they are at least partially hedged, as there is no telling when the market will suddenly jump to new highs or plummet to new lows. The same goes for stocks. The market always takes a dip once in awhile, just as it sometimes does a bull run. Isn't it nice to know that those 1,000 shares of IBM you own are insured by 10 puts that can quadruple in price if the stock falls 5 or 10 points? Isn't it also nice to know that short position in 1,000 shares of Merck is partially covered by 10 calls that will absorb some of your losses if the stock does a quick turnaround?

A good rule of thumb for the bull is to proceed on the basis that:

1. When the market falls, it usually falls at a higher percentage than it realizes when it's on the climb.

2. When the market falls, it falls with a vengeance. And it will dip and plunge at unexpected times.

3. Be prepared.

Many bulls were caught dusting their horns on Black Monday. This was the October 19, 1987, stock market collapse. It started on the New York Stock Exchange and dominoed through the other American and world financial markets. The Dow Jones Industrial Average fell more than 500 points, over 20 percent of its value. Though trading remained heavy, there was little that could be done to stop the decline.

Prior to this event, the last major upheaval in market prices was the great Crash of 1929. But that was nowhere as drastic as the 1987 crash. The Crash of 1929 represented only about 13 percent of the DJ Industrials.

The investment community still hasn't decided who or what was the culprit in the 1987 Crash. Many argue that portfolio insurance and index arbitrage may have started the slide. Others argue that the fault lay with the inherent volatility of all world markets at the time. There was too much leveraging all around; the world markets were not firmly based.

In any event, bulls running naked in the marketplace got caught with their pants down. Merck dropped 22 points, IBM 13 points—all in one single day. Investors owning those stocks who were also covering themselves with puts made out fairly well. Those with covered calls as hedges at least were able to offset some of their losses.

It can happen anytime. And to prove the point, look at October 13, 1989. Tremors again! The Dow Jones Industrials dropped 190 points that day, sending a cold wind throughout the world markets. After 1987, they said it couldn't happen again. But it did; and it will happen again.

The lesson: Don't run naked into the marketplace.

The Red and the Black

It is important, also, to always know exactly where your break-even point is so that you understand your possibilities and probabilities of turning a profit. On spreads and straddles, you must be sure you understand what it will take for you to move out of the red and into the black, and that immediately upon setting up a spread or straddle you are in the red. Brokerage commissions make sure of that.

If you buy 1,000 shares of Citicorp for $30,000 and pay a $300 commission, the stock only needs to move about $5/8$ of a point before you begin to profit (given another $300 in commissions on the sale side). But if you hedge your position by buying 10 out-of-the-money puts for $1,000 including commissions; then your stock must move a full $1\frac{5}{8}$ of a point before you break even.

For the Big Money, this is not a bad hedge, nor a particularly worrisome break-even point. However, for the Little Money that can only purchase a few round lots of the stock at a time, the cost of hedging can push the break-even point relatively high.

Consider, for example, an investor who buys 200 shares of Citicorp at $30 per share and pays $90 in commissions. Including the sell commissions to come, this means that the stock must move up roughly $1 per share before she can begin to profit. If she purchases two puts for $250 plus commissions, this means the stock must climb a full $2.25 per share before she will be in the black.

As you can see, the investment game favors the rich. The large amounts of money they can invest keeps their break-even points relatively low. The Smart Money above needed a mere $1\frac{5}{8}$ of a move in the stock to profit; the Little Money needed $2\frac{1}{4}$. The Really Big Money can profit on moves of even $\frac{1}{4}$ of a point or less.

Investment firms with millions of dollars to invest in any single security have inherent leverage. The big bucks they come in with allow them to keep their break-even points close to the entry point, as well as giving them great advantage in negotiating trading commissions when necessary. But they have a big disadvantage that the Little Money does not have—it's very hard for the Big Money to get in and out of stocks very quickly.

Even with their great financial strength and teams of investment researchers, the Big Money is still very leery about leaving their positions uncovered. They may not always hedge with the tools described, for at their level of sophistication they can make more subtle types of hedges work very well for them. For instance, they may constantly change their cash-to-investment ratios as the market rises and falls, or put equal amounts of money in varying stock groups. These are indeed effective ways in which to hedge one's bet.

Notes

1. Glenn G. Munn, F. L. Garcia, and Charles J. Woelfel, *Encyclopedia of Banking and Finance*, 9th ed. (Chicago: Probus, 1993), 910.

2. Ibid.

3. For instructions on additional hedging techniques, see T. Noddings, *Superhedging* (Chicago: Probus, 1986).

5

THE IMPORTANCE OF SMART ORDERS

A necessary part of any investment strategy is placing smart orders. In the stock and options markets, there are a number of types of orders that are especially suited to long buyers or to short sellers or to both. The bull usually has special considerations the bear does not have.

Major types of orders for stock and options traders are:

- Market orders
- Limit orders
- Discretionary orders
- Day orders
- Open orders
- Stop orders
- All or none
- Fill or kill
- Cancellation orders

Table 5–1 rates the types of orders in terms of their applicability to stock and options trading.

Market Orders

Market orders are those orders to be executed at the best obtainable price. Market orders apply to opening positions as well as closing positions. A market order is a default order. If no price is stated by the buyer or seller, the broker assumes the transaction is at the market price. Speculators looking for quick profits and ready to trade even on movements of less than a point are rarely interested in placing market orders. This type of order is generally for the long-term trader. By placing a market order, he is assured of ownership.

Table 5–1
Rating Stock and Option Orders

Type	Description	Options	Stock
Market	Immediately at the best price	2	2
Limit	At the price limit or better	1	1
Discretionary	Whenever the broker wants	2	3
Day orders	By the close of market	3	2
Open orders	Good-till-cancelled	3	2
Stop loss	Buy or sell when stock falls to, or reaches, a certain price	n/a	2
All or none	No partial orders	1	1
Fill or kill	Fill immediately or cancel	2	2

1 = recommended
2 = occasionally beneficial
3 = not recommended
n/a = not applicable

EXAMPLE #20. The Market Order

You call your broker and ask him to buy 100 shares of Grumman for $45 per share. Before the order is placed, Grumman advances to $46 per share; you will not be able to get the stock unless it rolls back in price during the term of your order, which may be a "day" or "good-till-canceled" order (also known as limit orders).

Sometimes, market orders work against you. You can very well wind up buying at the high of the day or the high for the rest of the life of the stock. Other times, market orders can work to your advantage, as in the case of a $6 stock that is at $25 when your order is placed.

Because market orders are executed shortly after they are received (as quickly as the broker can place them), they are not ideal for buyers of puts and calls. Put and call prices can fluctuate considerably in very short periods of time, and it is easy to wind up paying much more for an option than you had planned.

On the sell side, market orders are generally wise, as the rule of thumb for most trades is, "In slow, out fast."

Limit Orders

Limit orders are buy or sell orders for execution at a stated price. These are ideal for investors who have very specific goals as well as for speculators. The broker can only execute the trade at the specific price specified in the order.

EXAMPLE #21. The Limit Order

Assume that IBM is selling at $50 per share, but you are expecting a pull-back. So, you give a limit order to your broker to buy at $49⅛. If the stock drops "below" that price, your order will be executed. If your stock drops "to" that price, you may or may not get it, depending upon how many orders are ahead of yours.

Brokers vary in terms of the limit orders they will accept. Some will accept good-till-canceled and day orders only; others may accept weekly or monthly orders.

For long and short orders in puts and calls, consider limit orders an absolute necessity. The one exception may be in covered call writing.

Most independent traders deal in low-priced out-of-the-money options and tend to purchase them in quantity. For instance, they may order 10 puts at $¾, which means a $750 investment. If instead of a limit order, they were to use a market order, by the time the broker executes it, the puts may increase to $1. This means a $1,000 investment, now, instead of a $750 one.

Because of their low price, puts and calls have built-in leverage, so just a mere ¼ point movement in an option can mean a 100 percent gain or loss to the trader. The rule of thumb, then, for all trading in uncovered options is to use limit orders. It's easy for the price of the options to run away from you. When this happens, you can find your profits slashed drastically or your losses magnified.

Discretionary Orders

Discretionary orders are those that give authority to a broker to manage a portfolio at her own discretion, buying and selling as she may see fit to yield a profit for the account. She cannot be held responsible for losses to the account—theoretically, at least—but in the past few years courts have penalized brokers for mismanagement of discretionary accounts.

Discretionary accounts are moneymakers for brokers. If you have a highly skilled and experienced broker who has been building his own fortune by buying and selling stocks and options for his own account, he can be a big plus for you. But the majority of brokers are primarily order takers who have a great deal of knowledge about how the stock market works; they, however, rarely have the skill for building individual portfolios.

Discretionary privileges allow a broker to churn an account. Remember that a broker gets a commission on every buy and sell transaction. The more she buys and sells (churns), the more money she is going to make, whether or not her transactions are profitable to the customer.

One very unique and seemingly, but not necessarily, effective way brokers will churn an account is to set it up for covered call writing. The inherent safety of covered call writing brings additional income to the customer and lots of additional income to the broker, for every two or three months he is writing a new round of covered calls.

To very experienced brokers and other investment managers, covered call writing can be a program highly beneficial to the customer as well as to the broker. But many brokers get carried away and forget that, even in a covered call program, it is necessary to pay special attention to the underlying stock, for a covered call program entails selecting not only the right options but also the right underlying stocks. While it is unusual to lose money when writing out-of-the-money covered calls, it is not impossible to lose money in the underlying stock. By writing covered calls that are almost at-the-money, at-the-money, or in-the-money, the broker earns higher commissions, for the premiums are higher and the broker's commission is a percentage of the premiums. However, by writing at-the-monies and in-the-monies, the broker takes a covered call strategy from the realm of safety to the realm of speculation and puts the customer at risk. The risk can pay off, or it may not.

Most brokers wisely shy away from discretionary accounts and refuse to accept them. Still, there are some brokers who actively seek them, and if your name gets on a list of active traders, you are likely to receive a call from them. Just remember the following before you give anyone discretionary powers on your account: Few people will handle your money as wisely as you will, and brokers make money by buying and selling—whether you profit or lose.

The one exception may be in the case of options traders relatively new to the game. Timeliness is important for success in options trading, and most investors do not have access to up-to-the-minute quotes. It is impossible for them to be on top of the continuous movements in options prices. Additionally, many investors lack the experience with puts and calls and really need help in learning the game. In this case, it might, on occasion, be a good idea to set up a special discretionary account in addition to your regular cash or margin account. This discretionary account should also have limited funding and represent, perhaps, a quarter of your total investment program. In this way, your entire portfolio is not in someone else's hands, while at the same time you can take advantage of someone who has a lot more expertise than you. Just remember that all brokers are not equal. It takes a long time to develop the skills and knowledge necessary to manage any portfolio. If you do open a discretionary account, look for highly recommended brokers with a long track record of successes and for brokers who are willing to give you a written report of why they decided to take the positions they did.

Day Orders

Day orders are closed out when the market closes at the end of the day. Day orders are also default orders. If, when you place an order to buy or sell a stock or option, you do not specify its limit, the order is automatically a day order.

Day orders make a lot of sense for both option and stock traders. Every day brings new opportunities. Frequent traders like to check the early morning financial news before they take their positions in the market for the day. Leaving an order in "till canceled" or for any other length of time keeps open the possibility that they may forget they ever placed the order. This means they can find themselves buying or selling a security even when they changed their minds about doing so.

Except for covered call writers, day orders are almost a must for options and stock traders.

Open Orders

Open orders are also known as "good-till-canceled" orders. Well aware that traders sometimes forget they have placed open orders, the more ethical brokers will query their accounts on a weekly or monthly basis to make sure no orders are left open unintentionally. Few brokers will ever recommend that any options trader use open orders.

Stop Loss Orders

Stop orders are another way of hedging your bet. With the stop order, you state the price at which you want to either buy or sell a security. For example, suppose you have purchased 100 shares of A. H. Belo at $48 per share. You are expecting the stock to move substantially in the next few weeks, pending some very good news about its takeover plans. But you know that if the company does not expand as intended, the stock price might drop 10 points or more. So, you instruct your broker to put in a stop loss at $44 per share. If the stock drops to $44 per share, the broker will immediately execute your sell order, and you will be out of the stock before it falls any further. As practical as they are, stop loss orders can prove to be very disappointing, because once you have placed them you are not in a position to benefit if the drop in price is only temporary.

All or None Orders

This type of order is frequently used in stock and options trades. It specifies that a purchase or sale must be in the quantity specified, not for any number of stocks or options that may be marketable during the time limit of the order. For most stocks and options, an order can be completed for the quantities specified, but there are certainly enough times, particularly in the case of low-volume stocks or options, when an order cannot be completed in full. In this case, the broker purchases or sells only as many shares or options as he can. This means that it will take two or three trades—and two or three separate commissions—for the trader to complete his goals. However, if an order is given as "all or none," the broker cannot execute it except for the quantities specified.

Fill or Kill Orders

Fill or kill orders must be executed as soon as possible. These are recommended for the options trader. As "all or none" instructions are inherent in "fill or kill" orders, options traders need not worry about paying outrageous commissions for the purchase of a few options. They also assist stock traders who want to make sure they are able to buy or sell in the quantity necessary to increase profits or limit losses.

Cancellation Orders

There are three types of cancellation orders: straight, replacement, or "fill or kill." The straight cancellation occurs with instructions to the broker to cancel an order. The replacement order changes one order to another.

EXAMPLE #22. The Replacement Order

You place an order to buy 200 shares of CBS common at $256 per share. Hours later, you decide you are being too aggressive and would rather spread your risk. So you call your broker with a replacement order: "Mr. Broker, please change my order for 200 shares of CBS to 100 shares at market."

The "fill or kill" order must be executed immediately. If it cannot be, then it is automatically canceled. These cancellation orders add to the trader's flexibility in moving out of or changing positions that he may decide are unfavorable for him.

Other Order Data

The types of orders discussed above are qualifiers. They specify price, duration, and condition. Additionally, there are basic order instructions that must be delivered with all orders.

For stock investors, this includes specifying whether or not the trade is on margin, whether or not it is a short or regular-way sale, and the quantity involved. Table 5–2 is a checklist of considerations that are necessary for ordering stock.

EXAMPLE #23. Buying and Selling Stock

A typical stock order to your broker would read something like this:

"Mr. Broker, I would like to place a day order to buy on margin 200 shares of New York Times common at $33 per share—all or none. I'd also like to place a stop loss at $29 per share. My account number is 194456."

Or

"Mr. Broker, for my cash account, 194450, I'd like to place a market order to sell 200 shares of New York Times common-good-till-canceled and all-or-none."

Ordering options requires additional information. This includes striking price, expiration date, and whether or not this is an opening or closing transaction. Table 5–3 is a checklist for trading options. The example below shows how an instruction to a broker to execute an option order might read.

Table 5–2
Stock Order Checklist

ACCOUNT TYPE
        Cash? _____
        Margin? _____

SIZE OF ORDER
        Round lot?* _____
        Odd lot?** _____

PRICE LIMIT
        Market price? _____
        Specific price? _____

TIME LIMIT
        Day? _____
        Open? _____
        Other? _____

SPECIAL
        All or none? _____
        Fill or kill? _____
        Stop loss? _____

*A round lot is 100 shares.
**An odd lot is less than 100 shares.

EXAMPLE #24. Writing (Selling) and Buying Options

"Ms. Broker, I'd like to *write* 10 January 35 calls on Citicorp for $1. This is an opening position, all or none. My account number is 194456."

Or

"Ms. Broker, I would like to *buy* 10 January 25 puts on Citicorp for $1. Good for the day. This is an opening position, and all-or-none. My account number is 194456."

All option trades must be in cash, so there is no need to specify whether or not either transaction is on margin.

Table 5–3
Option Order Checklist

POSITION
        Opening?   _____
        Closing?   _____

SIZE OF ORDER
        Number of Options?   _____

OPTION I.D.
        Expiration date?   _____
        Strike price?   _____
        Underlying stock?   _____

PRICE LIMIT
        Market price?   _____
        Specific price?   _____

TIME LIMIT
        Day?   _____
        Open?   _____
        Other?   _____

SPECIAL
        All or none?   _____
        Fill or kill?   _____

When ordering stock or options, your broker, or account representative, as he or she may be called, will usually ask you for all required information. They sometimes forget, however, to ask whether or not your order is "all or none."

6

ECONOMIC PERSPECTIVES

Before you place your "smart" orders and trek into the marketplace, it is advisable to consider how you are going to manage your money. Being a good stock picker does not mean you are also a good money manager. To win in the stock and options markets, you absolutely have to know how to manage money: when to be in cash, when to be in stocks, when to be in money market instruments. Most investors are not very good money managers, regardless of their ability to pick a high percentage of winners. Few change the ratio of their holdings in money market instruments, equity investments, and cash for any other reason than they may need cash at certain milestones in their lives. But there are clearly times when the best place to be is in the market, and clearly times when it is the worst place to be.

Guiding Economic Principles

There is no single formula for success in managing investment dollars. A general rule is to stay informed and switch from equity investments to the money markets, or just stay in cash, as market projections or economic indicators may suggest.

There are, however, three economic principles that are as applicable to stock investors as they are to any business person or economist. These are the principles of supply and demand, of diminishing returns, and of economies of scale, briefly defined in Table 6–1 and discussed in following subsections.

Supply and Demand

There is something in economic theory called the law of supply and demand, which generally governs pricing systems. Fundamentally, the law tells us—or is supposed to tell us—how various markets generate order within their systems.[1] The law tells us that when prices go up, demand goes down; when prices go down, demand goes up. As Slavin puts it, "All other things being equal, price and quantity supplied are directly related."[2] All other things, however, are not always equal, so you must expect that the relationship between supply and demand is not consistent, though it is eventual. There are times when demand increases while prices increase, and when demand decreases while prices decrease.

Table 6–1
Guiding Economic Principles

Supply and Demand	The generally orderly system generated by markets as a result of the way demand and supply counter each other. The principle of supply and demand drives the stock market. Prices increase when demand is high, falter when demand is low.
Diminishing Returns	Successive increases or additions of variable production factors to some fixed factor results in declining returns. The principle applies to investment programs that offer too much diversification or keep adding to securities that cannot maintain their market or intrinsic value.
Economies of Scale	Increasing or expanding investments in people, capital, or systems to average out costs of production. The principle, as applied to stock investing, means that buying in bulk reduces break-even points.

In the stock market, this is best depicted when there is a run on a given stock. The more buyers that come in, the higher the price goes; the higher the price goes, the more buyers the stock attracts—until it reaches what is generally referred to as an "overbought condition." Then the price starts to decline. The decline in price scares investors, who feel the stock is going to tumble, so they stay away from it. Because they stay away from it, the stock continues to slide in price—until it reaches what the market believes is an "oversold condition."

Stock prices are governed by the forces of supply and demand. The more popular a stock, the greater its demand, the higher its price. This popularity is based on what investors believe the stock will be worth tomorrow—not what it was worth yesterday or is worth today. People buy or sell stocks based on what they believe its possibilities are at some future time—the investor looking six months or more down the line, the speculator sometimes just looking a few minutes from now.

Demand for a given stock is indicated by its volume. High volume flags a stock for further investigation as a possible buy; low volume flags it for further investigation as a possible short position. Generally, bull that you are, you will want to keep your money on the sidelines when volume is down and in the game when volume is climbing. You do not want to be long on a stock that is not generating much interest in the marketplace.

What kind of volume indicates a worthwhile candidate for further investigation? Certainly that which puts a stock on the "most active" list (Table 6–2), but aside from this, what kind of volume flags a stock as a potential money maker is highly relative. All stocks have trading ranges, some 40,000 to 50,000 shares a day, others much more. When they burst out of their normal trading ranges, then they are likely targets for your dollars. But nothing is simple in the stock market; there are no singularly dependable flags. High volume in itself is not indicative of a bull market,

Table 6–2
Most Active List

NYSE Stocks (Average price of 20 most active = $39)

Stock Name	Closing Price	Group Vol. Chg.	Str.	(mil)	Vol. % Chg.
Hanson PLC ADR	21⅛+	¼	C	7.87	+225
Telefonos De Mex L	61½–	¼	D	3.68	– 22
U S Surgical Corp	20+	1⅝	C	3.63	+176
Mylan Labs Inc	20⅜–	2⅜	E	3.04	+537
Amer Tel & Tel	53½+	¾	C	2.71	+ 30
Amoco Corp	55⅜+	¾	E	2.61	+283
Time Warner Inc	43⅛+	1⅞	E	2.51	+ 79
Chrysler Corp	58⅞–	1	B	2.44	+ 10
Merck & Co	31½+	¼	C	2.36	– 17
RJR Nabisco Hldgs	6⅜+	⅛	E	2.34	– 23
Wal–Mart Stores	27¼–	¼	E	2.32	– 8
E M C Corp Mass	23+	¾	A	2.03	+ 37
Coca-Cola Co	41½+	⅜	D	2.02	+ 24
Y P F Siciedad Anon	25½+	⅜	E	2.02	+ 69
Citicorp	40⅞–	¼	E	2.00	– 2
Philip Morris Cos	54⅞–	1	E	1.96	– 2
I B M	57⅞–	⅜	B	1.89	– 19
Ford Motor Co	62⅜–	1¼	B	1.86	– 2
Pepsico Inc	37⅞+	⅝	D	1.84	+ 23
Airborne Freight Cp	36¾–	1¼	B	1.82	+1330

The list of stocks most actively traded is a way of flagging stocks for further research. The most active stocks during any period of the current day may be gotten from your broker. The most active stocks of the previous day's trading on the major U.S. exchanges can be found in the financial sections of large city newspapers or in the major financial dailies such as *The Wall Street Journal.*

but only of present interest. Only time will tell whether or not there is sufficient reason for that interest. Volume statistics must be weighed with other fundamental and technical signals, such as those described in Chapter 9.

Diminishing Returns

Diminishing returns is an economic principle that states you cannot just add money or supplies or energy and expect increasing returns. A very simple example of this fundamental law is in the case of adding additional human resources to dig a hole three feet in diameter. One person may be able to do the job in an hour, and maybe two can cut that time in half. But add a third and everyone will start getting in each other's way so that maximum efficiency cannot be expected from each worker. You must, therefore, measure the cost of the additional worker against what may now be the expected output.

The law of diminishing returns also governs stock investment in a number of ways. The law applies to portfolio diversification. Many investors, following advice really designed for the Big Money, tend to spread their investments over a wide assortment of stocks. Portfolios valued at no more than $20,000 often contain nine or 10 stocks, sometimes more. In the process of spreading their risks, investors often cancel the advantage of being in the stock market in the first place. For the small investor, risk is best spread through combination plays, through positions represented by straddles and spreads.

The law applies to stockholding in a unique way we often do not consider. If you have $10,000 in American Cyanamid and the value of your holdings increases at a rate of $5,000 per year, during the first year, you will realize an increase in equity of 50 percent, in the second of $33\frac{1}{3}$ percent, in the third, 25 percent, in the fourth, 20 percent. As time goes by, given the same dollar increase in the value of the stock, the percentage of return decreases to a point where you are better off finding another stock. You are just not getting the return on your investment that you once did, although you continue to add your earnings to the principle. Put another way, your rate of return is decreasing with time.

Economies of Scale

Start up costs are always very heavy. Consider, for instance, the production of a book. The format must be designed, the copy must be typeset and proofread, illustrations must added, paper must be purchased for the printing, and then the book must go to press.

If only one copy of the book is going to be printed, then its cost may very well be $25,000. If two books are produced, then their average cost is $12,500. The more copies that are printed and published, the lower the unit cost. The lower the unit cost, the lower the break-even point, and the greater the profit that can be made on each and every book produced. There is, of course, a limit to how many books can be produced to realize economies of scale, for if there are only buyers for 20,000 copies, every additional book over this production number will go unsold—and its cost must be divided over the average unit cost for all books produced.

This same principle applies to the purchasing of stock, in which the cost of commissions must be included in determining the break-even point per share (Table 6–3). The greater the volume, the lower the break-even point, and the greater the profit (or loss) with each movement in the price of the stock.

Economic Forces and Controls

In addition to understanding the governing economic principles above, the stock investor should know how to respond to the business cycles and monetary and fiscal policies. This means understanding how to ride the business cycle; knowing the real meaning of GNP (Gross National Product) statistics; planning for recessions and

---

Table 6–3
Buying in Volume to Lower
Break-Even Point

EXAMPLE #1. You buy 100 shares of AT&T for $60 per share. The brokerage commission is $100. Assuming a sell commission also of $100, the break-even point may be determined by the following arithmetic (done the long way for clarification).

$60 × 100 = $6,000 (cost before commissions)
$6,000 + $200 = $6,200 (cost after buy/sell commissions)
$6,200 ÷ 100 = $62 (break-even point)

EXAMPLE #2. You buy 500 shares of AT&T for $60 per share. The commision rate goes down substantially and may even be negotiable. Assuming a buy-side commission of $300 and a sell-side of $300, the break-even point is now considerably reduced.

$60 × 500 = $30,000 (cost before commissions)
$30,000 + $600 = $30,600 (cost after buy/sell commissions)
$30,600 ÷ 500 = $61.20 (break-even point)

With the larger share purchase, the stock needs to move only 1¼ points before you will realize a profit; with the smaller share purchase, it must move 2 points.

---

depressions; managing investments in periods of inflation, stagflation, deflation, and flation; and reacting to the expected impact of fiscal and monetary policy.

Riding the Business Cycle

The astute investor pays heed to the economic news, ever alert to signals indicating that a new business phase is approaching. When business is booming, interest rates are low and money for expansion is easy to get. This is when the neophytes are chasing the bull and going heavily into those stocks that have been on the uptick. Not the smart money! The Smart Money knows that buying heavily well into an expansion phase is a loser's game. Instead, it holds its positions, taking new ones only if there are signs that interest rates will not rise and the money supply will continue to flow. If there is indication that rates will rise or money will dry up, then the Smart Money moves to the sidelines.

When interest rates begin to climb and money is harder to get, business will begin leveling off. The Smart Money stays on the sidelines, watching carefully to see if the government is smart enough to manage the economy into another phase of expansion. The not-so-smart money is caught in securities that aren't going any place, or are losing ground because there isn't enough money around to bid up prices and sustain a rally.

If the economy begins to contract, the smart money moves slowly, taking short positions and hedging with other techniques of the bear. Or it remains heavy in money market instruments. Most of all, it does not want to get caught in an avalanche of falling prices! Deeper into the contraction phase, the Smart Money waits for signs of easier money and coming reductions in interest rates. When the signs are clear, it takes positions in companies with strong fundamentals, good management, and impressive projected earnings.

The Smart Money will continue to be heavily invested throughout the recovery phase and most of the way through the new expansion period. Then it will unload its holdings again, standing on the sidelines throughout the necessary settlement phase, all the while looking for signs of whether the economy can be managed for new expansion or whether contraction is imminent.

In responding to the various phases of the business cycle (which are numbered and defined in various ways by different economists and interpreted by the author in Table 6–4), the Smart Money performs as the contrarian that it is. It looks at the GNP (Gross National Product), at GDP (Gross Domestic Product), at money supply figures, at interest rate predictions, and at other economic indicators. It wants to go against the tide. It wants to wait on the shore to catch the flood of money the tide brings in. And when the tide reverses, it'll rush out to the other coast, calculators ready, smiles aplenty. Meanwhile, everyone else is riding the tide, trying to scoop up the water rushing for shore—only to land head-first in the sand when the waves toss them to the beach and the tide pulls away.

The Smart Money carries this same contrariness into short-term plays in the stock markets. This is why the smart money likes to pay attention to short interest statistics on the New York Stock Exchange or the American Stock Exchange. Short interest statistics are simply lists of stocks on specific exchanges and the number of their shares that have been sold short. When the number of shares sold short is relatively high, this reflects the sentiment that a stock is in for a decline. When there are many stocks on the New York or American exchanges being sold short, this is an indication that the investment community is not too impressed by the economy's future and is expecting the stock markets to give ground. The Smart Money says they're probably wrong. This is because sentiment is rarely a scientific basis for making sound decisions, and the smart money knows this.

But there is a caveat about short interest that you need to understand. Short interest numbers are often interpreted differently, depending upon whether one is inherently bullish or inherently bearish at any given time. Because when an investor sells short, he must eventually buy back the stock to cut his losses or make his profit, the potential buy-backs set up a bullish sentiment for the market. On the other hand, if the masses are right for a change, then high interest in short selling may be indicative of a market about to plummet. Once again, there is no sure thing in the marketplace, which is why it is okay for financial experts to be wrong 50 percent of the time and still keep their jobs. (Just think how long you would keep your job if you did things wrong 50 percent of the time!)

When bulls interpret short interest statistics to be relatively high, then they sense that the contraction phase for the stock markets is nearing completion and a turnaround can be expected. While everyone maintains their short positions, the Smart Money is getting bullish—accumulating, possibly through dollar cost averaging: $2 million worth of shares on August 1; $2 million on September 1, $2 million on October 1, and so on. In this way if their selections are depreciating in value instead of increasing, they will be picking up greater numbers of shares with each purchase

Table 6–4
Major Phases in the Business Cycle

Phase	Description
1. Expansion	Business activity is growing and setting new records. Production increases to meet new demands. Profits increase and labor wants a bigger share; business responds by making new capital investments, hopefully to meet new wage demands and still turn a profit. The next phase may be phase 2 or 3. There are short-term periods of a) Settlement, b) Contraction, and c) Recovery.
2. Settlement	There is a general leveling of activity with occasional but short-lived spurts of expansion and contraction in various sectors of the marketplace. Depending upon government intervention or free-market forces, the next phase may be phase 1 or 3. Meanwhile, there are short-term periods of a) Contraction, b) Recovery, and c) Expansion.
3. Contraction	Production costs increase, materials and labor are in short supply, money becomes tight and prices are high. Supply begins to outweigh demand. There is stiff competition for every dollar. It's a buyer's market. Depending upon government intervention or free-market forces, the next stage will be phase 1 or 4. Meanwhile, there are short-term periods of a) Settlement, b) Recovery, and c) Expansion and/or crisis.
4. Crisis	Contraction accelerates. Business cannot recover from earlier capital overexpenditures and the credit market begins to collapse. The jobs are no longer there, and neither is the money to meet debt obligations. Chapter 11s and 13s begin. Bank failures increase. Crisis period may result in depression or deep recession. Phases 1 or 5 follow. Meanwhile, there are short-term periods of a) Settlement, b) Recovery, and c) Expansion.
5. Recovery	Business begins to recover, either because the government has initiated certain monetary or fiscal policies or because market forces stimulate new demand. Phase 4 or 1 can follow. Meanwhile, there are short-term periods of a) Settlement, b) Expansion, and c) Contraction.

while they wait for the turnaround. At the same time, their average cost per share will be lower. On the other hand, if their selections head north, with each purchase they are buying a fewer number of shares and their average cost per share will remain less than the current market price. This means they are in the black (profit zone).

It is important to understand that dollar cost averaging is not a fool-proof method for profiting from stocks. If you pick a loser—a stock that heads south and never returns home—losses will mount up as they do in any investment. Thus, even with dollar cost averaging, stock selection must be extremely careful. There are no sure plays in the stock market. (Dollar cost averaging is discussed in detail in Chapter 10.)

You can dollar cost average just as many of the professionals do, but in most cases, you will get eaten up by brokerage commissions. The big money gets all kinds of deals from brokers that you will never get; and their monetary muscle allows them to deal in such quantities that very little movement in stock price will put them in the black. Still, the dollar cost averaging method is the very best strategy for the independent investor. The method simply requires the same amount of money to be invested in a stock at definite intervals. Note that this does not mean that the same number of shares is purchased at each interval. There's a big difference. Purchasing the same number of shares each time means investing varying amounts of money. This strategy does not allow an investor to maintain the same relationships between average market price and average cost that he needs to minimize losses if the stock depreciates or to maximize gain if the stock appreciates.

An independent investor can also ride the business cycle just as the Big Money does. However, it takes a great deal of experience and special skills to do it successfully. The successful investor needs nerves of steel and eternal patience, qualities few independent investors have, mainly because they are always playing with their own money and they usually do not have very much of it. The independent also needs the strength of her convictions and faith in her ability (or that of her advisor) to interpret economic trends. It is very hard to go short on a stock or stand on the sidelines when its trading volume is soaring and its price skyrocketing. The temptation is to ride the wave of excitement, get in on the soaring prices. But this temptation can lead to a fool's journey, because if that stock becomes overbought, the bull is going to be pulled down by the horns.

But how does one know whether the economy is in expansion or contraction phases?

Gross National Product

Business expansion and contraction are measured by the change in the Gross National Product (GNP). The GNP (Table 6–5) represents the total of all goods and services produced by a country. In the last 45 years, every major business expansion has rewarded the investment community with higher average prices for stocks. When GNP is on the increase, the outlook for investors is usually highly bullish.

There is an important relationship between the GNP and economic upturns that every investor should understand. This is that increases in the GNP and increases in stock prices are not time dependable. The GNP can point north and the stock market south. Or they can both point in the same direction. Economic news and stock

Table 6–5
Gross National Product

Year	National GNP (billions$)	Real GNP (billions of 1987 $)
1960	513	1,973
1970	1,011	2,876
1980	2,708	3,776
1985	4,039	4,280
1988	4,900	4,719
1991	5,674	4,850

Above data is based on information published by the Department of Commerce. GNP is composed of four major components: consumption, investment, government purchases, and net exports. Real GNP is also referred to as the constant dollar measure of GNP, as it puts a consistant value on prices from year to year.

market news are usually on their own ferris wheel. However, sometimes they ride together.

Economists are now beginning to rely more heavily on Gross Domestic Product (see Chapter 9) than on GNP for short- and intermediate-term forecasting, but GNP will remain an important indicator.

Stock Market Cycles

While economists identify any number of phases in the business cycle, you must bear in mind that these need not occur in succession or with equal severity or intensity. Economists in government and private industry try their best to prevent the contracting phase of the cycle from developing into major recessions or depressions. Some form of recession must generally be expected because the economy will always go through a period of correction after any major advance, just as an individual stock that you own will fall back in price before it continues its advance—that advance depending upon, again, whether or not it is overbought.

When the national economy is tailspinning into excessive decline, attempts are made to shore it up through the implementation of various fiscal and monetary controls. Or, when it has been in an extended period of expansion, efforts will be made to assure that the settlement period is managed to avoid any contraction. Sometimes there is success; sometimes there is not. The important point is that you must stay alert to economic indicators. Do not guess that a period of expansion will automatically be followed by periods of settlement or contraction, otherwise you may lose everything you own by short selling in the wrong securities or missing a number of great opportunities because you have been waiting on the sidelines.

The stock market and the economy do not move in unison. The market is usually ahead of the economy by 6 to 12 months. Thus, the economic news may be bad, but the "stock market" is gaining new ground. This means that things are about to improve, and now is the time to start taking long positions. Sometimes, it is the economic news that may be good, but the stock market news that is bad. This means things are about to get worse, and now is the time to put your money in the bank.

While the stock market and the economy do not move in unison, it is important for every investor to be aware that stocks, as well as the stock market in general, have their own business cycles (as defined by the author in Table 6–6). The market is continually going through periods of expansion, settlement, contraction, and recovery. Stock market prices do not continue to soar forever. The Dow Jones Industrials may climb in price for a few days, then retreat, then go lower . . . or higher, depending upon how the investment community feels about market performance over the next few months. The stock market actually goes through minicycles each and every day.

Individual stocks have their own bear and bull phases, their own periods of expansion, settlement, contraction, and recovery. In its own bull market, a stock's recovery after each contraction will excite periods of expansion that bring its price per share to new ground. In its own bear market, a stock's recovery will only be

---

Table 6–6
Stock Market Cycles

Phase	Description
1. Expansion	Volume is extensive and prices are on the way up. There are short periods of reduced volume and declining prices, though not necessarily at the same time. There is general euphoria about the market, generally high activity in low-priced issues and wide use of margin. Regular-way buyers of stock and calls and writers of puts have been doing well. The next phase may be phase 2, 3, or 4.
2. Settlement	Prices begin to settle, and the market trades in a relatively short range. Volume is also relatively consistent. Bulls are doing some profit taking, writing calls, or starting to put money on the sidelines. Bears are taking cautious steps into short positions on stock or long positions on puts. The next phase may be 1 or 3.
3. Contraction	Prices are beginning to slide. Supply begins to outweigh demand. Bulls are losing, bears are gaining. Covered call writers are fighting to hold their own. The next phase may be 4, 5, 2, or 1.
4. Crisis	Volume is down and prices are down. The bears are winning big and the bulls are sustaining losses. Put buyers are realizing huge profits. The market is dropping quickly. The next phase may be 2 or 5.
5. Recovery	Volume begins to pick up. The bears are getting out of their positions and the bulls are moving slowly into stocks and options. Prices start to rise. The next phase may be 3 or 2.

short term before contraction resumes. Speculators have often pinpointed the stocks that will go through short-term cycles and they will continually go in and out of them to squeeze out every dollar they can. In this case, their philosophy is that the devil you know is better than the devil you don't, so it's better to play the cyclicals with which you have a strong history of experience. Some investors are so hooked on a few stocks that they stick with them even when their trading ranges remain shallow. Here they can squeeze out additional profit by selling (writing) covered calls.

Recessions and Depressions

Business contractions sometimes result in deep recessions or even depressions. Depressions and recessions can bring about such catastrophic results that businesses fail in great numbers. This creates a situation wherein both business and consumer outlook is so pessimistic that neither is willing to gamble on any upsurge. Production is down, no one wants to invest his or her money, and no one is willing to extend credit except under fail-safe conditions. Supplies have stockpiled and prices have been cut to give-away levels; industry has not been willing to invest in labor or capital; and unemployment is adding to the dilemma! This was the scenario for the Great Depression of 1929–1933, which some of you may have experienced. This was hardly the first in U.S. history, or the worst. There was an even longer depression beginning in 1873; it lasted for almost five and one-half years. In those days, however, people did not have as much to lose and were used to getting by with little.

Depressions are always a possibility. Generations that have not experienced them tend to live economic lives that are sloppy and wasteful; they generally set themselves up for very hard falls when tight money times come. Generations that have suffered depressions—had to stand in line for free food, live hand-to-mouth for extended periods of time—usually learn a lesson that serves them well for future years. Those investors that experienced the depression of the 1930s are the ones that managed to survive the crash of 1987 because their portfolios showed comparative spread expected of investors that know the market can turn on them.

The economic well-weathered may have been in the market in the technical crash of 1987, but they were probably in at least all-cash positions. Younger investors knowing only the higher side of life and easy money were well-leveraged; that is, they were in penny stocks, over-invested, or probably heavily margined.

Penny stocks are great when they rise in price, but when they plummet they need not fall far to rob an investor. A $20 stock needs to drop 10 points per share before its owner loses half his investment; a 50 cent stock only needs to lose 25 cents per share—one tiny quarter of a point—to do a lot of damage.

Stocks with poor fundamentals can often be pulled along in bull markets. But when the bull settles down, these stocks can lose ground very easily. If bears happen to claw their way into the marketplace, stocks with weak fundamentals—no matter how strong the technical indicators—will usually be adversely effected.

Using margin is like playing penny stocks or the weaker high-priced issues trading only on technical strength. It is a great means of profit and quicker wealth in a bull market, but when the market has fangs (bear) instead of horns (bull), the slashing is vicious. With margin, you can buy a stock by putting up only half the money. The broker covers the rest. Thus, if you purchase 100 shares of stock at $10 per share on 50 percent margin, you owe the broker $500. If the stock drops to $5 per share, you're broke. Why? That money is the broker's—and he has the legal right to force you to sell out so he can get his money before the stock depreciates any further.

Understanding that both the national economy and the stock market run in cycles is signal enough never to get too greedy. To the bullish investor, this means never being totally invested in stocks, always being ready to move money from stocks to money market instruments when economic indicators so direct, and always being covered to some degree by low-cost put options—just in case. The puts will sky-rocket in price during sharp declines in the underlying stock on which they were contracted.

Monetary and Fiscal Policy

Every administration fears depression. The current administration is no different. Mass unemployment means mass discontent. People are driven to extremes. Depressions underscore the need for new government. Politicians want to stay in office.

It is up to every government to effectively use the economic controls at its command. It is the only way to encourage periods of expansion and to control periods of contraction. The two means the United States government has to control business cycles are the Federal Reserve System and the Treasury Department.

Through the Federal Reserve System (Table 6–7), the government can manage the money supply and the cost of money. Through the Treasury Department, it can manage government spending and income.

Through the Treasury Department, the government works to control the business cycle in what is termed "fiscal policy." This is the raising and lowering of taxes and the increasing or decreasing of government spending.

Every investor needs to know the kind of stocks she should be in when cost of money or the money supply increases or decreases.

She needs to know what effects increased taxes will have on employment statistics as well as on demand and supply forces. If she does not, she is going to have her money in securities at the wrong time or in the bank at the wrong time. She's not going to be where she should be to profit handsomely.

Economic activity drives the stock markets. More specifically, *what the economy is expected to do* drives the stock markets. No matter how impressive the performance of a particular stock has been or looks to be, no matter how strong its fundamentals, it cannot go against economic tides. A stock is just a small ship in treacherous seas. Don't sail a ship in bad weather; don't buy stock long in an economic storm.

Inflation and Other Economic Pressures

One would think that, in any economy, high employment, rising wages, and an increasing money supply are sure signs of an economic "Camelot." But if there is too great a demand while industry is functioning at maximum capacity and increases in wages are out of proportion to the increase in productivity, new danger can threaten the economy. That danger is inflation. It also occurs when general sources of supply begin to decline or when an increase in the money supply occurs much more rapidly than an increase in productivity. Any of these situations result in higher prices.

Table 6–7
Federal Reserve System

Functioning Body	Description
Board of Governors	Seven members, serving 14 years. The board governs credit and monetary policies. It also supervises Reserve banks and bank holding companies.
Federal Open Market Committee	Sets Reserve open market policy, buys or sells government securities in the open market to control money and credit.
Federal Advisory Council	Made up of one banker from each Federal Reserve District. Confers with the Board of Governors on Reserve business.
Presidents' Conference	Made up of 12 presidents of Reserve banks. Meets frequently to coordinate Reserve operations.
Chairmen's Conference	Made up of 12 chairmen of Reserve banks, who meet informally to oversee matters to their responsibilities to Reserve banks.
12 Federal Reserve Banks	Apply the monetary and credit policies set forth by the Board of Governors through 25 branches and 9 suboffices. The 12 Reserve banks are located in Atlanta, Boston, Chicago, Cleveland, Dallas, Kansas City, Minneapolis, New York, Philadelphia, Richmond, St. Louis, and San Francisco.
Member Banks	All national banks by law and state banks by voluntary request and approval. Each member bank holds stock in the Reserve. They have access to Reserve credit facilities and Reserve services, including check clearance and fund transfers.

The purpose of the Federal Reserve System is to maintain economic stability by stabilizing the dollar, managing international payments, and encouraging incentives for business and employment.

Inflation

Consider the following. If there is too great a demand for the product being produced, a sellers' market occurs and prices accelerate for the product presently available. If wages accelerate beyond the economy's ability to produce, there is more money available to purchase from a limited supply. If sources of supply are greatly diminished, their prices will increase to match the lopsided demand. If the money supply increases out of proportion to the availability of the product, there is more money available to purchase less.

We learn this lesson early in buying and selling stocks or options. If there is too great a demand for a particular stock, the price of the shares begins to climb. As the demand increases, the supply diminishes, putting further upward pressure on the stock's prices. As the holders of the stock become greedy and decide to go for even greater profits, the situation intensifies. The money coming off the sidelines can now buy fewer and fewer shares. The price of the stock is inflated and ready to crash.

In very basic terms, then, inflation means there is more money after fewer goods. The purchasing power of each dollar is severely depreciated. Every bill and coin buys less. The average wage earner must work longer or harder to increase his income so he may continue to purchase the same quantity of goods as before.

Economists often point to the inflationary period in Germany after World War I, which helped sweep Hitler into power, as a prime example of what can happen when inflation is left uncontrolled. German citizens at one time during this period were paying outrageous percentages of their income simply for a loaf of bread. Money was depreciating so quickly that Germany could not print its paper fast enough. By the time a worker received a paycheck, he or she had to spend it immediately—what represented a loaf of bread last week now represented only half a loaf.

In the United States and other developed nations, thanks to economic watchdogs in both industry and government, one will never see such rampant inflation as Germany once experienced. But like it or not, inflation is a constant threat to American economic stability; and it often throws individuals and businesses alike into financial panic. As a matter of fact, it has been one of the major economic ills plaguing America since the Nixon administration. The period of heaviest impact was during the Carter administration, when many of us over the age of 17 were seeing oil prices eating up much of our disposable income and we were often in line for hours to get our ration of gasoline. Those with odd numbered license plates were allowed to buy gas for autos on odd numbered days of the month; those with even numbered license plates were allowed to buy on even numbered days.

Just think of what happens to your savings during a time of 10 percent inflation when the bank where you have placed your money is only paying 6 percent interest. Instead of increasing the value of your money by 6 percent, you are actually falling behind 4 percent per annum. And just think of what happens to the true value of your pay increase if it is only 7 percent in this time of 10 percent inflation.

Business managers are confronted with a number of special problems during times of high inflation. At first thought, it would seem they would profit greatly from inflation, for they can raise the prices of their products accordingly. But rather than realizing any gain, they find themselves caught in a serious economic dilemma. Periods of inflation mean rising wages and salaries in addition to rising prices. The business manager thus finds increased prices bringing about income sufficient only to support the next increases in wages, salaries, and production costs.

It may seem at first that businesses can easily respond by cutting wages. This, of course, creates another problem, unemployment, which we will look at later in this chapter. But cutting wages is no easy strategy. Only in the 1990s have we seen corporations in such panic that they have been able to do just that. Normally, however, pressures from unions and other managerial and marketing concerns often send wages north under almost any circumstances. Add to this the changing of the economic guard from a manufacturing to a less-productive, service-oriented economy and it makes it even more difficult to fight inflation.

Even the government cannot gain from inflation. The value of its currency becomes so eroded it loses its value in the international marketplace. The government winds up with a balance-of-payments deficit, must continually export to meet its monetary commitments, and before long can be operating with such deficits that its own citizens press for political reorganization.

Periods of inflation, however, can be of special advantage to the stock investor; but timing is a crucial element. The investor has to be able to use economic data to interpret that some of the elements leading to inflation are on the increase: high employment, increasing money supply, and falling interest rates.

Stock prices are going to increase during inflationary times; but not all stock prices will. Selectivity is always important. In times of inflation, regular-way investors (buy low first, sell high later) will generally do well, for awhile. They are helped by the technical analysts who generally zero in on stocks or stock groups showing excessive price and volume movement. Then, as inflationary pressures pad stock prices, the technicians get excited and start a seller's market; this starts the inevitable correction of stock prices.

This is why the "new-high" list and trading volume are important market indicators. The new-high list serves as a means for flagging possible market upswings. If the number of stocks setting new highs is continually greater that those setting new lows, then there is usually a sound basis for assuming a bull market is in progress. Overall market volume numbers are important because the smart money knows from experience that volume is a fairly dependable forecaster. They see low volume over extended periods as a sign that the market has bottomed out, and that the economy is ready to follow. However, they do not see high volume over extended periods as a sign that the market has peaked. This is because historians tell us that when volume reaches a relative high for an extended period, the market generally has another 30 percent of the way to go. After it peaks, it generally falls back rapidly. The smart money will be bailing out after 70 percent anyway, while the foolish money waits for the end of the rainbow, often to wind up with an empty pot.

The smart money also knows that price movement and volume by themselves cannot be considered sure signs that an individual stock is in a bull phase. Volume must be interpreted differently for individual stocks than it is for the market as a whole. Comparisons must be made. A stock's price and volume movement needs to be compared to some index, such as the Standard and Poor 100 or some stock exchange's composite, as well as to its movement relative to other stocks in its industry group. Still, it's easy to be fooled. In 1989, the stock of Dow Jones Company (publishers of *Barron's* and *The Wall Street Journal*) suddenly started to show rapid increases in price and volume. Technical analysts jumped on the bandwagon and poured more money into the stock. In short time, Dow Jones stock (common traded on the New York Stock Exchange, options traded on the Philadelphia Exchange) increased 25 percent, up to the low 40s. Unfounded rumors, which are always undermining the credibility of the market and are often started for personal gain, now began to pour in: A takeover was imminent. More money flooded into the stock. Then suddenly, price and volume began to fall back. Someone did some research. A foreign firm had a lot of money to invest during a certain fiscal period. It felt Dow Jones stock was the best gamble. When the investment plan was finally executed over the given time frame, volume and price began to dry up. Before long, Dow Jones was below the price at which all the frantic activity had begun. The stock lost more in the last weeks of the period then it had gained previously.

Here we have seen an example of inflationary pressure on one specific stock. Extend this example to the entire market and then to the national economy. Now you have an idea of how inflation can feed on itself until demand exhausts itself and periods of settlement and pull-back must necessarily follow. On a national scale, however, the government tries to intervene before the marketplace self-destructs.

When the economic news begins to indicate that the government is going to begin tightening up the money supply or business in general is going to reduce its labor force, then it's time for the regular-way investors to rethink their positions. Tight money puts upward pressure on interest rates. The first impact is on preferred issues and on interest-sensitive stocks.

When interest rates begin to climb, as you learned in the previous chapter, there comes a point when the safety of the money markets and other fixed-income vehicles becomes more attractive than stock, which is always a gamble, and this puts further downside pressure on stock prices. The smart money is now chasing after items such as treasury bills and treasury notes (see next chapter) or certificates of deposit.

There are a number of types of inflation:

- Creeping inflation.

- Chronic inflation.

- Hyperinflation.

Generally, each of these provide opportunities for stock and options investors. The types of inflation and perspectives for investors follow.

Creeping Inflation

Creeping inflation generally applies to a rise in the general price index level of no less than 1 percent and no more than 3 percent, although some economists would put the maximum at 3 percent. But these percents are simply relative guidelines. What is considered creeping inflation in one economic arena might be considered major panic in another. To understand this, consider the United States in the late 1970s to early 1980, when the inflation rate was in the double-digits. Under these circumstances, 5 or 6 percent rates would have been considered creeping inflation.

Creeping inflation at the rates given above (1–3%) describes the economic situation that prevailed in the United States during much of the 1950s and 1960s. During these times, the increase in the general price index level never averaged more than 2 percent per year. Periods of creeping inflation usually result in high-priced securities but relatively stable yields.

What this means is that a stock selling at $10 per share and offering a dividend of $1 may, during times of creeping inflation, still maintain the same price-to-dividend ratio (or yield) even though the stock increases in price. For instance, when the stock increases to $20 per share, the dividend may increase to $2 per share. The yield, or return on investment, is the same: 10 percent. (Please understand that the arithmetic here has been simplified to get the point across. Yields will rarely, if ever, stay exactly or nearly exactly the same as stock prices increase.)

Times of creeping inflation are good times for the regular-way investor who does not like to keep constant tabs on his investment and likes to play total yield stocks— that is, stocks that will show good capital appreciation while maintaining or increasing the dividend payout. This type of investor is not really as interested in playing the market as in finding a place to invest his money for the long, long term. He does not want to make an occupation or game out of stock investing. He wants no part of dealing in puts or calls. He's quite content to look at the *New York Times* once a week to see how his investments are doing, and leave it at that.

Put writers may also do well in times of creeping inflation. But, again, it is important to be selective. (Actually, it is always important to be selective, regardless of the economic climate, because there are never any guarantees in the stock market.)

The put writer is usually after the income the put premium affords. As long as the underlying stock on which the put contract is written does not fall below the exercise price by a given date, the put writer can profit handsomely.

Put writing is a bull play and speculative, as you have learned earlier; many investment experts would be cautious about recommending shorting puts. Their perspective is appreciated and respected, because losses can mount up easily if a stock suddenly plummets in price. But on the other hand, if someone is bullish on a stock, writing the put can mean extra income from her portfolio.

A put will, if all other market forces do not counter its movement, go up in price as the price of the underlying stock decreases, and go down in price as the underlying stock increases. When you sell a put, you want the underlying stock to stay the same or go up in price throughout the contract period (a day to a few months). In this way, you profit nicely from your sale. If you sell five puts on Citicorp for $1,000, and Citicorp maintains its current price or increases in value through the contract period, you earn $1,000. The only cost to you is the broker commission on the sale of the puts, maybe $100.

That's the good side. Here's the bad side: As the writer of the puts, you are really a short seller and will have to cover your position if the underlying stock drops too much. As the stock drops and comes closer to what is called the striking price (the price at which the buyer of your put can exercise his option to have you deliver the stock), the puts become more valuable and increase in price. If the underlying stock actually falls below that striking price, you will probably be forced to buy back your puts at a higher price and possibly lose hundreds or thousands of dollars. This is why it is especially important to be highly selective about the underlying stock you select for your put writing program and to make sure you can depend on the current inflationary period to continue to place upward pressure on stock prices.

EXAMPLE #25. Put Writing in a Period of Creeping Inflation

You sell short 10 June Citicorp puts at $2 each. The stock is selling for $32 per share. Each put is equivalent to 100 shares of stock, so the puts actually represent 1,000 shares (10 puts x 100 shares). You receive $2,000 from your broker, which is kept in your account until the end of the contract period or until you close out your option position. The stock goes up $1 per share, and the puts go down 50 cents each. You buy them back at their new price of $1.50 each. Your cost is $1,500 ($1.50 x 1000 shares). Your

profit is $500 (as you sold them for $2,000 and bought them back for
$1,500).

The above plan works well as long as the stock continues to move up. But it's
unfair to just give the good news. You know something already about puts and their
risk, but let's emphasize the risk even further by offering another example of how
you can lose your money very quickly when a put writing strategy does not work.

EXAMPLE # 26. A Put Writing Strategy That Backfires

You sell short 10 June Citicorp puts at $2 each. You receive $2,000. The
stock is selling for $32 per share. The stock goes down $1 in price, and the
puts go up 50 cents in price. You buy the puts back to cut your losses. Your
cost is $2,500. You bought them for $2,000, so you have a $500 loss.
(Remember, as explained in the first example, each put represents 100
shares of stock.)

In the above example, you will have noticed how a one-point change in the price
of the stock (about a 3 percent change) resulted in a 25 percent gain or loss to the put
writer. Put writing is quick income when it works, but can result in severe losses
when it doesn't. Put writing strategies are not for the weak of heart or poor of cash.

Chronic Inflation

Chronic inflation, also a relative term, occurs when the rise in the general price index
exceeds the range defined for creeping inflation in any economic system. It is no
stranger to the United States economy or to many of the other major world economic
powers. However, the United States, most European nations, and Canada will probably never see the chronic inflation that has in recent times swept away the purchasing power of citizens of South American countries. In those countries, inflation, even
since the 1970s, has at times risen to 70 percent or more. But even such a high rate of
inflation as this can be dealt with successfully over the long term through strategic
economic controls.

Periods of chronic inflation are a serious hazard for market bulls. As long as
money remains widely available and interest rates are low, stock prices will march
north. However, sooner or later, the investment community will become scared; it
will worry about government fiscal and monetary revisions coming into play and
begin to back out of its positions. This will reduce demand for stocks and other
securities and start the market south. Warning signs that the market is no place for
bulls are such economic developments as a rise in unemployment, a tightening of
money, and increasing interest rates. Any of these signal tougher times ahead for the
regular-way investor.

Hyperinflation

Hyperinflation is the extreme form of the problem. Prices increase to such a degree
that the national currency actually becomes worthless. Prices double every six

months. This usually occurs only in time of war, and people, gifted with a unique instinct for survival, generally respond by reverting to a barter economy: "Forget the money, I'll give you a cow for two of those goats and use of your well."

The smart money will find another country.

Controlling Inflation

One of the ways in which a government attempts to fight off inflation is through the implementation of a tight-money program. Tight-money policies are instituted specifically to control credit and interest rates, two significant factors contributing to the inflationary spiral. The actual effect is a reduction in credit and upward pressure on interest rates. With credit not only hard to come by and expensive when it is available, demand for goods is reduced.

Tight-money policies do not always accomplish the intended goals. Large industrial nations are not so easily managed. There are just too many variables to consider. Billions of transactions at all levels occur each and every day. An economy like that of the United States is a living, breathing thing in which mass communications and mass psychology also play a significant part. In one era, certain controls might work; in another, they may not. People learn how to react. There is an educational evolution.

As time passes, they react more swiftly to controls or learn to foresee them; they establish new patterns of economic activity (such as switching from stocks to bonds) so early, so quickly, and in such great numbers that by the time the controls are in effect they create new problems instead. Economists, therefore, must be continually tuned to microeconomic and macroeconomic developments so they may be ready with alternate plans if current ones show signs of failure.

The government does have powerful fiscal and monetary authority to move against inflation. There remains, however, no one single method with which inflation can be managed. Sometimes a combination of controls must be used—all at once or in succession. But success always comes at a price. Arresting inflation can mean an increase in unemployment.

When tight money times appear to be looming in the not-so-distant future, it is generally the time to begin backing out of the marketplace and stashing money in fixed-income securities or in savings plans. This is not always easy to do because investors are always afraid of missing the boat or missing the last great gasp of the stock markets before they fall back. Stock investors are generally gamesmen. They are in the stock market because they like the challenge, like the chance for extra bucks. They actually sleep better knowing they can become wealthier with tomorrow's advances. If you find yourself unable to sleep because you have money in the stock market, it's a sure sign this is not your game. Get out quick and put your money into a mutual fund or into the money markets.

Actually, mutual funds are probably the best bet for small investors. They get to have high-priced and successful money managers invest their money for them, and they are freed from any temptation to get speculative and chance margin purchases, options plays, or penny stock gambles. Most of all, many of these funds are no-load, meaning there is no commission paid to join them. Additionally, it's easy to dollar cost average by depositing money into the funds at fixed intervals. At this writing, many mutual funds have been showing average annual returns for the past five years that are well above 20 percent. Some have shown 40 percent advances in just the last year.

Deflation

The problem that economists often confront is that in putting into effect stringent monetary and fiscal policies, they may very well force a decline in the general price index level at the same time that there is a tightening of the money supply and of credit. Now the problem becomes one of deflation instead of inflation. In this case, there is too little money seeking an overabundant supply. Business now sees no need to keep up production schedules and begins to slow down operations. A slow-down means less need for labor. This means higher unemployment.

Think about it. There has been a decrease in production and, as a result, a decrease in employment. Less production and increasing unemployment are sure signs of an economy going into the contraction phase. The smart money will already see this and begin dumping the stocks everyone else is holding—or will cover itself by writing covered calls or buying puts long.

Some individuals automatically gain from periods of deflation; these are the same people who ordinarily suffer heavily in inflationary times. They are usually the elderly who usually remain ahead of the game during periods of deflation because they are generally fixed-income investors. But they must be in true fixed-income investment. For instance, we tend to think of dividends from preferred stock as fixed income. But a corporation is under no legal obligation to pay dividends on its preferred stock. In souring times, they sometimes elect not to do so—or to reduce those dividends. When they do, stockholders have no legal recourse, unless a company actually declares a dividend and then does not pay it.

Dividends are a suspect form of income anyway. They are really marketing and bookkeeping games, in my opinion. They are marketing games because corporations know that people like to receive dividends; dividends reinforce the investors' feelings that their money is working for them and help keep demand and prices up for stocks that pay them. But dividends are actually the *net earnings* of a corporation that are paid out to stockholders. From an accounting perspective, dividends reduce the value of each share of stock. This means that when a stockholder receives a dividend, he is actually borrowing some of his own money back from the corporation and paying taxes on the borrowed money as though it were income.

Flation

On the one hand there is inflation, and on the other there is deflation. Inflation means a decrease in the purchasing power of wages and other income, whereas deflation means increased purchasing power—providing one has a steady source of income.

Inflation usually occurs within the expansion phase of a business cycle, and deflation usually occurs during the contraction phase.

Right smack in the middle of inflation and deflation is something else again: flation, a period of generally stable prices—not perfectly stable, but generally so. Flation does not occur very often in the complex industrial societies of today. The United States last experienced it in the 1950s and 1960s when the wholesale price index varied only $4/10$ of a point. Periods of flation are probably ideal for the covered call writer (Table 2–12). And if they are writing covered calls on stocks that are paying impressive dividends, they stand to have an unusually high income from their portfolios.

Covered call writers understand that the game they play will never make them rich. They are not after capital gains—although they may realize them—as much as they are after income. This makes flationary periods highly suitable for them.

Stagflation

Finally, there is stagflation, a strange hybrid. It is a period of high inflation at the same time that there is little economic growth and/or high levels of unemployment. This is a time for extreme cautiousness for the smart money. If they are in the market, they are hedging strongly, using option calls, or employing stop/loss orders. The stop/loss orders leave them a safety net: If their stocks fall to a certain price, they will automatically be sold, thereby cutting their losses.

Effects of Unemployment

It seems to be a Catch 22. Fighting off inflation means unemployment; fighting off deflation means unemployment.

The record has hardly been impressive. Capitalistic economies have never really been able to manage inflation so that the unemployment rate remains low during periods of stable prices. Of course, governments can play with the statistics to make it look like they are doing this, but the informed investor can see through their ploy.

Regardless of the political jargon that defines types of unemployment and establishes the unemployment rate, the smart money needs to heed the published statistics. Whether unemployment is high or low is of less importance than whether it is on the increase or decrease. If it is on the increase, then it is time to back out of securities or employ tools of the bear (buying puts, short selling stock, short selling calls). If it is on the decrease, then it is time to start climbing back into securities.

Why? Because inflation and unemployment are often on opposite sides of an economic seesaw. When unemployment is low, inflation is usually on the rise, and so are stock prices. When unemployment is on the rise, inflation is soon to be on the decline, and the price of stocks will probably be turning south, unless there are special economic or market forces that are countering the effects of either inflationary or unemployment changes. Countering economic forces may be such things as changes in tax or interest rates, wars, announcements of huge federal deficits; countering market forces may be such things as short sellers covering their positions, technical frenzies (self-perpetuating price and volume movements), takeovers, or unexpected bankruptcy filings.

There is really no one single economic flag that an investor can count on. He has to look at the gamut of economic indicators and constantly evaluate their relationships. Some investors just throw up their hands and say it is all impossible. There is just too much to weigh. Let me just find a few good stocks and pour money into them during the good times and stop pouring money into them in the bad times.

This is also why many investors simply turn to market indicators, which they figure respond to economic developments anyway. It is easier to just round up a few indicators that are easy to follow and offer a means of checks and balances for market predictions and run with them. They look at things like the CBOE Put-Call ratio, Closing Tick Indicator, Arms Index, and the Advance/Decline Indicator, which are discussed in Chapter 9.

Notes

1.   Robert L. Heilbroner and Lester C. Thurow, *Economics Explained* (New York: Simon and Schuster, 1987), 156.

2.   Stephen L. Slavin, *Economics: A Self-Teaching Guide* (New York: John Wiley & Sons, 1988), 194.

7

OPPORTUNITY COST ANALYSIS

Opportunity cost is an important concept because it helps every stock and options investor to realize that it not only costs you when you lose on a transaction, but it also costs you when you do not make as much money on an investment as you could have made elsewhere.

Often we hear about the investor who has never made a bad pick. Every stock he has ever selected has come out a winner. He's not lying. It happens. Some people are not only great stock pickers, but also are in the financial position to hold on to that stock until it sows a profit—whether it be one month from now or 10 years. But often this same whiz could have done much better if he were not in the stock market in the first place but in the money markets, or in real estate, as opportunity cost might dictate.

Being a successful money manager is as important as being able to pick the right stocks and options.

Opportunity Cost

From the perspective of the economist, opportunity cost represents the dollar value of resources needed to develop one product of service or another. Another way of defining opportunity cost is thinking of it as the value of that which must be disregarded because some other good or service is to be produced.

A very simple example of how the principle relates to the investor is illustrated in the following example.

EXAMPLE #27. Opportunity Cost Analysis

You are interested in income opportunities, so you purchase 100 shares of Public Service of Colorado common for $6,000, paying a $2 per share dividend. Yield on the stock at that price is 6.2 percent. You guess that the stock will maintain a very narrow trading range. Twelve months later, after receiving four dividend payments, you decide to sell the stock when it is has dropped to $58.

Dividend Income: $200
Loss of Capital: −200
Return on Investment (ROI): $000

If during this same period you had, instead, purchased a Certificate of Deposit paying 4 percent simple interest (to simplify the math), your return on investment is the interest received:

Interest Income: $240
Change in Capital: 000
Return on Investment: $240

Your opportunity cost for having purchased the stock is:

Projected income from CD: $240

To say, then, that you broke even on your stock transactions, is a very optimistic statement. You actually lost at least $240. At least? Yes. Suppose, instead, you had the opportunity to invest in another stock which eventually showed a 125 percent return while you were holding Public Service of Colorado. In this case, your opportunity cost would be even more—$7,500.

Return on Investment

It is imperative that every investor weigh the opportunity costs involved before deciding to put money in stocks, options, bonds, commodities, money markets, or mutual funds. The questions to ask are: Is there a better place to put my money? What are the risk/reward factors to be considered?

The objective is maximum return. The whole idea of investing in the stock and options markets, in any equity or money markets, is to increase your income and capital. But stocks are unpredictable. The whole market is, ultimately, unpredictable on the short and intermediate terms. Companies can go bankrupt, dividends can be canceled, any series of national or international economic forces can drive prices south. That's good news for the bear but very bad news for the bull.

There are never guarantees, of course, except, perhaps for the income from covered options, and there will always be something better you could have done with your money. You could have invested in better stock; you could have stayed safely in the money markets or some mutual fund that is outperforming not only you but all the popular averages.

Because there is always uncertainty related to stock and option picks, every investor must select opportunities that can reward her handsomely for taking the risks associated with that uncertainty. Thus, one of the underlying themes of this book: Don't go after stocks that can only give you a probable return that is not much better than you can get from interest-bearing certificates that preserve your principle. This also means do not spread your risk so thin that any savings bank can give you a better return on your money. If you are going into the stock market, go for the money. Hedge as necessary, but go for the money. Or get out.

It is no easy task to determine the amount of true return that common stocks will produce or the time it will take to produce that return. Even preferred stocks will sometimes fluctuate considerably, a point many investors fail to consider. Stock investing is a gamble. The expected return must make the gamble worthwhile.

How much of a gamble an investor should be willing to take depends upon a number of factors. These include the percentage of total capital she is gambling with, the possibility of needing that capital before the term of the investment is over, and whether or not the return on investment is worth the risk.

Other Opportunities

So where does the bull put his money when the stock and options markets are about to start working against him, or where does he put it once these markets have already started working against him?

From the standpoint of relative safety, the answers are government securities and the money markets; surprisingly, a large percentage of investors have no idea of what types of investments comprise these markets.

Now it takes a great deal of money to invest in some government securities and also to invest in other money market instruments. Eventually you might have enough money to do so by yourself, but in the beginning of your reach for a million, you will have to invest indirectly in these markets. You can do this by investing in any number of funds that specialize in government and other instruments making up the money markets.

These funds are the money market mutual funds, which have become very popular with both individuals and corporations in the last decade. (See Table 7–1 for a list of benefits.) These mutual funds deal primarily in short-term U.S. Government securities, banker's acceptances, broker/dealer loans, commercial paper, federal funds, Eurodollar certificates of deposit, negotiable certificates of deposit, and repurchase agreements. These securities are collectively known as the money market.

The money market is not a market in the sense that the stock markets are. The money market actually consists of a matrix of banks, financially secure corporations, and federal and local governments. The market extends to major financial centers outside the United States.

The mutual funds that specialize in this market become popular because they offer the small investor not only a chance to get into the money markets, but the chance to have the privilege of an investment that is very safe and liquid. (Table 7–2

Table 7–1
Advantages of Money Market Funds

1. Offer the small investor opportunities normally only available to the Big Money.
2. Pay yields that are usually higher than bank yields.
3. Provide daily income.
4. Are highly liquid.
5. Invest only in high-grade, short-term securities.
6. Pay frequent dividends.
7. Invest mainly in government-backed securities.

Chapter Seven

Table 7–2
Principal Money Market Securities

Name	Summary
Treasury Bills (T-Bills)	3, 6, 9, or 12 months; purchased at discount from face value; minimum $10,000.
Treasury Notes	Quoted on some percentage of their par value ($1,000); fixed rates of interest paid semiannually; quoted in $\frac{1}{32}$s.
Treasury Bonds	Mature in 5–35 years; pay fixed rate of interest; issued at $1,000 par; quoted in $\frac{1}{32}$s.
U.S. Savings Bonds	Primary market only; cannot be transferred to someone else.
Ginnie Maes (Government National Mortgage Association— GNMA)	Sold like treasury bonds at $25,000 minimum, then $5,000 increments.
Fannie Maes (Federal National Mortgage Association—FNMA)	Publicly held; common stock sold on N.Y. Stock Exchange; raises money to purchase FHA and VA residential mortgages.
Federal Home Loan Banks (FHLB)	Mature in 30 to 270 days; $100,000 minimum; pay interest at maturity.
Co-ops (13 Banks for Cooperatives)	Issued by federally charted banks and supervised by U.S. government. Minimum of $5,000; state and local tax exempt.
FCIBs (Federal Intermediate Credit Banks)	Supervised by Farm Credit Association; provide funds to lending institutions making short-term loans to farmers.
FLBs (Federal Land Banks)	Provide first mortgages for farming; $1,000 minimum.

Money market securities are ideal for bulls who want to wait out bear markets. These funds have as their primary objectives investment in high-interest securities providing immediate income and high investment safety.

provides a list of money market securities.) The yields they offer are usually more than can be obtained from a bank, though not always more than longer-term CDs.

Money market yields fluctuate continuously. The rates are never fixed or guaranteed for any length of time. Whatever the yield available from the underlying securities is, is what the investors get, less the net expenses of the fund.

These mutual funds are able to provide investors with daily income, because the purchasing strategy of the funds is to invest deposits on a daily basis. Dividends are usually made available to the recipient on a monthly basis, although most investors just prefer to have the money reinvested, withdrawing it only as needed. Leaving the money in their accounts gives investors the privilege of monthly compounding of interest, a nice way to increase their holdings at a relatively rapid pace.

Liquidity, a very important plus to small investors, is a highlight of money market mutual funds. Investors can usually get their money by simply making a phone call or, in many cases, by simply writing a check, as the funds provide check writing services. In the case of check writing privileges, there is usually a minimum amount that can be withdrawn at one time. Checking is not the same as it would be at your local bank, savings and loan, or credit union.

There is, of course, some risk associated with any investment, and in the case of the money market mutual funds you must understand that they are not insured by any federal agency. Yet the risk is minimal for a number of reasons. The investments are in high-grade, short-term securities selected by professional money managers familiar with government and other securities. Additionally, the funds are regulated by the Securities and Exchange Commission (SEC), are audited by certified public accounting firms, and are required to periodically issue financial status reports to account holders.

Also, the fact that a good part of their investments are in government-backed securities underscores the safety net they provide investors. Government securities were a particularly good idea in the late 80s and early 90s when the banking industry in the United States was in relatively poor shape, but now that U.S. bonds have made a noticeable turnaround, opportunity costs must be more carefully weighed.

The U.S. government depends upon government securities to raise the money it needs to meet its expenses. Because these securities are backed by the full financial might of the U.S. government, they are favored by investors for their combination of safety and tax-free yields; the U.S. government has never once defaulted on any of its securities. They are also appreciated because they are short-term investments, and so large amounts of money need not be tied up for lengthy periods of time; investors can stay relatively liquid.

Government securities are marketed in a very different way. There are a number of financial firms that qualify as primary dealers and who alone are allowed to deal directly with the Federal Reserve to initiate the public market in these securities. These primary dealers trade not only among themselves but also with the general public. In addition to these privileged dealers, there are also banks and securities firms that create a secondary market for these same securities.

The government's shortest-term security is the T-bill (Treasury bill). If you want to buy these directly, you would need a minimum of $10,000; this is why you will buy them indirectly through some fund specializing in these types of investments. The fund will require only a few hundred dollars in investment from you.

T-bills are issued for 3, 6, 9, or 12 months. Three- and six-month bills are auctioned each Monday, with the amount of bills to be auctioned published on the previous Tuesday. All bids are required to be made at any of the Federal Reserve Banks by one p.m. on the day of auction.

T-bills are popular with businesses, commercial banks, the Federal Reserve System, and foreigners, as well as with money market mutual funds. They offer investors some unique benefits. These include high liquidity, exemption from state and local taxes, and no risk to principle. Because they are basically risk free, the bills offer lower interest rates than other money market instruments.

You generally buy these bills at a discount from their face value, and then you redeem them at their full value. For example, you might purchase a $10,000 bill for $9,750, then 91 days later cash it in for its face value. It would be too expensive for the government to make interest payments; discounting the bills at sale is a far more expedient and economical way of allowing the buyer profit. Actually, there is no redeeming the bills because they are never really issued to the buyer. All trading in Treasury bills is done via a bookkeeping entry; there are no certificates for issue. This helps to reduce the cost of issuing these bills in the tremendous volume required.

A secondary market exists for T-bills, and here the bills may be purchased in addition to, or instead of, the primary auction. This secondary market also allows investors the opportunity to sell the bills prior to maturity.

Besides Treasury bills, the government also issues other securities: TABS, Treasury notes, and Treasury bonds. Treasury notes are interest-bearing debt obligations that are quoted and traded on some percentage of their par value ($1,000) and in $\frac{1}{32}$s. (Thus, a bid of 99.16 is actually a bid of $99\frac{16}{32}$, or $99\frac{1}{2}$.) They have fixed rates of interest that are paid on a semiannual basis. They are issued in minimum denominations of $5,000 when maturity is under four years, and in denominations of $1,000 when maturity is in four years. Higher denominations are also available, with interest rates varying from issue to issue.

Treasury bonds are U.S. bonds with maturities from five to 35 years. They pay a fixed-rate of interest and are issued in $1,000, $5,000, $10,000, $100,000, and $1 million denominations. Like Treasury notes, they are quoted in $\frac{1}{32}$s. Most of these bonds have a maximum interest rate of $4\frac{1}{4}$ percent but are offered at a discount from face value so that they will be competitive with other interest rates. The bonds are subject to all federal taxes, including not only income taxes but capital gains, estate, and gift taxes. They are, however, free of all state taxes. The bonds are issued in book-entry form just as T-bills are.

U.S. Savings Bonds are also government securities, but they differ markedly from Treasury bills and bonds in that they are not tradeable securities. There is no secondary market for them. Whoever buys them, owns them; they cannot be transferred to someone else, although a beneficiary may be named in case of death of the owner.

Savings bonds have come a long way; today it is possible to buy them for relatively competitive interest rates. But there are a lot of qualifiers that leave the general public uninterested.

Take, for instance, Series EE bonds, which are purchased at a discount from their face value, and which mature in 10 years. If you cash them in early, you will not earn the full annual rate of interest that the discount would have guaranteed if you held the bond until maturity. These bonds, which are available in many denominations from $50 to $10,000, do not pay interest as do Series HH bonds, for which they may be exchanged. Your profit comes from the difference between the purchase price and the cash-in value. (Series HH bonds, which are available in many denominations from $500 to $50,000, cannot be purchased with money, but only with EE bonds.)

Ginnie Maes (issued by the Government National Mortgage Association—GNMA) have as their only purpose residential financing. Backed by the U.S. government, Ginnie Maes are sold like Treasury bonds and bills—that is, they are auctioned off to the highest bidders. They are purchased for a minimum of $25,000 and then in $5,000 increments thereafter. These are relatively risky securities compared to Treasury bonds and notes because the GNMA must continually reinvest its principal. As the mortgage market is rarely steady, re-investments can quite easily occur at risky times. But investors like the idea that the GNMA pays relatively high dividends on a monthly basis regardless of the collectibility of its mortgages, though its distributions are taxable at federal, state, and city levels.

Co-ops are short-term debt obligations available at a minimum price of $5,000. Unlike the bonds and notes described above, these are not government securities in the direct sense of the word. The 13 banks that issue the securities, however, are federally chartered and supervised by the U.S. government. This makes the co-ops relatively safe investments; and state and local tax exemption make them additionally attractive to large investment institutions.

Unlike Co-ops, Fannie Maes are long-term investments. They are issued by the Federal National Mortgage Association (FNMA), which engages in the purchase of insured FHA (Federal Housing Authority) and VA (Veteran's Administration) residential mortgages. Noncallable debentures and short-term notes, they are purchased at a discount from face value. Like Co-ops, Fannie Maes are not direct government securities, though they are sponsored by the government.

The Federal National Mortgage Association is actually a publicly held company, and its stock is listed on the New York Stock Exchange. You may buy and sell the stock just as you would buy and sell IBM or any other listed stock. But the difference between the FNMA and IBM is that the U.S. government oversees FNMA management and operation and allows it the privilege of borrowing from the U.S. Treasury. However, this privilege does not give the FNMA any special tax privileges; interest it pays out is taxable just like interest from a bank or from corporate bonds.

FICBs are securities issued by the 12 Federal Intermediate Credit Banks which fall under the jurisdiction of the Farm Credit Administration. These securities have maturities that range from nine months to five years, and their purpose is to provide short-term loans to farmers. These securities are exempt from state and local taxes.

FLBs are securities issued by the 12 Federal Land Banks that also fall under the jurisdiction of the Farm Credit Administration. Sold in minimum denominations of $1,000, they mature in one to 10 years and are free of state and city taxes. These securities, however, are not backed by the U.S. government.

Listings

The money market funds dealing in the securities described above may be found in the financial sections of daily newspapers or in the major financial dailies such as *Investor's Business Daily*. Table 7–3 provides a sample listing.

Table 7–3. Money Market Fund Listings

Mutual Fund	1994 Total % Change	Last 4 Week % Change	Net Asset Value	N.A.V. Change
Dreyfus				
A Bonds Plus	− 6	− 1	13.92	.05
Appreciation b	− 4	+ 1	14.30	.05
Asset Allocation b	− 2	0	12.42	.01
Balanced	− 2	0	13.06	.01
Calf. Tax Exempt	− 6	0	14.40	.02
CA Intm Muni	− 6	0	12.98	.02
CT Intm Muni	− 5	0	12.84	.02
Dreyfus Fund	− 5	− 2	12.45	.02
Edison Elec Index	−19	− 8	11.09	.08
FL Intm Muni	− 5	0	12.97	.03
General CA Muni b	− 7	0	12.96	.03
General Municipl b	− 7	0	14.49	.02
General NY Muni b	− 6	0	19.49	.02
Global Growth m	− 4	+ 1	34.22	.07
Growth & Income	− 6	− 2	16.02	—
Grwth Opportnity	− 7	− 2	9.95	.07
GNMA b	− 3	− 1	14.34	.04
Insurd Municipal b	− 8	− 1	17.29	.02
Intermed Muni	− 5	0	13.69	.02
Intl Equity b	− 1	+ 1	15.26	—
Investors GNMA	− 3	− 1	14.61	.03
Muni Bond	− 7	0	12.25	.02
MA Intm Muni	− 5	0	12.78	.02

Mutual funds specializing in government or other money market securities are easily identified among the mutual funds listed in the financial dailies. Here we see a listing of some Dreyfus funds, some specializing, for instance, in Ginnie Maes.

Source: *Investor's Business Daily,* May 19, 1994.

PART TWO

BUYING STOCKS

CONTENTS

8

THE MARKET

The market is in common and preferred shares of stock, either of which can be played for capital gains, although most investors are interested in the preferreds for dividend income as well as preservation of principal, and the common for capital gains or total yield.

Preferred Stock

Preferred stocks are hybrid securities sometimes popular with corporations, which may offer many classes of preferred stock. In this case, dividends must be paid on the first class of preferred before any can be paid on subsequent classes. If you check the listings for General Motors, for instance, you will see various classes of preferreds offered, perhaps class D,G, or P preferred stock. In this case, all dividends must be paid on class D before class G, and on class G before class P.

Preferred stocks represent additional financing flexibility to a corporation. They are a source for additional money with which to operate and expand. At the same time, they attract money that buys no voting power or the chance to share in the profits of a corporation.

Yet they have their appeal. Preferred stocks carry legal right to dividend payments before common stock. Additionally, in those cases where a corporation falls into bankruptcy, preferred stockholders almost always have priority over common stockholders during the distribution of assets. This does not mean, however, that the preferreds are top priority in the distribution of assets, for bondholders and other creditors must be reconciled first.

Preferred stocks are issued with a par value and this par value represents the liquidating value of the stock. For instance, the stock may be issued as 6 percent ($100 par) preferred, or 5¼ percent ($50 par) preferred. These par values represent the maximum entitlement of each share of preferred on the assets of the company.

The par value is also used to calculate the dividends to be received on each share of preferred stock. For example, if you own 100 shares of 5 percent preferred, with a par value of $100, your annual dividend will be $50. If the market value of the stock is $80, $90, $110, or any other amount, the dividend is still calculated based on the par value. There is an exception to this that has to do with participating preferreds. Owners of participating preferreds are entitled not only to dividends based on a percentage of par but also to any special dividends the board of directors of the issuing corporation may decide to pay out. These special dividends, however, cannot be paid until all payments owed to common shareholders are distributed. But not one cent of any of these dividends is ever guaranteed. At any time, the board of directors of the corporation can elect not to declare a dividend—and this happens in hard times. However, once they declare the dividend, they must pay it. This is also true for common stocks.

Dividends on preferreds are defined as being cumulative (wherein the dividend is carried from one dividend period to another, accumulating if not previously paid) or noncumulative. Unless otherwise stated, all preferred stocks are cumulative, and are entitled to all dividends that may be due prior to any dividend payments on common. Nonpayment is unusual but not rare. Corporations do not always make the kind of profit needed to meet their planned dividend disbursements.

Noncumulative preferreds have prior claim to any dividends that may be paid during the year, but in the case of partial payments due to the lack of funds, balances due are lost forever when not paid in the year they are due.

Though the appeal of preferred stocks has mainly to do with the high yield they offer, you will notice in scanning the day's stock listings that some preferreds offer extremely low yields. In fact, some common stocks offer a much better yield. These low-yielding preferreds are usually the convertible preferreds, but not necessarily so, for the range of available yields will vary depending upon the financial strength of the issuing corporation. This convertibility feature offers the owners the ability to turn in their preferred stock for common stock whenever they feel that the common may offer greater potential. (See Table 8–1 for advantages and disadvantages of preferred stock and Table 8–2 for the arithmetic of determining annual dividends.)

While convertible preferred stock may be of interest to the bull who wants to protect his principle and earn a competitive yield while waiting for an opportunity in the object common stock, for the most part you will want to be dealing in common stock.

Common Stock

Common stocks represent a completely different ball game than preferred stock. Common stocks represent ownership. A common share carries with it the legal right to vote for members of the board of directors and to share in the profits of the corporation.

There are other advantages to common stock, as Table 8–3 indicates. Common shareholders have the privilege of ownership with limited liability. They are liable only to the extent of their investment except in one unusual case. This is when the par value of the common stock is higher than the price paid for it. In this case, if the company goes into bankruptcy, the stockholders who paid under par for their stock are liable for the difference to par for each share they own. Corporations usually circumvent this problem of additional liability by fixing the par value on each share of stock at some extremely low rate. Par value on common stocks is really just a bookkeeping entry; par value has no intrinsic meaning, as it once did when its value was determined by the net worth of the corporation backing it. (This does not hold true for preferred stocks, however, because preferreds are, in part, debt instruments and the par value is an important base for determining entitlement when the stock is

Table 8–1
Some Advantages and Disadvantages
of Preferred Stocks

Advantages	Disadvantages
Dividend rate is usually competitive and often cumulative.	Dividends are never guaranteed unless declared.
Dividends are paid prior to distributions on common.	Unless there is a sinking fund provision, no eventual payment to par is required.
Sometimes are participating, which means they can earn additional dividends.	Highly sensitive to interest rate movements.
Offer less risk than common.	Not likely to show competitive price movement on the short or intermediate term.
Sometimes are convertible to common, giving owner advantages of higher income as well as a chance for capital gains.	Offer holders no right to participate in management.

Table 8–2
Determining Annual Dividends
on Preferreds

Preferred Stock Par Value	Dividend Rate	Annual Dividend
$100	6.0%	$60
100	5.5	55
50	6.0	30
50	5.5	27.50

Dividend rates may be any percent. Neither the par value nor the dividend rate ever changes. Thus, whether the above stocks move up or down in price, the annual dividend is always the same.

Table 8–3
Some Advantages and Disadvantages
of Common Stocks

Advantages	Disadvantages
Offer opportunity for excessive and frequent capital gains.	Can fluctuate widely in price.
Give legal right to vote for corporate officers.	Receive dividends only after preferred stock has been paid.
Give right to share in dividends declared.	In the event of liquidation, are last to receive what is left of corporate assets.
Limit legal liability.	

---

being recalled. The par value of preferreds also serves as the basis upon which the dividend of a preferred stock is based.)

Common stock represents risk. Have no doubt about it! Prices of common can fluctuate widely and in very short spans of time. Other risks are inherent in common stock ownership. Common is entitled to dividends only after distributions to creditors and preferred stockholders. Additionally, common shareholders are the last to receive their share of assets when the corporation is liquidated, whatever the reason.

There are classes of common stock just as there are classes of preferred stock. Each class entitles owners to special rights and privileges. Most of these rights and privileges, however, are related to voting rights. (See Table 8–4.) Thus, when you

---

Table 8–4
Voting Rights

Statutory Method	Cumulative Method
One vote for each share of stock owned.	Number of votes is determined by formula.
Majority vote determines election.	Minority vote can determine the election.

In the cumulative method, the minority holders benefit because now each share is determined by the following mathematical steps:

1. Shares outstanding are multiplied by the number of directors desired.
2. The result is divided by the total number of directors to be elected.
3. A value of 1 is added, and the result represents the vote for each minority share.

---

buy common stock in a corporation issuing more than one type of common, be sure you understand the rights and privileges that come with your investment. (Most small investors, however, care little about voting rights.)

Market Value

The market value of common stock is determined strictly by the law of supply and demand, as discussed in Chapter 6. If there is a great deal of demand for a certain stock, you can be sure the price will eventually go up. If there is a great deal of supply with little demand, then the price of the stock will eventually go down.

You will be surprised to learn, however, that the direction of a stock's price may not be coincidental with the financial fortunes or misfortunes of the issuing corporation. This is because the market price of stock usually reflects future corporate financial potential. People buy stock for what they feel it will be worth tomorrow. They sell it for the same reason. AT&T may be announcing record earnings, but the stock may be heading south. This may be because the marketplace feels the company has had its run, reached its peak, and has nowhere to go but downhill.

This is a very different valuation than we find for preferred stock, the price of which moves up or down mainly in relationship to interest rates. This does not mean, however, that the fiscal performance of the issuing corporation is an influence on market value of preferreds. It only means that preferreds appeal to fixed-income investors and, therefore, are in constant competition with other fixed-income instruments, such as Treasury bonds and bills. The potential increase in principal plus the dividend income must be enough to make an investor want to gamble on the preferreds rather than corporate bonds, CDs, notes, or other interest-bearing securities such as those Treasury bonds and notes. Common stocks are also interest-rate sensitive, as is the entire stock market, but not as much so as the preferreds. The price of common reflects mainly investor confidence in its future. This is why even though many common stocks pay no dividend at all, they are highly active in terms of both volume and price movement. Generally, one would expect that common prices reflect some ratio to book value—or liquidating value—but this is rarely the case.

Book Value

Book value is the same as stockholders' equity. It is generally arrived at by finding the difference between assets and liabilities. Thus, if a corporation has assets of $100 million and liabilities of $80 million, its book value is $20 million. Sometimes this value is expressed in terms of dollars per share. Thus, if there were 100 million shares outstanding for our current example, book value would be expressed as 20 cents per share.

It is not uncommon to confuse the terms book value, par value, and liquidating value. These terms, however, have completely different meanings. Par value, as noted earlier, is an arbitrary value placed on common stock solely for bookkeeping purposes, although some common stock carries no par value, mainly to reduce stockholders' liability.

Liquidating value is the net value realized when a business is closed down and its assets are sold. Generally, we would guess this to be the same as book value, but in reality it cannot be. This is because liquidation carries its own substantial costs that reduce the average value of the assets, and because assets are never really sold for their estimated value. For instance, a hotel may carry its facilities on the books for an estimated worth of $30 million, but during liquidation it may find that there are absolutely no buyers interested in the structure for half that price, because of repair costs, competition, changing neighborhood, or any other number of considerations. On the other hand, there are cases when the liquidating value will be much more than bookkeeping values. This applies in the case of companies with large real estate holdings who may find that the market for the underlying properties has skyrocketed.

Of these three methods of estimating what might be the value of a corporation's market worth, book value is still an important factor. The rule of thumb is that a stock should be selling at least at book value. There are securities researchers who do nothing but search to find these companies for the Smart Money. So if you come across one that has a market value 10 percent or 20 percent below book, take a position and hold on—unless there is good reason why the rest of the investment community has not been bidding up the stock.

Categories of Stock

There can be no standard guideline for selecting stocks, for there are a number of categories that stocks fall into, and in each category you can expect different types of activity. Some of the major categories are banking, insurance, industrial, investment, transportation, and utilities. These can be further broken down into subcategories and then groups and subgroups, but for our purposes a high-level review will be sufficient. (See Table 8–5.)

Bank Stocks

Banks generally do not lean toward the issuance of preferred stock, and the marketplace is generally not eager to consider bank preferreds unless they have a convertibility feature. This is because they are so adversely affected by upward movements in interest rates that they become more volatile and more of a gamble than bank common.

Bank common, however, is generally well-received by the investment community, particularly when it is issued by those banks with aggressive and knowledgeable management. Mergers, diversification into other financial markets where and when possible, and expansion through branches can produce income and balance sheets that will attract investors and bid up the price of the common. In the past few years we've seen some bank stocks skyrocket in price, not the least of which were Bank of America and Citicorp, although the latter took an incredible dive from over $30 per share to under $10 before returning to the mid-30s.

Bank stocks are usually highly leveraged instruments, and where there is a great deal of leverage, there is great opportunity for either high returns or incredible losses. Until 1980, bank stocks were relatively safe and generally predictable investments, but when deregulation took effect many things began to change. For one thing, banks found themselves in a new marketplace in which they did not have the

Table 8–5
Dow Jones World Industry Groups

Groups Leading

GROUP Strongest Stocks	CLOSE		CHG.		PCT. CHG.
Entertainment	157.00	+	4.61	+	3.03
King Wld Pd (US)	36.75	+	1.50	+	4.26
Time Warner (US)	42.88	+	1.63	+	3.94
Parmnt Cmm (US)	45.38	+	1.25	+	2.83
Oil Drilling	115.60	+	3.09	+	2.75
Global Marine (US)	4.50	+	0.25	+	5.88
RossOffshere (NW)	52.00	+	2.00	+	4.00
Energy Svc (US)	3.81	+	0.13	+	3.39
Coal	109.16	+	2.04	+	1.90
Cyprus Amax (US)	31.63	+	1.25	+	4.12
Addngtn Res (US)	17.00	+	0.50	+	3.03
SumitCoal (JP)	820.00	+	20.00	+	2.50
Oilfield Equip	104.73	+	1.62	+	1.57
Baker Hughes (US)	20.38	+	0.75	+	3.82
McDermt Int (US)	23.88	+	0.75	+	3.24
NowscoWell (CA)	21.00	+	0.50	+	2.44
Media: Brdcast	154.72	+	1.95	+	1.28
Tele-Comm A (US)	24.25	+	1.25	+	5.44
Cablevis Sys (US)	58.63	+	1.38	+	2.40
CBS Inc (US)	321.00	+	5.50	+	1.74
Commodity Chem	127.57	+	1.57	+	1.25
MitsuiPtchm (JP)	847.00	+	37.00	+	4.57
MitsubPtchm (JP	678.00	+	29.00	+	4.47
Monsanto Co (US)	79.88	+	2.63	+	3.40

Groups Lagging

GROUP Weakest Stocks	CLOSE		CHG.		PCT. CHG.
Plantations	214.27	–	3.97	–	1.82
ConsolPlant (MA)	3.76	–	0.18	–	4.57
Perlis (MA)	7.75	–	0.35	–	4.32
Dunlop (MA)	9.20	–	0.40	–	4.17
Real Estate	129.45	–	1.52	–	1.16
SiamFortune (TH)	123.00	–	11.00	–	8.21
HemarLndDv (TH)	188.00	–	11.00	–	5.53
AmoyProp (HK)	10.90	–	0.60	–	5.22
Consumer Svc	137.15	–	1.44	–	1.04
ChinaMotor (HK)	65.00	–	1.50	–	2.26
Service Intl (US)	27.38	–	0.63	–	2.23
Actava Gp (US)	6.50	–	0.13	–	1.89
Hm Construct	143.90	–	1.48	–	1.02
Pelangi (MA)	2.75	–	0.12	–	4.18
Persimmon (UK)	3.19	–	0.10	–	3.04
HasekoCp (JP)	700.00	–	20.00	–	2.78
Casinos	198.67	–	2.02	–	1.01
MultiPur (MA)	4.80	–	0.20	–	4.00
Genting (MA)	28.00	–	1.00	–	3.45
CasMuni (FR)	4290.00	–	110.00	–	2.50
Advertising	134.94	–	1.36	–	1.00
Intrpblc Gp (US)	30.63	–	0.50	–	1.61
Foote Cone (US)	41.88	–	0.38	–	0.89
WppGp (UK)	1.20	–	0.01	–	0.83

AU - Australia	FI - Finland	IT - Italy	NV - Netherlands	SW - Sweden
AS - Austria	FR - France	JP - Japan	NZ - New Zealand	SZ - Switzerland
BE - Belgium	GR - Germany	MA - Malaysia	NW - Norway	TH - Thailand
CA - Canada	HK - Hong Kong	MX - Mexico	SI - Singapore	UK - United Kingdom
DK - Denmark	IR - Ireland		SP - Spain	US - United States

Various investment research firms or publications will group what they feel are representative stocks to determine international financial direction.

experience to compete efficiently. Second, they no longer had the monopolies on certain financial products that provided them with dependable and predictable income. A lot of banks were not prepared for the 1980s, and a lot of them went under. Those that survived were the ones, such as Bank of America, that knew how to juggle new opportunities and produce a marketing mix that would drive them ahead of the herd, even though the high interest rates prevailing during the early part of the 1980s were driving a lot of banks out of business. Some of these banks managed to weather the financial storm, but from about 1990 until 1992, the weaker members of the banking community were finally closed down by the FDIC.

Bank stocks are worth your consideration. They generally pay a dividend equivalent to what you might receive from a passbook account and at the same time offer the possibility of greatly increasing your principal. But all bank stocks are not equally attractive—nor are the common stocks of bank holding companies, also usually highly leveraged—and you will want to approach them cautiously. Some of the big guys, like Bank of America, are ideal covered call candidates. The out-of-the-money calls offer high premiums, the stocks pay competitive dividends, and there is upside potential in the common.

Industrial Stocks

Industrial stocks is a vast category that includes the stocks of companies such as General Motors, IBM, Eastman Kodak, Grumman, Goodyear, and Texaco. The category includes such industries as aerospace, building materials, containers, gold mining, home building, machinery, office and business equipment, mobile homes, paper, publishing, retailing, textiles, tobacco, and toys—to name just a few.

Most of the stocks you will buy during your investment programs will probably be industrials. They represent a vast range of businesses and markets, and this tremendous diversity necessitates that their plans, procedures, personnel, products, accounting, and management be unique to their special situations. Your criteria for determining what tools to use to play Ford stock (i.e., options or short positions in stock, etc.) will not be the same as the criteria you use to determine the tools you use to play Boeing for maximum gain or safety. Not only are the companies very different, but so are their markets, their historical price-to-earnings ratios, and their future prospects.

Many of these industrials are giant conglomerates that have positions in a number of industries. This provides them with a relatively dependable rate of return on their capital despite the swallowing of one market segment or another. Still, many of these industrials are highly cyclical in nature, so you will find that their preferreds are generally not in great demand and their common is often for speculators.

Industrials usually drive the market in one direction or another. When these stocks are doing well, usually the market is doing well, too. When they are on the decline, so, too, is the market. If you buy their common, bear in mind that you will have to keep a watchful eye on the stock and be very careful about being uncovered. When these stocks hit hard times, they are usually very hard times and their stocks will drop rapidly. If you are long on any industrial stocks, it is always wise to be "insured" with low-priced puts. If you decide to sell the stock short, at least be partially covered with long positions in calls.

Insurance Stocks

Many insurance companies are stock companies. They may be listed on any of the American or foreign exchanges like any other stock.

Insurance companies vary in terms of the products they offer and in terms of their potential as investments. Some specialize in life insurance, others in fire and marine, and others in casualty and surety.

Life insurance companies have generally benefited from annually increasing returns from bonds, stock, and real estate. These are wealthy companies that benefit, strangely enough, from regulatory limitations, which serve to prohibit speculation and focus the companies on investment-grade securities.

Activity last year easily demonstrates the potential that insurance stocks offer. Stocks like Aetna and Travelers common had seen over a 50 percent increase while paying dividends that far exceed those of the bank stocks. In the case of Travelers, however, there were other forces at work. Primerica, a rapidly growing financial giant, was after Travelers. Sanford Weill, chairman of Primerica had, for some time, been interested in acquiring another company, preferably an insurance or financial services company that would give him a second chance at building a financial services company able to play in the same league as companies such as Aetna Life and Casualty and some of the giant brokerage firms. Weill's intentions were no secret on Wall Street, and this encouraged trading in many insurance stocks. Usually takeover speculation or news about a stock, even if fabricated, excites interest throughout that stock's industry. In this case, rumor was truth. Primerica took over Travelers.

Insurance companies, however, can be adversely affected by natural and human-made disasters. Losses can sometimes be in the billions of dollars. Overall, however, the stocks offer good potential for those investors, such as yourself, who may be looking for stocks offering a good total return (dividends plus capital appreciation). Many of these stocks, however, are currently near their highs and may see a pull-back. They might be good candidates for aggressive dollar cost averaging programs that are covered by low-priced puts, just in case there is any substantial pull-back.

Investment Companies

Investment companies are primarily involved in the very business of investing. They are periodically in and out of favor with investors; in recent years, they have very much been in favor. These investment companies usually maintain highly balanced portfolios that provide you with a relative amount of safety. This does not mean, however, that they guarantee you will profit or that they are always the best place to put your money. Much depends upon what your investment objectives are.

Investment companies register their investment policies and may specialize in specific markets (such as overseas growth companies) or diversify their funds over any number of markets, depending upon where they feel the risk/reward ratio is compatible with their goals. Some are highly speculative, some extremely conservative. In recent years, some of these companies have been bringing in returns averaging over 15 to 20 percent per year, with a few occasionally bringing in a return of 30 to 40 percent for their stockholders.

Publications such as *Money* magazine offer periodical review of the returns these companies bring in, as well as their average rate of return over the past five or 10 years. Just remember that past performance is no indication of future performance, so always be on your toes when you are tempted to buy into an investment company that has recently been among the top 10 performers. Next year it could just as well be among the 10 lowest performers.

Some of these companies are no-load funds, which means that you can buy into them without having to pay any commissions. Many of these no-load funds are also top performers. But do not pick an investment company solely because there is no sales charge. Buy the ones that have had a good performance record, have the same management team that was in office during this performance period, and have portfolios consistent with your own objectives.

The funds offer a great deal of financial flexibility. Some provide checking accounts so you can withdraw portions of your money when needed. Or they provide the choice of either receiving dividend and capital gains or reinvesting them. Most of all, they are particularly beneficial because most people dollar average their way into them, buying many dollars of shares periodically.

Transportation Stocks

Transportation stocks include such companies as airlines, rail freight systems, transportation equipment leasing, trucking, and shipping, to name just a few. Some of these stocks are highly recognizable: AMR (holding company for American Airlines), Burlington Northern (railroads, pipelines), Delta Airlines, and Union Pacific.

At this writing, most of these stocks are on the uptick. Not many offer preferred stocks, but their common is generally popular with the investment community. Stocks like AMR, Delta, and Ryder have daily volume in the hundreds of thousands of shares.

Government regulations and pricing wars can wreak havoc on these stocks, so if you decide to take positions in any of the common or preferreds, proceed with caution. Research with great effort not only the stocks but also their particular industry. Find out what's happening, for instance, in the airline industry and whether price wars are imminent, or new markets are suddenly opening up for certain companies.

These stocks do not normally pay high dividends, so there is little incentive to chance getting caught when they are stagnant or falling. Also, these stocks seem to be very slow on the uptick but always very quick on the downtick. Many, however, are optionable, which means you can do some covered call writing. The best bet, however, is to clearly lay out your investment objectives and weigh these against the market forecasts for specific transportation stocks. Keep yourself covered.

Utility Stocks

Utility stocks are stocks for those companies that provide light, power, or water. They include gas and electric utilities, steam utilities, and water companies, as well as gas line operators and the various utility holding companies. Stocks in this category have names that are familiar to the general public, including Consolidated Edison (Con Edison), Detroit Edison, Houston Industries, Pacific Gas and Electric, and Public Service Enterprises (holding company for Public Service Electric and Gas).

Utility stocks are mainly income plays for people whose portfolios consist mainly of high interest and high dividend rate securities or investors who want to balance their otherwise speculative portfolios with more conservative stocks.

Utility stocks are usually very sensitive to interest rates. When interest rates are high, investors will be much more interested in interest-bearing certificates, which also assure preservation of principle. Why go to utility stocks for income if that same income is available in safer instruments?

When interest rates are on the rise, the price of utility stocks will be under tremendous pressure to make the yield attractive to the investment community. When interest rates are on the decline, these stocks can advance and still keep the dividend rate highly competitive. Other forces also influence utility stocks, and these include the same fundamental forces that drive other regulated industries and some of the same fundamental forces that drive unregulated industries. These include price regulation, market limitations, financial stability, and projected stock price-to-earnings ratios.

These stocks would be of interest to you if you are trying to balance your portfolio for a reasonable trade-off between total yield and capital appreciation. Probably the best way to play these stocks is to dollar cost average your way into them, selling covered calls when you have enough shares to do so. In this way, you can squeeze additional income from your portfolio (in addition to dividends) and provide yourself with some downside protection. If you sense, however, that interest rates will be on the rise, then consider moving out of the utilities and into interest-bearing securities.

Dividends

If your goal is to find stocks that offer high dividend yields, you need not limit yourself to utility stocks. Transportation, telephone, and many industrials and other stocks also offer high dividend rates. But before you go after stocks with high dividends, you must understand the conundrum that dividends are to the Smart Money.

Dividends are actually that part of the net earnings of a corporation that are distributed to the shareholders. Dividends are the profits the corporation makes. You are taxed on dividends as you would be on ordinary income. If, on the other hand, the corporation did not distribute the dividends, that money would be distributed over the outstanding shares in the corporation and stockholders' equity would increase tax free. What this means is that you really do not get anything extra from high-dividend-paying stocks, except extra taxes. Dividends are popular with many investors, however, regardless of this fact. They like the idea of periodic income from their portfolios and generally feel they may as well get the money while they can, taxes or no taxes. The real movers on the stock exchanges, however, are usually the stocks that do not pay high dividends, but reinvest profits into their own business.

What actually constitutes profits for the purpose of determining dividend payouts is a tricky legal question. For instance, can money be borrowed to pay dividends on profits earned but not received? Can money received from the sale of fixed assets be available for dividend payments?

Stockholders can not only reap the benefits of cash dividends, but can also benefit by qualifying for stock splits and stock dividends. There are some major differences between stock splits and stock dividends, although they both represent additional distributions of stock to stockholders. Stock dividends are additional payments in stock instead of cash. The par value of the stock is not affected (though the market price will be), and the percentage of ownership that the stockholder has in the company remains unchanged. Stock splits are additional payments of stock. The payments are not in lieu of cash, and the par value changes, though the percentage of ownership the stockholder has in the company remains unchanged.

It sounds as though we are splitting hairs here, but the closer you look, the more clearly you see the difference between stock splits and stock dividends.

EXAMPLE #28. Effect of a Stock Dividend

You own 200 shares of stock in Glow Cinema. The directors declare a 50 percent stock dividend. How many shares of stock will you now own?

100 shares × .50 (50%) = 50 shares
100 + 50 = 150 shares

You now have 150 shares. But will these 150 shares be worth as much as the 100 shares you had?

Let's see.

The stock dividend requires that Glow Cinema readjust its earnings per share accordingly. If it had an earnings record of $6 per share, that would now have to be reduced.

Think about it. If the company earned $6 per share, the 100 shares you own would represent $600 in corporate earnings. But now you are given an additional 50 shares. The earnings per share, then, cannot remain the same. You now have 150 shares representing $600 in corporate profits instead of 100. Each share is now worth less, and the marketplace will bring down the value of the stock accordingly. A little grammar school division tells you that after the stock dividend, each share now represents $4 in earnings to the corporation instead of $6.

Although the par value of the stock is not reduced, when a stock dividend is distributed, investors are receiving no more than a piece of paper acknowledging their ownership of additional shares and the corresponding reduction in the value of all their shares. It is all a bookkeeping game—but one that can pay off. If the cash dividend for each share of stock remains the same, the investor is getting greater income from the same amount of money he has invested in the corporation. Additionally, if the market value of the stock goes up, the investor has more shares of stock to increase in value. (If the market value of the stock goes down, then he has more shares of stock to lose money on.)

EXAMPLE #29. Effect of a Stock Split

You have 300 shares (market value $3,000) in the American Book Company. The directors declare a 2-for-1 stock split. What is the value of your holdings after the split?

Before the split – 300 shares = $3,000
After the split – 600 shares = $3,000

As you can see, you have gained no more money. You only have additional shares of stock. Twice as many, as a matter of fact. But now each share is worth half of what it was worth before the split. The par value for each share of stock will be cut in half and so, probably, will be its market value.

You receive nothing from the stock split except potential—the potential to earn a greater amount of money or to lose a great amount of money. Why? Because you now have twice as many shares.

If you feel that the stock has potential, you are going to like the idea of a split. If you feel the stock has no potential, you might want to sell the stock as soon as possible.

Perspectives of directors of a company and of stockholders will often differ markedly on the benefits of stock splits and stock dividends. The shareholder is interested in additional income or capital gains. The directors are interested in conserving cash yet giving something to the stockholders (in this case, additional profit potential) and in keeping the market value of the shares at a more attractive trading level.

Reverse splits sometimes occur. Corporations consider these in order to reduce the number of shares they have outstanding. Thus, instead of a 2-for-1 split, they might offer a 1-for-2 split. In this case, the value of each share is worth more, but you would, of course, have fewer shares, so everything balances out to zero. You have neither made nor lost money on the deal, but the company has been able to raise the market value of its stock to twice what it was. When stock prices get too low, corporations worry that investors might lose interest. So, the reverse split is their answer.

9

MARKET VIEWS

Investors employ a number of strategies to get a fix on the market.

It is very important for them to have a clear view of what has been happening, what is currently happening, and what will probably happen in the future. Unfortunately, no one has yet devised a crystal ball that will let you see what the stock listings in *The Wall Street Journal* or *Investor's Business Daily* will be six months down the line. The more eccentric investors may sometimes resort to forms of magic or rely on psychics to help them stay in the black, but the more sober members of the investment scene tend to rely on economic, business, and market statistics and forecasts to help them get a good feel for where the market is and where it is going. As business activity drives the economy, they look to a number of business barometers to analyze general economic trends. To determine when the market is ready for up or down swings, they next look at important market indicators so they know when stocks are fertile enough to respond to their bull or bear strategies.[1]

Business Barometers

Business barometers are made up of a number of industrial indices and statistics that can be used to forecast general business activity. The barometers used by both business and government are extensive. There is no need for the independent investor to know each and every one of them, but there are a few that are popular with the press and investment community, and these need reviewing, for they help you to understand what's happening in the corporate world. (See Table 9–1 for summary.)

However, there are two very important considerations you must bear in mind. The first is that if you took the time to study all this data, you would never have time to place a buy or sell order with your broker. The second is that you invest in selective stocks, not index options or the stock market in general, so whatever good news the barometers may indicate, you can still find your investments saturated with red ink.

Gross Domestic Product

In Chapter 6, you were introduced to GNP (Gross National Product) and what it represents. The GNP has in the past been considered a very important business

Table 9–1
Widely Referenced Business Barometers

Name or Category	Description
Gross Domestic Product (GDP)	Measures all services produced by labor and property on a national basis, even if this production is not originated by U.S. residents.
Corporate Profits	Measures financial and marketing strength of private "for profit" industries and mutual financial institutions.
Disposable Personal Income	Measures the amount of money available to purchase goods and services.
Capacity Utilization Rate	Measures whether or not businesses are operating at full capacity in order to predict employment trends.
Consumer Price Indexes	Measures price changes for specific consumer groups.
Producers' Price Indexes	Measures price changes in selected markets.
Consumer Installment Credit	Measures consumer borrowing activity.
Interest Rates	Determine the cost of money which, in turn, drives the price of common stocks but mostly prefereds.

barometer. However, it has never been as functional for measuring national income as something called the Gross Domestic Product (GDP). That is why you were introduced to GNP in Chapter 6 in the discussions on economic forces and are being introduced to GDP here.

GDP is a measure of all services produced by labor and property on a national basis. This labor and property need not be supplied only by U.S. residents. It may also be supplied by residents of foreign countries.

GDP has now replaced GNP as the preferred measure of U.S. business and economic activity. Economists like it mainly because it is a short-term rather than long-term system of measurement and also because it allows a direct comparison with the national product of other countries. GDP measures personal consumption expenditures, gross private domestic investment, government purchase of goods and services, and net exports.

Personal consumption expenditures represent the dollar value of all services, and durable and nondurable goods provided. This includes goods and services provided to individuals, the operating expenditures of nonprofit institutions, the dollar value of financial services received by individuals, and the dollar value for basic needs supplied to individuals. These basic needs include food, clothing, and housing.

Gross private domestic investment is a measure of all privately purchased dwellings, fixed capital goods purchased by profit and nonprofit institutions, and the delta of private business inventories.

Government purchase of goods and services represents all government purchases, including state and local governments.

And net exports is a measure of all exports less imports.

You will hear the GDP being referred to constantly in the financial news and financial broadcasts. It serves as a comprehensive depiction of national business trends and the relative growth in national income. When the forecasts for GDP are favorable, bulls have the added advantage of possibly having their stocks move on market current as well as on their own fundamentals.

Corporate Profits

Understandably, any investor would be interested in corporate profits. This indicator measures the health of private for-profit industries as well as for mutual financial institutions. This barometer is an integral part of a larger business measure, that of national income. National income is the aggregate of earnings produced by labor and property. Besides corporate profits, the barometer is also made up of the following components: compensation for employees, proprietor's income, rental income, and net interest.

While corporate profits are an important indicator, as Munn points out, certain caveats are tagged to this statistic.[2]

- The estimates measure only corporate profits, not the profits of all businesses.

- The estimates are broad aggregates and need supplementing by industry-specific data.

- Capital gains and losses are not included in the profit statement because they do not result from current production.

- Bad debt expenses are measured by actual losses, not additions to reserves.

- Unpaid debts are considered profits in the case of bankrupt firms.

When corporate profits are up, the financial community is generally bullish. Their bullishness drives up volume, which, in turn, drives up price—or should.

Disposable Personal Income

Disposable personal income is the income that individuals may either spend or save. This economic measure helps to determine the amount of money available to purchase goods and services, including financial instruments, or to save. When disposable income is down, the economy is bound to suffer, for people will be hoarding money or using it only to buy staples. For the business community, this means that supplies are going to outweigh demands, and profits are going to bottom out. When disposable income is up, there is a market for the supply of goods available today and possibly tomorrow. This, in turn, gives impetus to the business community to increase supply. To increase supply, they must purchase goods and labor. This means more people in the work force and more tax income for governments, also.

Capacity Utilization Rate

This is another very significant indicator, for it is a useful tool in forecasting employment rates. As the theory goes, when businesses are operating at full capacity, they are capable of supporting high levels of employment. However, when they are operating at less than maximum capacity, there is no motivation to increase the labor supply and, more than likely, unemployment will increase. The capacity utilization rate should point to oncoming bull or bear markets. High capacity, bull markets; low capacity, bear markets.

Consumer and Producers' Price Indexes

Consumer price indexes (CPIs) provide measures of price changes for selected consumer groups. These groups include wage earners and clerical workers, and all urban consumers. The latter category is the more broadly based index, as its name would imply, and the one that carries the greater weight with economic analysts.

The consumer price index for all urban consumers measures the average change in the cost of goods and services made available to consumers. It is also called the cost of living index, for it represents changes in pricing for consumer goods—goods such as food, clothing, dwellings, automobiles, fuel, transportation, utilities, and medicine. Taxes may or may not be included as components depending upon their nature. If a tax is directly related to the purchase of goods or services, it is included as a component of the price index.

The index considers almost all consumer groups a part of its population. These groups include not only wage earners but also salaried personnel, self-employed professionals and other service workers, retired individuals, and even the unemployed. Some of the exceptions are farm and military families, and institutionalized persons.

The index is an important reference base in labor negotiations as well as in economic forecasting. This economic forecasting must necessarily include the development and implementation of corporate business strategies, as economic policy and business planning are interdependent. It is important to note, however, that the CPI really only measures changes in consumer prices, nothing else. That is, the index is not a measure of changes in spending habits or family makeup, or what it actually costs consumers to live. Thus, "cost of living" is not really an appropriate title for this index.

While the index can herald oncoming periods of inflation, you must not believe that, simply because it continues to rise month after month or year after year, you must change your investment strategies markedly. It is simply an economic fact that, while consumer prices in selected markets may fall, generally consumer prices flow one way—uphill. Thus, it is not the general direction of the CPI that forecasts inflation but, rather, its rate of increase. Inflation is a constant presence in almost every major country, although there have been periods of deflation. As long as inflation rambles along at a 2 to 4 percent rate, there is generally little need to alter investment strategies. However, when there are signs that inflation rates may be in the double digits, it is time to adjust your investment strategies according to the guidelines in Chapter 6.

Producers' price indexes are also highly valued by economic analysts and are widely used in both government and private industry. The most comprehensive of the indexes is the producers' price index for finished goods, which measures price changes in all primary U.S. markets. It is probably as important, if not more so, in depicting inflationary tendencies at the primary market level than the major consumer price index described above.

Consumer Installment Credit

Another series of indexes that will be an important economic flag for you are those measuring consumer installment credit. Consumer borrowing activity always creates a great deal of interest in both government and business because it measures purchasing power. It also indicates what the market activity may be for the types of goods that consumers traditionally buy on installment plans.

These indexes can also signal possible economic downturns. For example, an index for the percentage of consumer installment loans delinquent 30 days and over indicates that the money flow is tightening up and business activity cannot continue at the pace at which it has been marching. Like it or not, credit is an integral part of our economic system. Think of what would happen to the auto industry, for instance, if we had to pay cash for our cars.[3]

Interest Rates

The significance of interest rates can never be underestimated. Interest rates determine the cost of money. When the cost of money is high, demand for money is low; when the cost is low, demand is high. We see, again, the law of supply and demand in action.

The price-to-earnings (PE) ratio of stocks generally decreases as interest rates begin to climb, particularly on those stocks that market themselves, by paying dividend rates competitive with rates of return available from the various money markets. Preferred stocks qualify under this category. Because they are purchased mainly for income purposes, their price generally depreciates when interest rates rise. This is the way the marketplace adjusts the dividend-to-stock ratio to keep the stocks competitive. The effect of changing interest rates on common stock is not as predictable as it may be on preferred, because there are so many other variables that affect common stock prices. But when the cost of money is on the rise, the general environment is usually bearish.

The key figure you will be interested in is the prime rate. Its up or down movement generally affects the outlook on the market, with a falling prime signaling the bulls to run and a rising prime signaling the bears to come out of hibernation.

The prime rate represents the interest rate that comes as close as possible to representing riskless money. This is the rate at which the most creditworthy customers are able to borrow. It is not available to you unless you are borrowing from Mom or Dad, but it is available to important money or businesses that qualify under a bank's lending policies. Changes in the prime rate are sometimes very frequent, at other times only occasional.

The prime rate directly affects the call money rate, which is the rate banks charge brokers for the collateral they need for their stock exchange operations. This means that staying tuned to changes in the prime, which always make the financial news, is a way to feel out coming bull or bear markets. A climbing prime is good news for the bears; a falling prime is good news for the bulls.

Market Averages and Indexes

The chief barometers that investors use to reconcile projected stock prices with business and economic trends are the market averages and indexes measured by the activity of representative stocks tracked by financial service organizations. Among the more widely quoted averages in daily financial broadcasts and publications are the following:

- Dow Jones Averages
- Dow Jones World Index
- Standard & Poor's Averages
- New York Stock Exchange Indexes
- American Stock Exchange Indexes
- NASDAQ Index

These are just a few of the available averages and indexes. They are important to market watchers who put a great deal of emphasis on price and volume movement. Some averages are simple averages, such as the Dow Jones Averages, and these must be constantly adjusted to compensate for special distributions or splits. Some are weighted, as for instance, the NASDAQ Indexes, and in this case the weight of individual components making up the index must be reevaluated. (They are summarized in Table 9–2 and are discussed below.)

Dow Jones Averages and World Index

There is a company called Dow Jones, that, among other business enterprises, publishes *The Wall Street Journal* and *Barron's*. In the beginning of this century, one of the founders of Dow Jones Co., Charles H. Dow, developed what came to be known as the Dow theory of stock price movement. It was based on stock market averages of representative industrial and transportation stocks. Originally the transportation stock average was derived from the activity of 20 railroad stocks, but in 1970 Dow Jones revised the list to include companies offering other forms of commercial transportation.

The Dow Jones Averages now include 15 utility stocks in addition to 20 transportation and 30 industrial stocks. The averages are still made up of a relatively small sampling of stocks in the three selected categories. Many of the other indexes or averages include hundreds of stocks in comparison to the 65 used in the Dow Jones Averages. Yet the Dow Jones Averages still command a great deal of respect from

Table 9–2
Widely Referenced Market Averages and Indexes

Name or Type	Description
Dow Jones Averages	Tracks the price activity of 15 utility, 20 transportation, and 30 industrial stocks. Dow theory is based on the relative performance of these three groups.
Standard & Poor's Averages	Tracks the price activity of selected stocks. The S&P 500 and the S&P 100 are the most popular of the averages and are used as the basis for index options.
New York Stock Exchange Index	Tracks the price activity of all common stocks on the NY exchange.
American Stock Exchange Index	Measures the price levels, market breadth, and price/earnings of its common listings.
National Association of Securities Dealers Index	Tracks the price activity of thousands of stocks on its market quotation system.
Moody's Averages	Tracks the price activity of selected industrial, rail, and electric utilities.
Value Line Stock Average	Tracks the price activity of the almost 2,000 stocks supervised by the Value Line Investment survey.
Russell 2000	Tracks the price activity of 2,000 selected stocks.
Wilshire 5000	Tracks the price activity of 5,000 selected stocks.

stock market technicians, although debate continues to explode occasionally on just how representative these averages are.

The Dow theory as it is now expressed is based on the activity of the three averages. If the industrials, utilities, and transportation stocks reach new highs for consecutive periods, a bull market is on its way or already here. If, however, they all reach new lows, a bear market is coming or already here.

Dow Jones also publishes a world stock index, which measures market activity on four continents: North America, Europe, Australia, and Asia. For convenience, the index lists Australia under the heading of Asia/Pacific. Stock markets from the following countries make up the index: Belgium, Canada, France, Germany, Hong

Kong, Italy, Japan, Malaysia, New Zealand, Netherlands, Spain, Singapore, Switzer-
land, United Kingdom, and United States.

Standard & Poor's Averages

Standard & Poor's (S&P) is a statistical and financial publishing giant that offers a
full range of business and economic data to the investment community, the government, and the public at large. It has also constructed an index consisting of the
majority of stocks listed on the New York Stock Exchange. The core indexes consist
of industrial, transportation, utilities, and financial stocks. Many market technicians
prefer the S&P Averages over the Dow Jones Averages, but, generally, the DJ Averages and the S&P Averages are more in than out of sync. The most popular of the
S&P indexes is probably Standard & Poor's 500. High, low, and closing prices for the
S&P Averages are easily found in any of the financial newspapers, such as *Investor's
Business Daily*, and in the financial section of large city newspapers.

Stock Exchange Indexes

Other frequently quoted indexes are the New York Stock Exchange, American Stock
Exchange, and NASDAQ indexes. All three have a far more extended base than is
used for the Dow Jones or Standard & Poor's averages.

The New York Stock Exchange Index is based on the total value of every common
stock on the exchange, which means that probably over 2,000 stocks make up the
index. Because stocks are constantly being listed or delisted and there are periods of
recapitalization for many of the issues, adjustments are continually made to manage
the integrity of the index, as the index is expressed in relation to a base period
market value.

The American Stock Exchange compiles three separate indexes, one dealing with
price levels, the second with market breadth, and the third with price/earnings. The
first is the more commonly referenced and indicates the current price levels, and
changes in those price levels, of American Exchange issues. The second indicates the
way in which price changes have been distributed over exchange listings, and the
third looks at price-to-earnings ratios.

The NASDAQ (National Association of Security Dealers Automated Quotations)
Index is based on a sampling of almost 5,000 domestic stocks in its quotation system.
This index is like all others in that it is expressed in relation to a base period market
value and adjustments in the data are continually being made to assure the integrity
of the index.

Other Market Barometers

While the above remain the most widely referenced indexes or averages by the
broadcast and news media, there are other market barometers that in combination
weigh heavily with private and government economic groups. These include
Moody's Averages, Value Line Stock Average, Russell 2000, Wilshire 5000, and the
many foreign stock exchange indexes, all of which are listed in publications such as
The Wall Street Journal, Investor's Business Daily, Barron's, and other financial news
publications.

Investment Indicators

When economic and business barometers are relatively coincident and consistent, investors next look at a number of indicators that help them determine their strategies and time their orders. These include the new high/new low list, short interest, advance/decline indicator, short-term trading index (Arms Index), and the closing tick indicator, which are summarized in Table 9–3 and discussed below. These statistics are published regularly. Bear in mind that there is no single indicator that predicts market performance. They must all be constantly weighed, and they still do not offer any guarantees.

New High/New Low List

This list is simply a record of the stocks reaching new highs and new lows for whatever period is identified. There are usually daily, weekly, monthly, and annual lists, depending upon the source. The list contains preferred stocks as well as common.

As the theory goes, when the number of new highs is greater than the number of new lows over a period of time a bull market is in the making. Just what that "period of time" is will vary depending upon how technicians interpret the economic and business barometers that support the market. You can readily understand that regardless of by how much the new highs outnumber the new lows, there is a length of time after which a bear market may be in the development.

Table 9–3
Popular Investment Indicators

Name	Description
New High/New Low List	Record of stocks reaching new highs or lows during the identified period.
Short Interest Tables	Record of shares sold short but not yet covered.
Advance/Decline Indicator	Specifies the number of stocks that have advanced, declined, or remained unchanged for the identified period.
Short-Term Trading Index (ARMS Index)	Computes the average volume of declining issues on the New York and American exchanges and on the NASDAQ trading system. (See Table 9–4.)
Closing Tick Indicator	Shows the strength of individual exchanges in terms of stock price activity, and the relative strength of the Dow Jones Industrials. (See Table 9–5.)

Short Interest

Short interest statistics are simply a record of the number of shares sold short for specific stocks and not yet covered. The statistics are usually for the New York and American stock exchanges and serve more as a "sentiment indicator" than a technical directive. When the tables indicate a relatively high level of short selling, this indicates a bearish sentiment. When the tables indicate a relatively low level of short selling, this indicates bullish sentiment.

This indicator is generally used in conjunction with the put-call ratio, which looks at options trading on the Standard & Poor's 100 Index (S&P 100) and compares it with the Chicago Board Options Exchange (CBOE) equity ratio. The theory is that if the ratio of puts to calls on the S&P 100 is $70/100$ and on the CBOE is $65/100$ the outlook is bullish.

The word "sentiment" must be emphasized, for what the short interest tables do is simply indicate how investors are playing individual stocks and the major market movers. Whether or not their short positions are on the mark, only time will tell. Many investors will go against the tide. That is, if the short interest lists are lengthy, they are interpreted as being a bullish signal. If they are brief, they are interpreted as being a bearish signal.

Advance/Decline Indicator

The advance/decline indicator gives the number of stocks that have advanced, declined, or remained unchanged for whatever period is being measured. It is simply a numerical indicator; it does not list specific stocks. This indicator is used in conjunction with the Dow Jones Averages. When the latter are up and the advance/decline indicator is showing more advances than declines, this is considered the heralding of a bull phase. When the Dow Jones Averages are down and the advance/decline indicator is showing more declines than advances, this is considered the heralding of a bear phase.

Short-Term Trading Index

The short-term trading index identifies where most of the action in the market has been. It is computed by taking the average volume of declining issues on the New York and American exchanges and the NASDAQ system, this last being the computerized trading arm of the National Association of Securities Dealers (which makes the market for over-the-counter stocks). Whenever the result is less than one, then most of the action has been in rising stocks. If more than one, then most of the action has been in declining stocks. (See Table 9–4.)

Closing Tick Indicator

The closing tick indicator (Table 9–5) shows the strength of individual exchanges as well as the Dow Jones Industrials. When the numbers are positive, related markets are showing strength. When they are negative, related markets are showing weakness. It is not a widely published indicator, but a call to your broker will get you a quote.

Table 9–4
Short-Term Trading Index
(ARMS Index)

Market	MON	TUES	WED	THUR	FRI
NYSE	.85	1.20	.50	.72	1.20
AMEX	.90	.90	.60	.82	.90
NASDAQ	.87	1.10	.55	.72	.85

This indicator is used to spot market action. Whenever the value is greater than 1, most of the action is in stocks heading north. In the above example, Tuesday and Friday have high activity in rising stocks. This would generally indicate a bull phase, except we see that the markets are unable to sustain any bull run. NYSE and NASDAQ looked hot on Tuesday but faltered on the next two days. It's likely that the Friday trend will continue on the next Monday.

Table 9–5
Closing Tick Indicator

Market	MON	TUES	WED	THUR	FRI
NYSE	−250	−220	+300	+255	+300
AMEX	−42	−90	+85	−12	+120
NASDAQ	−15	−15	+20	+10	+20

If the closing tick figures are positive, the underlying market is showing strength. If they are negative, the underlying market is showing weakness. Figures are derived by subtracting the number of stocks in which the last change in price was downward from the number of stocks in which the last change in price was upward.

Notes

1. These categories are arbitrary. For instance, any of the averages and indexes discussed can also be considered economic barometers or market indicators.

2. Glenn G. Munn, F. L. Garcia, and Charles J. Woelfel, *Encyclopedia of Banking and Finance,* 9th ed. (Chicago: Probus, 1993), 141–142.

3. For a comprehensive guide to economic and business barometers, see George Hildebrand, *Business Cycle Indicators and Measures: A Complete Guide to Interpreting the Key Economic Indicators* (Chicago: Probus, 1993).

10

BASIC STRATEGIES

Professional stock pickers use a number of methods to select stocks. Even the Big Money employs its own strategies, but most of them are variations, combinations, or extensions of the two "classical" methods: fundamental analysis and technical analysis. The independent investor, like yourself, usually has a number of unique methods that, while they would make the pros cringe, are sometimes very effective.

The type of strategy you may use for stock picking will depend a great deal upon whether you are investing or speculating whether or not you are going to cover your positions, and the degree to which you are going to cover them. If you are not going to hedge, but simply play for the long term, you must learn to become a fundamentalist who resorts to technical strategies only to determine when to go in or out of a stock or stock option. In this case, portfolio mix and diversification will be of special interest to you. However, if you are going to hedge and employ the different tools described in this text, you can practice guerrilla stock selection; that is, you can devise your own independent strategies for quick and "relatively safe" selects and sells.

Formal Methods of Stock Selection

In the fundamentalist method, analysts look at such things as current assets and liabilities, projected assets and liabilities, projected earnings, historical and projected price-to-earnings ratios, management, and labor relations. These six fundamentals are probably included in every analysis, though they will be added to and weighed differently by researchers. (See Table 10–1 for a comparison of technical and fundamental analyses.)

Additional data often included on top of these six fundamentals are current inventories, sales stability, new competition, copyrights and patents, liquidity, pending law suits, and developing competitive technology or products. You do not have to do this type of investigation yourself. If you have a full service broker, he or she can usually supply you with fundamental information on the stocks you may be interested in, as well as give you a final evaluation of the relative strength of the stock.

Table 10-1
Major Elements of Formal Stock Selection Methods

Method	Elements
Technical Analysis	Volume, price, price-volume relationships, short interest, stock distribution, shares outstanding, investor interest, public thinking, gain/loss record
Fundamental Analysis	Current assets and liabilities, projected assets and liabilities, projected earnings, management, labor relations

In the technical (or chartist) method, analysts rely almost exclusively upon price and volume data. Their argument is that the market will already have considered the fundamentals of various stocks, and interpreting market statistics gives them a much more three-dimensional and active picture of what is and will be happening in the marketplace.

To gauge the general market, technicians look at market breadth, market and stock volume-price relationships, advance/decline indicators, short interest, OTC-to-major exchange relative movements, new highs/lows indicators, selected averages and indexes, margin statistics, money statistics, closing tick indicators, insider trading and, generally, any measure of price or volume movements that indicates a trend.

To gauge individual stock performance, technicians look at short interest in the stock, the extent of public participation, volume, price, volume-price relationships, general public and Big Money interest, and the extent to which the stock may have advanced or declined without major bear or bull phases taking place in its trading.

While technical analysis is an often overrated method of stock selection, volume and price statistics have often been early-warning flags for takeover or Chapter 11 candidates, as well as for coming bull or bear phases in specific stocks or the market in general. However, there is nothing more dangerous than something that works some of the time. If it never works, you know to stay away from it. If it always works, you know to stay with it. But if it only works sometimes, what do you do?

The fundamentalist method, by the way, also carries no guarantees.

Random walkers pay conditional respect to technical and fundamental analysis but hold primarily that prices are relatively unpredictable through volume and price analysis. Their philosophy is known as the random walk theory, which is based on the theory that the stock market is, finally, an efficient market.

Because it is an efficient market, as the theory goes, price and volume patterns are an undependable predictor of future prices. Additionally, most of the players in the stock and options markets are experienced professionals who have access to software encyclopedias of current and historical data and will compete to assure that prices currently reflect true worth—which, ultimately, is what the marketplace is willing to pay for a stock. Each and every one of these competitors stands ready to adjust his or her holdings to reflect random developments that will affect the worth of a stock. The conclusion is that unless you are privy to inside information, even if you are the most informed and experienced investor, you are unlikely to benefit from any type of analysis unless you are willing to take great risk.

Stock Investing

As an investor, you are interested in long-term commitments. You are not generally looking for quick returns but rather a good total yield over extended periods. You will be interested in stocks with strong fundamentals, stocks with good balance sheets, good profit and loss statements, and good projected earnings. But, like most if not all independent investors, you are rarely going to give in-depth study to the financial or technical strength of stocks, though you will not ignore the data. You will rely on popular or highly recommended stocks by investment newsletters and brokers or those that make up the Dow Jones Industrials, Standard & Poor's 100, and various safety lists such as the most widely owned stocks. Nothing beats detailed fundamental and technical analysis and a lot of luck, but the fact of life is that most independent investors make their stock selections from secondary research.

To make big money in the market requires a great deal of risk. Because you are the little guy trying to build your fortune and not the big guy with money to lose, you must necessarily limit risk. You want a return on your investment from stock investing that will add to the average return from all your investments. That fortune you will build someday, by the way, will not come just from successful stock investing but from many sources including a good salaried job, smart real estate investments, and all around good money management.

Not every investor has the same goals. Some investors never set goals at all, though they should. One recommendation for investment-class stock players is that they look for stocks that will give them an opportunity to double their money within six years. This is not an unrealistic goal for an investor. Many stocks have the chance of performing this well in a predominately bullish period.

Note the word "chance." Stock picking, despite the possibilities and flag waving, is still a game of chance. The chances of you picking winners are very slim. The chances of your broker always picking winners for you are also very slim.

So what do you do? You hedge, meaning—for your specific case, that of the long-term investor—you go after quality stocks in a way that protects you as much as possible from losses that can be incurred if your stock should fall in price.

The professionals have many ways to hedge their bets. For your purposes, and your means and goals, there are two you might want to adapt:

- Dollar cost averaging.

- Covered calls.

In both cases, you will want to concentrate on quality stocks, and preferably quality stocks that pay a reasonable dividend. If these stocks also have dividend reinvestment plans, take advantage of them.

The stocks appearing in Table 10–2 are considered some of the better quality stocks listed on the various exchanges because they have great earnings records in relation to their current price, great management, are well situated in their markets, and have a chance for future growth. They also represent a large share of the market and large general ownership.

By the time you read this book, their fundamentals may have changed. So do not go out and buy the stocks just because they are listed here. Select the ones that may interest you, check with your broker about how his research department feels about

Table 10–2
Popular Stocks

The following stocks are selected because of the large share of the market they represent plus the number of shareholders owning their stock.

Allied Signal	General Mills
Amoco Corp.	General Motors
American Express	GTE
AT&T	Kellogg Co.
Anheuser-Busch Cos.	McDonald's Corp.
Bell Atlantic	NYNEX
Chevron	PepsiCo
Coca-Cola Co.	Philip Morris
Eastman Kodak	Public Service Enterprises
Eli Lilly	Schering Plough
Exxon Corp.	Texaco
Federal National Mortgage Assoc.	Walt Disney Co.
General Electric	

them, and look for good press on them in prestigious financial newspapers such as *Barron's, Investor's Business Daily, The Wall Street Journal,* and others.

Sometimes a stock that's doing well can plummet in price right after you buy it, despite the fact that nothing has happened to affect the corporation's profits or future performance. This is because the value of a corporation's stock is worth only what people will pay for it. People will pay for it whatever they figure it's worth based on future dividends and/or future growth potential. It is the future worth of a stock that is important to investors, and if they feel there are better places to put their money, no matter how well that corporation is doing, its stock will fall in price as demand for it decreases. The stock market is an auction market governed by the laws of supply and demand.

Stocks rarely go straight up or down. A falling stock occasionally rebounds before it falls again, and a climbing stock occasionally falls before it climbs again.

Your objective must be to find a way to cover yourself during the downward swings. You are not a market watcher; you do not watch the stock market every minute trying to determine when to buy and sell and possibly buy back again. What you need is a system that covers you during temporary bear phases. There are two systems of investing you might want to consider as part of your long-term investment strategy: dollar cost averaging and covered calls. Through dollar cost averaging investors try to take advantage of the "law of averages." They hope that the average price they invest over a long period of time will eventually put them in the profit zone. An equal amount of money is invested in a stock each week or month or at some other interval. Brokerage- or employer-sponsored plans in corporate stock allow the purchase of partial shares, as often occurs during dividend reinvestment programs you may join.

From investment to investment, the stock continues to swing in whatever trading range has been established for it as the law of supply and demand begins to govern.

Your advantage is realized because when the stock is at a higher price, that $500 you may be investing periodically buys fewer shares; and when the stock is lower in price, that $500 is buying more shares, as Table 10–3, 10–4, and 10–5 indicate.

Can you lose? Yes. If the stock heads south in price and you sell at a time when your total investments exceed the market value of the stock less buy and sell commissions over the period of the program, you lose.

Additional protection can be managed through the second of the two systems, covered calls. But as you have had only a preliminary introduction to calls and still need to understand money positions, the topic will be covered in Chapter 22.

Stock Speculation

As a speculator, you are on a different track than the investor, though your goals are the same: profits. But you are willing to take risks to get those profits frequently and in greater quantity.

Most investors who speculate in the market rarely take the time to do any detailed technical analysis except perhaps when they first enter the marketplace and

Table 10–3
Winning at Dollar Cost Averaging

Date	Cost Per Share	No. Bought	Buy Price	Total Shares	Total Invst.	Total Mkt. Value
5/95	$10	60	$600	60	$ 600	$ 600
6/95	12	50	600	110	1,200	1,320
7/95	10	60	600	170	1,800	1,700
8/95	10	60	600	230	2,400	2,300
9/95	6	100	600	330	3,000	1,980
10/95	6	100	600	430	3,600	2,580
11/95	5	120	600	550	4,200	2,750
12/95	6	100	600	650	4,800	3,900
1/96	6	100	600	750	5,400	4,500
2/96	10	60	600	810	6,000	8,100

By 2/96, you have invested a total of $6,000 in stock which now has a market value of $8,100. Your gain, then, is $2,100.

In this example, you come out a winner even though the stock had some serious slides in price, at one point even declining as much as 50 percent. This is because in your program, you were able to accumulate more stock at the lower prices than at the higher prices. In every case you invested the same amount of money. But bear these two things in mind: 1) you always invested the same amount of money, not bought the same amount of stock, and 2) dollar cost averaging does not guarantee profit, as Tables 10–4 and 10–5 will show.

Table 10–4
Losing at Dollar Cost Averaging

Date	Cost Per Share	No. Bought	Buy Price	Total Shares	Total Invest.	Total Mkt. Value
5/95	$10	60	$600	60	$ 600	$ 600
6/95	12	50	600	110	1,200	1,320
7/95	10	60	600	170	1,800	1,700
8/95	10	60	600	230	2,400	2,300
9/95	6	100	600	330	3,000	1,980
10/95	6	100	600	430	3,600	2,580
11/95	5	120	600	550	4,200	2,750
12/95	4	150	600	700	4,800	2,800
1/96	4	150	600	850	5,400	3,400
2/96	5	120	600	970	6,000	4,850

By 2/96, you have invested a total of $6,000 in stock, which now has a market value of $4,800. Your loss, then, is $1,150.

In this example, if you sell out on 2/94 at $5 per share, you will come out a loser. You need to continue your program in hopes that the stock will start to rise again—or you have to take your lumps and get out. There are no guarantees in stock investing, and even though dollar cost averaging is a conservative method of investing, you still have to be either lucky or skilled in picking the right stock to average on.

become enthralled with learning as much as they can. This is when they select stocks for fundamental and technical study; this is when they embark on their own charting program, charting the price of stock after stock—until they realize the task is too much for them. There are too many stocks and not enough time in the day.

Besides, by the time the speculator has done a little study and made a few trades, he quickly realizes there is no single analytical technique he can depend upon. He knows that the Smart Money will have all the important data long before he does. He knows that fundamental analysis can show how strong a stock is today but it can only speculate about how strong it will be tomorrow—and it definitely cannot predict how the investment public is going to feel about it. He knows that technical analysis only tells what is happening and cannot guarantee future performance. And he also soon begins to learn that the stock market is hardly efficient: Price and volume movements can gyrate in response to wars, weather, media hype, and false reports; statistics show that prices do not always go up when volume goes up; and government fiscal and monetary policy changes can render all your fundamental and technical analysis obsolete. In short, all the indicators discussed in the previous chapter can say "time to buy" when it is actually "time to sell."

This is why many investors design their own analytical tools. They surmise that if all the professionals with all their data, computers, and fancy algorithms cannot

Table 10–5
Breaking Even at Dollar Cost Averaging

Date	Cost Per Share	No. Bought	Buy Price	Total Shares	Total Invest.	Total Mkt. Value
5/95	$10	60	$600	60	$ 600	$ 600
6/95	12	50	600	110	1,200	1,320
7/95	10	60	600	170	1,800	1,700
8/95	10	60	600	230	2,400	2,300
9/95	12	50	600	280	3,000	3,360
10/95	15	40	600	320	3,600	4,800
11/95	20	30	600	350	4,200	7,000
12/95	15	40	600	390	4,800	5,850
1/96	10	60	600	450	5,400	4,500
2/96	12	50	600	500	6,000	6,000

In this example, you break even. There were a number of decision points during the program, but in every case you opted to stay in the stock. If you sold in 9/95, you would have realized a $360 profit. On 11/95, you could have realized a $2,800 profit. The lesson here is that even with dollar-cost averaging you still have to know your stock and be prepared to make decisions along the way. No matter what anyone tells you, dollar cost averaging takes alert management to be successful.

Note the irony here. While the stock was up $2 per share on 2/96 from what you paid for it, you still could not make money. This can happen during dollar cost averaging programs when there are wide swings in price over short periods of time.

---

consistently outperform the market averages, such Dow Jones and Standard & Poor's, they may as well go their own way.

Some of the methods are worth considering, though they offer no guarantees. Now, in evaluating some of them, you may say that they are after the fact. But you must understand that the independent investor like you and I do not have the timing advantages of professional money managers, nor their money; what works for the big guys does not work for us.

The stock selection techniques described below are not recommendations. They are methods that independent speculators, and occasionally professional portfolio managers, use, and that you may find useful or inspirational in forming your own combined strategies. What is additionally important is that you begin to realize the importance of staying covered, at least to some degree.

Stock Splits and Stock Dividend Announcements

Some investors play stock splits or stock dividends. When a stock split is announced, the split affects stockholders of record at some future date, which may be weeks or months away. This means that the announcement itself is the flag to begin taking positions. As you have learned in Chapter 8, stock splits and dividends are book-keeping games. However, they usually generate a great deal of buying interest. Long before the split or dividend is announced, the news leaks to the right people, so by the time of the announcement, the stock may already be overbought. Not knowing if this is the case, the investor goes in and plays the stock both ways.

If the price is relatively high compared to pre-announcement prices, she can expect that the market will adjust itself soon or right after the split. In this case, she goes short on the stock but long on lower-priced calls. If the stock goes up she wins on the calls; if the stock goes down, she wins on the stock. If the price is not much higher than pre-announcement prices, she might go long on the stock and long on puts.

She has other tools to use, of course. Rather than stock and options combinations, she might want to consider buying puts and buying calls on the stock. But this can result in greater risk, although she will not need to put up as much money because of the low price of stock options. The greater risk comes in because of the time-decay factor. As the calendar marches toward the expiration date of options contracts, puts and calls decay unless there is substantial movement in the price of the stock.

Let's look at two examples, each representing stock selection because of an announced split. Please bear in mind that there is much more for you to learn about puts, so the examples are not designed to include all the specifics, only to illustrate the potential that puts have as a hedging tool. You will learn more about put transactions in Chapter 16.

EXAMPLE #30. Playing a Stock Split: Stock and Options

On July 25, C&S Corporation announces a 2-for-1 stock split to holders-of-record on August 15. The stock is at $60 at the time of announcement, and had been at $48 just one month previously, indicating that the market has adjusted the price in anticipation of the slip. You know that there is usually a big swing in a stock's price before and after a stock split, so you decide to take your positions, leaning toward a bullish position, as you expect the stock to climb further.

You buy 200 shares at $60 and buy two October 55 puts for $250 (2 1/2). Total cost (commissions excluded) is $500 for the options and $12,000 for the stock.

Just prior to the split, the stock moves to $65 per share and the options decrease to 50 cents each. You decide to get out, so you sell your stock for $13,000 and your options for $100.

A. Sale of stock:	$13,000	
Purchase of stock:	−12,000	
Profit:	$ 1,000	
B. Cost of puts:	$ 500	
Sale of puts:	− 100	
Loss:	$ 400	

Gain: $600 [Profit from stock ($1,000)
less loss from options ($400)]

You might believe that it would have been better to just short the stock, but that's Monday-morning quarterbacking. There is no possibility you could have been sure of which way the stock was going at the time you took your positions.

The stock could have risen to $65 and the calls to $6, in which case you would have seen a loss of $1,000 on the stock but a $700 gain on the calls. On the other hand, the stock could have stayed at $60 through the expiration of the calls, and you would have lost $500 on the calls and broken even on the stock. But because there is no expiration date on the short position, you could have held it until it finally went down—if it went down.

In our second example, only the options are played.

EXAMPLE #31. Playing a Stock Split: Puts and Calls

Assume the same conditions. C&S announces a split. The stock is at $60, higher than in preceding weeks. You buy four October 65 calls at $2½ and four October 55 puts at $2½. Cost of puts is $1,000 and of calls $1,000.

The stock climbs to $65 per share within a week or two. The calls are now worth $6 and the puts 25 cents. You close out your positions. $2,400 is received from the sale of the calls, and $100 from the sale of puts.

A. Sale of puts and calls:	$2,500
B. Cost of puts and calls:	−2,000
C. Profit:	$ 500

In this case, you chose to sell out-of-the-money puts and calls, a somewhat risky procedure because if the stock did not move, you would be assured a loss as time decayed the value of the puts and calls. If you sold in-the-monies, you would necessarily have to buy fewer puts and calls because of the expense of the options, but you would always have the option of preserving some of your holdings by exercising your options to take positions in the stock. Other alternatives are also open to you. You could purchase in-the-money calls and out-of-the-money puts or vice versa. You could purchase the next series of options as soon as the current ones expire so that you stay in the game as long as necessary. Never think of stock options as short-term investments just because they expire within months. When the October 65 calls expire, then go to the November 65 calls, and so on.

Corporate Takeover Announcements

Playing takeover announcements is little different than playing stock split and stock dividend announcements, except here your strategy is based on the fact that after the initial surge in price on takeover news, there are usually secondary and tertiary surges as the negotiations continue.

The strategy necessitates using stock and options combinations or put and call combinations, because hedging assures some insurance against negative developments. If negotiations continue and a bidding war ensures, the price will certainly go up. But if the negotiations fall apart, the stock will tumble.

Investors who play this game usually like to load up on puts but, for this example, the safer way to play the game is illustrated.

EXAMPLE #32. Playing Takeover News

Rigg Systems Integrations announces that it intends to take over Sheen Telecommunications. This is your flag to take positions in stocks and options. By the time you get the news, the stock has already moved to $50 per share. Undaunted, you buy 200 shares of the stock and insure your position with two December $45 puts which you get at $1 (for a total of $1,000).

The fight is on. A white knight, Kingsley Inc., comes along and drives the price up another $10. You decide to take your profits. The puts, however, are off the board and worthless, or else worth less than the cost of commissions to sell them.

A. Sale of stock:	$12,000	
Cost of stock:	−10,000	
Profit:	$ 2,000	
B. Cost of puts:	$ 250	
Sale of puts:	− 000	
Loss:	$ 250	
C. Profit:	$ 1,750	

The number of puts purchased does not necessarily have to correspond to the number of shares purchased. That is, instead of one put for every 100 shares, other ratios can be used. For instance, in the above examples, 10 or 20 puts could have been purchased. This necessarily requires the stock to move a great many more points before the strategy can prove profitable. If the stock falls in good time and far enough, the puts can pay off handsomely. In the above example, if the takeover attempts fall apart because of stockholder challenge or antitrust laws and the stock tumbles to $40, the puts can have intrinsic value of about $5 each (give or take ½ point). This means while the stock may depreciate by $2,000, the puts will have a total value of $5,000 (if you have 10) or $10,000 (if you have 20).

Other Speculative Stock Selection Techniques

The dividend and takeover examples above serve as the basis for understanding how to play stocks selected by relatively random means. You have the option of doing one of the following:

- Buying stock long and buying puts.
- Selling stock short and buying calls.

- Buying puts and calls.

Understanding this, you may consider the following speculative stock selection techniques, further understanding that technical analysts and fundamentalists might very well dismiss them as "lazy, random methods." The major problem with each of them is that they rely on just one or two indicators and are therefore considered extremely chancy, for there is no one market indicator that can be depended upon to gauge the potential of a stock. Nevertheless, independent investors find that having their own mix of just a few indicators to watch simplifies the game for them and allows them the ability to make their moves as quickly as possible. The Big Money often does not have such flexibility and also has many people to answer to, so it needs to prove all indicators were weighed before taking a position.

New highs. Investors will watch the daily list of stocks breaking new highs and then move in to play them both ways, more often than not by purchasing the stock and buying low-priced puts. Many who play this game will take their positions the first time a stock breaks new high ground; others prefer to wait for the second or third thrust into higher territory before they buy in. Additional criteria is often required. The stocks, first of all, must be optionable; that is, options must be available on them. Additionally, there may be the requirement that the stocks be one of the S&P 100 or 500, one of the Dow Jones Industrials, or one of the 20 most active stocks for the previous day or week.

Most active. The most active issues list published daily is another source for quick plays. Many investors understand that this list serves to point out where investor interest lies. Thus, if they see a stock making the most active list two or three times in a week or two, they will consider this a highly bullish signal. Other criteria may also be necessary, such as the stock being on a particular exchange, included in a major index, being a part of a particular industry, and being optionable.

Volume percentage leaders. This list appears daily in all major newspapers and financial dailies. In the *Wall Street Journal*, the list is of stocks priced $5 or more that have also maintained a trading average of over 5,000 in the past 65 trading days. Some speculators see this list as a primary indicator of special situations. Other criteria for the stock they pick may include that the most recent price change be positive, that the percentage difference should be at least 500 percent, that the stock is also a member of a particular growth industry, and that it is optionable.

Price percentage leaders. This is also a daily listing and a primary flag for some investors. Other criteria for target stocks on this list may include the price change being more than 20 percent, the stock also being included on the most active list, a member of a growth industry, and, of course, optionable.

Newsletters. Many investment newsletters have a "stock of the week" or "stock of the month" selection. Many speculators will play these stocks both ways, assuming that the newsletter itself creates the market for the stocks and that there will be a short-term run-up before the stocks eventually fall to their preselection prices. This strategy sometimes works, but timing is difficult for a number of reasons. Word usually leaks out before press time, and the stock has usually already had most of its run-up. When the newsletter reaches its subscribers, there are usually additional price gains, but these are often relatively small. Most investors who play this game say they do not really care, for they can profit on the puts when the stock prices slide back to reality. This entails, however, always maintaining a position in puts. Over time, the cost can add up so that eventual profits are not very impressive if they occur at all.

Money Management

Money management is extremely important in stock investing but it is where many investors lack knowledge and skill.

"How much should I invest?"

"Should I reinvest all my dividends and capital gains?"

"When do I take my profits?"

These are frequent questions investors ask. And they are important questions that require different answers according to individual investment goals. But here's a four-step strategy that everyone can employ:

1. Set up a margin account so you have the flexibility of always buying in round lots and are able to hedge your positions immediately—if you so wish—with puts and calls, each put and each call representing 100 shares of stock.

2. Set up a monthly budget for investing. Assume it is $500. You do not have to buy stock with it each month. You can just have your broker deposit it in an interest-bearing account until you are ready to invest.

3. Buy outright or dollar cost your way into selected stocks, depending upon whether you are investing or speculating, as you see fit.

4. Every time you sell your holdings, it goes back into the bank, whether you make a profit or a loss. Meanwhile, you continue to deposit your $500 every month and to invest accumulated sums as you prefer. But every time you sell, you withdraw the money. In this way, you remain liquid, never go to extremes, and are never in a position to lose everything in the market. You may at anytime increase your monthly deposits to your brokerage account. But that monthly deposit should always be what you can afford to keep putting in for the long term.

It is not a complicated scheme. Once you put it into effect, you will realize the comfort and consistency it brings to your investment program.

11

SAMPLE TRANSACTIONS

Every investor has his or her own agenda. Some are interested mainly in income, others in capital appreciation, others in both. Trade-offs always have to be made. A stock providing high income is not going to provide high capital appreciation; a stock providing high potential for capital gains does not usually pay high dividends.

The fund managers who are able to successfully navigate their extensive portfolios through bad times as well as good times have skills that are rarely appreciated by independent investors until the latter have had their share of disappointments in the few stocks that they manage. Peter Lynch (of Fidelity Magellan fame) and a Stephen Lieber (of Evergreen Foundation) are masters of their trade; until you are up against them, you have no idea how special their skills and knowledge are. Providing income, safety, and capital appreciation all at once is close to impossible. So, the trade-offs start. Which is more important? Every investor has to know the answer before beginning to build a portfolio.

Portfolio Mix

In this book, the emphasis is on stock and options trading and the combinations that will bring safety and capital appreciation. It is taken for granted that readers realize they will rarely, if ever, want all of their investment dollars just in stock and options. For instance, for most of 1994 and into 1995, they will want to have at least 25 percent of their portfolios in U.S. Treasury bonds, the other 75 percent in stocks and options—but not too many different stocks and options. The more conservative will want to have stocks and options make up even less of a percentage of their total investment dollars (or net assets). In the years 1996 and beyond, the proportion of investment dollars to be assigned to stocks and options must be determined by the investment climate, which is pretty much orchestrated by which way the investment community expects interest rates to go. If interest rates are expected to decline, the market will be bullish and prices will climb. If interest rates are expected to increase, the market will be bearish and stocks will fall.

For those of you who will be trading mainly in stocks and not using any of the hedging strategies discussed in this book, it is wise to spread your risk over a number of stocks, with some mix of government and money market instruments to limit risk factors and provide some steady income as well as back-up money.

For those of you who will hedge, or use options, a few well-chosen stocks and a mix of options will give you the same level of safety; and at the same time, these positions will allow you greater liquidity, for you can effect the same results with less investment. This will become even more evident in coming chapters on puts and calls.

Buying In

Whatever strategy you may decide to use for selecting stocks, always be sure that you get two additional opinions besides your own. These other opinions may come from your broker, some investment newsletter, or some stock picker interviewed by, or writing in, *Barron's* or one of the other financial newspapers.

Table 11–1 gives stock listings that may be found in *The Wall Street Journal* and Table 11–2 gives listings that may be found in *Investor's Business Daily*. There is a tendency on the part of investors to make their stock selections from these tables— but this is old information even if it does appear daily. These tables provide nothing more than a snapshot of the previous day's or year's activity.

Investor's Business Daily has made great strides in developing tables that can help you select a stock that is worth *further investigation*. As a matter of fact, this little financial newspaper is strong on all types of statistics. It does not have the editorial strength of *The Wall Street Journal* or *Barron's*, but this newspaper understands its audience much better than *The Journal*. It knows that the investor is basically a sportsman, and like all sportsmen he delights in statistics. Tables are not just tables to the small investor—they are action figures. But they are not meant to provide the basis for stock selection, only to flag stocks that may be worth further research.

A glance at Tables 11–1 and 11–2 immediately tells you that you have to go much deeper than such superficial data as current P/E ratios and 52-week high/lows. What is more important to you are such things as *projected* earnings, *projected* P/E ratios, and *future* high-lows, more of which are available from the tables.

For all practical purposes, pricing and other data presented in these tables represent what the Smart Money expected them to be six months or more before. As the random walkers tell us, the Smart Money has already seized any nonrandom price fluctuations, and what is left for you and me is nothing short of hope—that some definable but unexpected event will send the price of the underlying stock the way we want it to go.

Assume, for example, that you are interested in buying stock in a major oil company. This oil company, which we will call Stock One, has been on a capital spending program that has totaled some $10 billion. The company recently declared a stock split, and because this is a Blue Chip company, you feel it's worth the investment. It is also paying a 75 cent per share dividend every quarter. So, you decide to buy 1,000 shares at $30 per share. First you check with your broker or other financial counselor to find out if he has any "show-stoppers" that might make you rethink your strategy. If not, you look for a third recommendation, even if it may be indirect. This may come from the financial newsletter to which you subscribe or to some positive reference that may be received from the media.

Table 11–1
Stock Tables

-L-L-L-

	10⅝	6¾	LAC Min g	LAC	.06e	...	...	584	8⅝	8⅜	8½	...
	13⅜	**6½**	**LAGear**	**LA**		**...**	**dd**	**2146**	**7½**	**7⅛**	**7½**	**+ ½**
	43⅜	34⅜	LGE Energy	LGE	2.08	5.6	14	180	37¼	37⅛	37¼	+ ¼
	5⅝	4¼	LLE RoyalTr	LRT	.42e	8.6	...	411	5	4⅝	4⅞	+ ⅛
	9⅝	7⅝	LNH REIT	LHC	.56a	6.9	dd	2	8⅛	8⅛	8⅛	...
	22	**10½**	**LSI Logic**	**LSI**		**...**	**20**	**14742**	**22**	**20½**	**21⅞**	**+ 1½**
	14⅜	11½	LTC Prop	LTC	1.08	7.9	18	1289	13⅝	13⅜	13⅝	+ ¼
n	18¼	10	LTV Cp	LTV		...	3	1140	17¾	17½	17⅝	...
n	6¼	3	LTV Cp wt			...	...	151	5	4⅞	4⅞	– ⅛
	1¼	9/16	LVI Gp	LVI		...	dd	1061	1¼	15/16	1	– ⅛
s▲	28⅝	11⅞	LaQuinta	LQI	.10	.3	48	1535	30	28⅝	29⅝	+ 1
	40	25⅜	LaZ Boy	LZB	.68	2.0	18	273	34½	34⅜	34⅜	...
s	25⅝	21½	LacledeGas	LG	1.22	5.0	16	72	25	24⅝	24⅝	– ¼
	27¼	15	Lafarge	LAF	.30	1.2	cc	2165	26	25¼	25⅞	+ ⅝
	8⅞	5⅜	LaidlawA g	LDWA	.16	...	...	6	6¼	6⅛	6⅛	...
	9	5⅜	LaidlawB g	LDWB	.16	...	...	828	6⅜	6¼	6¼	...
	34	25⅝	LakheadPipe	LHP	2.36	7.6	13	298	31½	31	31¼	– ⅛
	7⅝	4½	LamsonSes	LMS		...	dd	628	7⅛	6¾	7	+ ⅛
	52¾	27	LandsEnd	LE	.20	.4	21	783	50¾	49¾	50⅜	– ⅜
n	7⅝	4⅝	LASMO	LSO	.08e	1.3	...	201	6⅛	6	6	...
n	26	21¾	LASMO A	LSOA	.83p	3.8	...	182	22½	21⅞	22	– ¼
	17⅛	13⅝	LatinAmDllr	LBF	1.50a	9.9	...	129	15⅜	15⅛	15⅛	– ¼
	31⅝	13½	LatinAmEqty	LAQ	.75e	2.8	...	212	27⅜	26⅝	26¾	+ ⅛
	30¼	14	LatinAmDiscv	LDF	1.57e	6.4	...	279	24⅞	24⅜	24⅜	...
	35⅞	17⅛	LatinAmFd	LAM	2.81e	10.7	...	644	26¾	26¼	26⅜	+ ⅛
	15½	11¼	LawterInt	LAW	.40	3.4	cc	3824	11¾	11½	11⅝	– ⅛
	17¼	14⅜	LeaRonal	LRI	.52	3.4	15	63	15⅜	15¼	15¼	...
	38¼	27	Lee Ent	LEE	.84	2.4	19	592	34¾	34	34¾	+ ⅝
s	25¼	19⅜	LeggMason	LM	.40	1.8	7	177	22⅜	22¼	22¼	– ⅛
	50⅛	32¾	LeggetPlat	LEG	.60f	1.3	22	2205	45⅜	45	45¼	+ ¼
	37¾	27	Lennar	LEN	.12	.4	15	425	33⅝	33¼	33⅜	– ⅛
	5¾	2⅝	vjLeslieFay	LES		...	...	99	3⅝	3½	3½	– ⅛
	47¾	36	LeucdaNat	LUK	.25i	.6	8	197	40½	40	40⅜	+ ⅜
	32¼	23½	Leviathan un	LEV	2.00e	6.6	...	102	30¼	30	30¼	+ ¼
n	20¼	10⅞	LevitzFurn	LFI		...	...	125	17⅛	16⅝	16⅞	– ⅛
n	11⅜	8¼	LexngtnPrpty	LXP	1.08	10.7	...	79	10⅜	10⅛	10⅛	– ¼
n	18⅞	11⅞	Libbey	LBY	.15e	.8	...	209	18⅜	18	18¼	+ ⅛
	2⅝	**½**	**vjLiberteInv**	**LBI**		**...**	**...**	**114**	**2⅜**	**2¼**	**2⅜**	**+ ⅛**
	11⅜	10⅝	LibtyAS	USA	1.06e	9.7	...	609	10⅞	10¾	10⅞	+ ⅛
	34¾	23¾	LibtyCp	LC	.62f	2.3	11	75	28	27¼	27¼	– ½
	10¼	8	LibtyTrmTr	LTT	.72e	8.6	...	50	8⅜	8⅛	8⅜	+ ⅜
n	23⅜	16¾	LifePartnrs	LPG	.08f	.5	9	1782	17⅞	17½	17½	– ⅜
	37½	19⅛	LifeReCp	LRE	.24f	1.2	8	70	20⅜	20⅛	20⅛	– ⅛
	61⅞	43⅝	LillyEli	LLY	2.50f	4.8	31	6014	52⅜	51	52¼	+ 1
	25¼	16⅝	Limited Inc	LTD	.36	1.8	16	10240	19¾	19⅛	19⅝	+ ⅛
	21¼	17⅞	LincNatSec	LNV	.96a	4.9	...	61	19⅝	19½	19½	...
s	48¼	37	LincNatCp	LNC	1.64	3.9	9	1624	42½	41⅞	41⅞	– ¾
s	17⅜	14¼	LincNatInco	LND	1.28a	8.3	...	12	15⅜	15¼	15⅜	+ ⅛
	74¾	51	Litton	LIT		...	dd	6172	74¼	72	74¼	+ 1¼
n	34⅞	28¼	Litton wi			...	...	10789	32½	31¾	32¼	– ⅝

This is a typical listing from *The Wall Street Journal.* At best, the information represents a snapshot of the previous day's activity for listed stocks. None of the information provided should be the basis for stock trading.

Table 11–2
Specialized Stock Tables

EPS/ RelSt		Acc. Dis.	52-Week High	Low	Stock	Symbol	Closing Price	Chg.	Vol.% Change	Vol. 100s	% Yld.	Day's Price High	Low	
					— A —									
16	**30**	**B**	**12¾**	**4¾**	**APeainPod**	**APOD**	**9½**	**+1¼**	**+65**	**160**		**9½**	**8½**	
64	10	B	19	10¾	APlusComm	ACOM	12	....	−40	306		12¼	11¼	
93	99	A	14⅜	2⅜	AAONInc	AAON	13⅞	− ⅛	−75	161		13⅞	13½	
91	92	B	20½	12	ABCRailPdts	ABCR	19⅝	....	−94	35		19⅝	19¼	
96	86	A	15¾	7⅛	ABSIndsInc	ABSI	15	+ ¼	−36	46	1.3	15¾	14¾	
81	86	E	30	15	ABTBldgPrd	ABTC	26½	− ⅜	+315	4090		27	26	
34	71	A	22½	10½	ACC Corp	ACCC	20¾	+ ¾	+179	2064	.6	21	20	
57	98	C	24	3⅞	ACSEnter	ACSE	18¼	+ ¾	−58	356		19½	18	k
91	46	C	46¾	21¼	ACXTech	ACXT	34¾	− ¼	−54	235		35¼	34	
79	**78**	**B**	**44**	**18¾**	**ADCTelecom**	**ADCT**	**40**	**+1½**	**−37**	**1543**		**40**	**38½**	o
96	65	D	19½	6¾	ADESACorp	SOLD	13¾	....	−62	244		13¾	13½	
91	74	B	10¼	5	AELIndsClA	AELNA	8½	− ½	−72	10		8½	8½	
95	96	A	21	7⅛	AEPIndsInc	AEPI	19½	− ¼	−57	110	.4	20¾	19½	
13	62	B	11¼	7	AEREnergy	AERN	9⅞	+ ⅛	−27	92		10¼	9¾	
3	1	.	17¼	15	AESChina	CHGNF	16	....	−87	705		16⅛	16	
58	61	B	23¾	18⅜	AESCorp	AESC	22¾	....	+705	6644	3.0	22¾	22¼	
80	69	B	12½	9¼	AFCCbleSys	AFCX	11¼	− ¼	−95	18		11¾	11¼	
93	97	C	44¾	14	AGCOCorp	AGCO	44	+ ¾	−29	1472	.1	44¼	43¼	
46	79	B	22⅛	15¼	APSHoldings	APSI	21¾	+ ⅝	−10	540		21¾	21	
50	19	B	5½	1⅞	ARINetwkSv	ARIS	4⅛	+ ¼	−49	54		4⅛	3⅞	-
23	1	E	26¼	NL	ASKCmptr	ASKI	6¾	− ¼	−28	1962		7⅛	6¾	o
59	85	B	33	12¾	ASTResrch	ASTA	23¾	....	−48	6505		24	23½	o
76	8	B	8¾	4½	ATSMedical	ATSI	5	....	−49	106		5	4½	
67	1	D	5⅞	1½	AWCompA	AWCSA	2 5/16	+ 5/16	−96	4		2 5/16	2	k
51	**4**	**D**	**13⅛**	**7**	**AamesFncl**	**AAMS**	**8**	**+1**	**+999**	**6666**	**3.8**	**8**	**7**	
22	77	B	8½	4	AbaxisInc	ABAX	8	+ ⅜	−59	171		8¼	7⅝	
32	78	B	29½	17	AbbeyHlthcr	ABBY	26⅜	− ⅞	+24	2285		27½	26¼	
74	71	B	12½	8½	AbingtonSvg	ABBK	12	− ¼	+93	205		12¼	11¾	k
62	**82**	**B**	**NH**	**7**	**AbraxasPetr**	**AXAS**	**13½**	**+1½**	**−34**	**109**		**13½**	**12½**	
38	2	D	16½	3⅛	AbsoluteEnt	ABSO	4	....	−37	128		4⅛	3⅞	
12	**92**	**B**	**NH**	**6¼**	**AccessHlth**	**ACCS**	**13⅝**	**+ ¼**	**−10**	**273**		**13¾**	**13**	
91	71	B	31¾	10⅝	AcclaimEntn	AKLM	22¼	− ¾	+250	3.9m		23¼	21⅛	k o
42	64	B	15⅞	6¾	AceCash	AACE	12	+ ¾	−98	2		12	12	
64	64	B	15½	12¾	AcetoCorp	ACET	15⅛	− ⅜	−97	3	2.1	15⅛	15⅛	
92	90	B	27¼	13	AcmeSteel	ACME	24½	....	−24	470		25	24¼	
50	53	B	20½	9	ActelCorp	ACTL	13¼	....	+6	2015		13¾	13	
12	20	B	7	3	ActionPerfrm	ACTN	4¼	+ 3/16	+160	369		4⅜	4⅛	
..	..	.	1¾	7/16	ActPr wt	ACTNW	13/16	+ 1/16	....	171		⅞	13/16	
99	69	C	24¾	16½	ActiveVoice	ACVC	22	+ ¾	+161	771		22	21¼	
76	66	B	24½	14¾	AcxiomCorp	ACXM	22	− ¼	−89	36		22¼	21¾	
72	17	B	16¾	9¼	Adac Labs	ADAC	11⅝	− ¼	+49	1254	4.1	12	11¼	
55	68	B	7½	3¼	AdageInc	ADGE	6	....	−82	47		6	6	
70	89	B	22½	9¼	Adaptec	ADPT	21¾	+ ⅜	−42	4443		21¾	21¼	o
16	38	D	20	12¼	AddingtnRes	ADDR	17	+ ½	−94	17		17	17	k
19	28	C	26½	11½	AdelphiaCm	ADLAC	16⅝	− ⅛	−81	154		17½	16½	
70	72	B	27	17½	AdiaServices	ADIA	26	....	−57	65	.6	26	25	
98	**84**	**B**	**37**	**16¼**	**AdobeSystm**	**ADBE**	**30⅞**	**+1⅜**	**+122**	**2.6m**	**.6**	**31¼**	**29½**	k o

This table from *Investor's Business Daily* shows an expanded listing designed to help select a stock that is worth further research. But no matter how extensive a stock table may be in terms of the statistical data it provides, stock tables are only reports, not analyses.

Reprinted with permission from *Investor's Business Daily*, May 19, 1994.

EXAMPLE #33. Bidding on a Stock

"Mr. Broker, please put in a cash order for 1,000 shares of Stock One common at $35 per share, good-till-canceled, all or none."

Now you begin to watch the paper every day to check the price and any news. Much to your chagrin, the stock begins to go south in price shortly after you take your position. Uh, oh! Did you make a mistake? Did you interpret the financial data incorrectly? What's going wrong? Should you bail out?

Well, a lot of things could have gone wrong. The stock split could have created a "fool's market" in the stock, and a price adjustment was to be expected. On the other hand, perhaps some of the fundamentals were changing, mainly because of the tremendous spending and exploration program.

You may have been too absorbed in current and past statistical data and not enough in projected statistics. What a stock has done in the past, or is doing in the present, is not necessarily indicative of what it will do in the intermediate and long term. The company may be planning to issue millions in company guaranteed debt securities and be planning to cut back staff. Security analysts may be projecting declining earnings. Insider trading might have the investment community highly nervous about the stock. Almost anything can be putting downside pressure on the stock.

But do you stay with it or bail out? Tough decision.

If it's a Blue Chip, it has come-back power. If volume is consistent and heavy, it has come-back power. If sale and P/E projections are strong, it has come-back power. But there are no guarantees. The decisions get a bit easier when you are hedging with options, and you will see this in coming chapters. But here, where you are limited to only playing the stock, options are very limited.

Selling Off

Table 11–3 shows the price movement for the stock. While the real name of the stock is not given, the price movement in the table is actual.

You can see that the stock has declined from $35, where you purchased it, to $26⅛ in a period of roughly 13 months. That's over a $9,000 loss in principal when broker commissions are included. Dividends of $2,600 for the same period will partially offset the loss.

What would you do? Would you have placed a stop-loss order ($30 or $28?) at the same time you took your initial position? Would you panic and sell after 13 months, taking your losses before they may get worse? Or would you hold on and pray? How bad can it get?

The first thing to look at is your objective.

If you purchased the stock for income, stay with it, unless the dividend is in danger of being canceled.

If you purchased the stock primarily for capital appreciation, you must have had either long-term or short-term goals. If they were short term, the answer is to get out. If they were long term, hold on, as long as the fundamentals are still strong.

Table 11–3
Stock One Price Performance
Shares Owned: 1,000

Month/Day	Stock Price	Dividends Received
1/16	$34⅜	$750
4/18	32½	750
7/19	28⅛	750
10/18	26⅛	750

Over a 10-month period, Stock One has depreciated 8¼ points, or $8,250. Dividends for the same period have totaled $2,600. What would you do, hold or sell? Table11–4 tells you what the stock did over the next 12 months.

Table 11–4 shows what finally happened 25 months later. The stock finished at $37.25.

If you held and decided to sell now, you would place the following order:

EXAMPLE #34. Selling a Stock

"Mr. Broker, please sell 1,000 shares of Stock One at market and put the proceeds in my money market account."

Table 11–4
Stock One Price Performance, Continued
Shares Owned: 1,000
Original Cost: $34⅜

Month/Day	Stock Price	Dividends Received
13/13	$30¾	$750
16/10	30¾	750
19/10	33⅜	750
22/10	37⅜	750

As this table shows, if you held the stock for 22 months, you would have realized total capital gains of $3,000 plus total income of $5,200. That's an $8,200 total return on a $34,375 investment for a period of 22 months. Whether or not this represents a competitive return depends upon what government and money market instruments are yielding and what the stocks making up the Dow Jones and other popular averages are doing.

In the money market account, your proceeds will collect interest until you are ready for another stock transaction.

You will find that sell decisions are harder than buy decisions. Take a look at the market performance of the stock in Table 11–5. These are actual price movements over the given time period for actual stocks. The names of the stocks are not given so that you are not prejudiced for or against the stocks in your future trading.

How long would you have held on in each of these cases?

In both buy and sell decisions, you will want to be especially eager for financial forecasts. The price of a stock is always based on expectations of the performance of the issuing corporation and on the usual multiples at which the stock is expected to sell.

Financial forecasts are estimates of performance over established periods They are usually conditional and may be absolutely hypothetical, so it is very important to pay careful attention to wording. For instance, Stock One may have had projected earnings of $10 per share for the coming year, provided that explorations at offshore sites in western Canada produced so many barrels of oil. If drilling, however, should turn out to be unproductive, the entire forecast can be useless. Generally, however, financial forecasts give alternative scenarios so that an analyst can determine returns on investment that may result under various conditions.

Easy Hedges

From the very start, the position in Stock One was uncovered. There was no "insurance" in case the stock fell in price. Yet very easy hedges could have been put in place for some protection in case Stock One turned out to be a bad pick. These "easy hedges" are stop loss orders, covered calls, and puts.

Table 11–5
Stock Two Price Performance
Shares Owned: 500

Number of Days	Stock Price	Dividends Received
5	$34	$80
30	31½	$80
60	30⅝	$80
90	32¼	$85
120	36⅜	$85
150	38¼	$85
180	38⅛	$85

At what point would you have sold? It is not always difficult to determine whether or not you should cut your losses, take your profits, or stay with a stock for the long term.

Stop Loss

The stop loss order would work in the following fashion.

EXAMPLE #35. Placing a Stop Loss Order During Initial Bid

"Ms. Broker, please put in a cash order for 1,000 shares of Stock One common at $35 per share, good-till-canceled, all or none. Put in a stop-loss at $30 per share."

The stop loss order is just what its name implies. It is an order to stop any further losses in principal that may occur beyond $5 per share.

You do not have to place the stop loss order at bid time. It may be placed anytime you feel such an order may be necessary. The order is used to both ensure a profit created by an advance as well as to reduce any losses that may result from a rapid decline in the stock.

Bear in mind that a stop loss order is actually a market order, and the broker is not legally obligated to unload Stock One should it fall to $30 per share. Like any market order it has to wait its turn to be executed, and there may be thousands of orders ahead of it.

You may change your stop loss order at any time, and when your stock is on the upswing, you will want to do this often.

EXAMPLE #36. Changing a Stop Loss Order Rolling Up

A. Stock One advances to $40 per share
"Mr. Broker, please put in a stop loss on Stock One at $39 per share."

B. Stock One advances to $44 per share.

"Mr. Broker, please cancel my stop loss at $39 per share on Stock One and place another stop loss at $42 per share."

In Example 36, you are constantly making trade-offs. You are saying to yourself, "Well, the stock still has potential, and I don't want to lose out on any continued upswing. However, the run may be over, and the stock may fall back. I'll go for a trade-off. I'll chance a $1 or $2 loss to stay in position for further gains. But no more."

You are not limited to changing stop loss orders when your stock is on the way up. You may change or cancel them as many times as you feel necessary.

EXAMPLE #37. Changing a Stop Loss Order Rolling Down

A. Stock One declines to $30 per share.
"Mr. Broker, please put in a stop loss on Stock One at $28 per share."

B. Stock One declines to $28½ per share.

"Mr. Broker, please cancel my stop loss at $28 per share on Stock One and place another stop loss at $26 per share."

In Example #37, changing the stop loss orders allowed you to adjust to changing news and expectations.

Covered Calls

Covered calls also provide an easy way of hedging as well as producing additional income.

EXAMPLE #38. Bidding on a Stock and Writing Covered Calls

"Ms. Broker, please put in a cash order for 1,000 shares of Stock One common at $35 per share, good-till-canceled, all or none. Also sell 10 July 40 calls at $1½."

The calls provide immediate income of $1,500 (as each call represents 100 shares and a $1½ listed premium actually represents $150) as well as "insurance" against a $1,500 loss in capital should the stock depreciate in price.

The stock and the call may be listed on different exchanges. For instance, Dow Jones stock is listed on the New York Stock Exchange, but options for the stock are listed on the Philadelphia Exchange. However, your broker can execute both orders.

When you become a covered call writer, you are at the same time a stock trader and an options trader, and you may play both together or separately. For instance, other things being equal, the call will depreciate in price as time goes by and the contract approaches the expiration date, as you have already learned. Understanding this, consider the following example.

EXAMPLE #39. Selling Only Covered Calls

Stock One holds at $35 per share, but as the expiration date is only one week away, the calls have depreciated in value to $¼. Rather than chance the stock suddenly moving to the striking price, you decide to buy back your calls at a profit.

"Mr. Broker, I'd like to buy 10 July 40 calls on Stock One at $¼. All or none. This is a closing transaction."

The broker buys the calls and you have a profit of $1,250—and still own your stock, and, therefore, are still eligible for dividends, participation in capital gains, and writing additional calls with other expiration dates.

The advantages of writing covered calls lie mainly in the fact that you can easily cover your position if called because you already own the underlying stock, and because the calls decay with time—which means you are in the unique situation of having time work for you for a change. But writing covered calls is not as easy as it appears. There are hidden traps. Writing covered calls is the safest game in the options market, but the covered call writer must also be a highly skilled stock picker. Gains from writing calls can be offset by losses in the underlying stock.[1]

Puts

Buying puts against your position in the underlying stock is also an easy way to hedge.

EXAMPLE #40. Bidding on a Stock and Buying Puts

"Mr. Broker, please put in a cash order for 1,000 shares of Stock One common at $35 per share, good-till-canceled, all or none. Also buy 10 July 30 puts at $1½ all or none."

The puts are an additional expense of $1,500 but they provide "insurance" against a $1,500 loss in capital should the stock depreciate in price.

As with the call, the stock and the put may be listed on different exchanges.

When you become a put trader, you are also a stock trader and an options trader, and you may play the stock and the put either together or separately. But note that in the case of a long position in puts, time is against you. You own the puts, so as they depreciate so does your capital.

EXAMPLE #41. Trading Only Puts

Stock One falls to $25 per share; as the expiration date approaches, the puts have actually advanced to $5. You decide to sell the puts for $5,000 (a $3,500 gain) and sell the stock for a $1,000 loss.

"Mr. Broker, please sell 1,000 shares of Stock One at $25 per share. Also sell 10 July 30 puts on Stock One at $5. All or none. This is a closing transaction."

The broker executes the order and you take your profit.

Now, you have a taxable gain of only $2,500. Puts provide a great deal of flexibility just as calls do, but they also have their disadvantages. As they are primarily a tool used by bears, buying puts is not discussed in detail in this book, but detailed discussions of put buying may be found in *Tools of the Bear*.[2]

Other Hedges

The Big Money has another means of hedging that you may have heard about. It's called *portfolio insurance*, and it goes through stages of varying popularity with brokerages, banks, and other financial institutions.

Portfolio insurance is a method of counterbalancing stock holdings with stock index futures and index options. The strategy is to hedge against falling stock prices either by selling stock index futures or buying stock index put options, which are listed in the financial papers just as stock prices are. As the market falls, greater numbers of the futures and options contracts are sold. It works a bit like buying stock and buying puts on that stock, although portfolio insurance is a lot more sophisticated—and, actually, a lot more dangerous. This is because portfolio insurance does not really provide substantial protection during sudden and deep market drops. The pension and mutual funds found this out during the market crash of 1987 when many of the portfolio insurance programs were shut down, and they found this out again when the programs were actually blamed for much of the trading volatility that followed the October 1987 crash.

Portfolio insurance is a form of programmed trading. It has its advantages because it allows hedging strategies for big-time portfolios. But when Wall Street lets computers do the thinking instead of the well-trained, well-heeled, responsive, and responsible professionals it has in its arena, when things go wrong, they can go very wrong. Computers follow programs, right or wrong. The human mind follows programs when they are right but can ignore or change them when they are proving wrong.

Certificates and Contracts

When a broker holds your securities he does so in "street name." This means there is no stock certificate in your name, but rather in the name of the broker or his nominee.

Generally, when you first open your account with a broker, you will specify whether or not you want your certificates sent to you or held in your account. If the stock is held in your account, it will be done so in street name.

Leaving your stock with your broker is the easiest strategy if you are going to trade stock often or deal in covered calls. You will not be able to write covered calls unless your stock is being held by the broker.

There are no certificates issued when puts or calls are purchased. And you will never see a copy of the contract. What you will see, however, is a transaction statement from the broker that specifies the details of your opening or closing transaction. This is perfectly legal and also perfectly necessary to maintain the level of economy and speed required for options trading.

Trading for Big Profits

Now that you understand the importance and basics of hedging on long positions in stock, you are ready to trade for bigger profits (or losses). To do this, you want to leverage as much as possible and hedge very strategically. Reward depends upon risk.

This is where margin comes in. If you can make every dollar you invest do the work of two or more, you are playing the game in earnest; you are doing what you came into the stock market to do in the first place: make big money.

Let's assume, for instance, that you purchase Stock Four on margin, something you would not do if puts were not available.

EXAMPLE #42. Leveraging with Margin

"Mr. Broker, I'd like to place an order for 1,000 shares of Stock Four for $10 per share, good-till-canceled, all or none. This is for my margin account." At 50 percent margin, the cost to you is $5,000 before commissions.

In two years, the stock climbs to $20 per share, and you decide to take your profits, so you sell. "Mr. Broker, please sell 1,000 shares of Stock Four at $20 per share, all or none." Your proceeds: $20,000.

Your $5,000 investment became $20,000. You actually quadrupled your money in two years, less commissions and any margin interest. Without margin, you would have only doubled your money.

But what if the stock goes down?

Then, each dollar it goes down in price, you lose $2. On the way down, you will be flooded with margin calls to beef up your equity so the broker is out of harm's way. If the stock suddenly drops to $5 per share, you will in fact have lost all of your principal. This is why you will want to cover yourself with puts.

EXAMPLE #43. Leveraging with Margin and Hedging with Puts

"Ms. Broker, I'd like to place an order for 1,000 shares of Stock Four for $10 per share, good-till-canceled, all or none. This is for my margin account. I'd like to purchase 20 August 7½ puts at $¼, all or none." The cost of the puts will affect your break-even point.

If the stock begins to drop, the puts will increase in price but not point-by-point with the stock, for these are out-of-the-money puts. However, if the stock drops to, for example, $5 per share, the puts will most certainly be worth about $5,000 ($2½ x 20 x 100).

The puts do not offer perfect insurance. For instance, if the stock drops to $8 1/2 or $9 per share, there may not be any noticeable movement in the puts, in which case you would lose on the stocks and the puts. But the puts would provide some insurance if there are more serious drops in price on the very short term. (Remember that the puts are a decaying asset and worthless at expiration date.)

Another scenario presents itself. The stock may drop and you hold your position but take profits on the puts. If the stock climbs back in price, you stand to realize additional capital gains—or at least capital appreciation.

Greater insurance would be provided by at-the-money or slightly in-the-money puts, but these are generally very expensive. What you have to do is weigh your rewards against possible risk and then determine how much you feel you should pay for put "insurance." This is a decision only you can make. But when you are leveraging extensively, as in this case, be sure to hedge in some way.

Covered calls may also be considered in this instance, but they will severely inhibit the extent of your capital gains. And in the case of covered calls, you will want to limit the number that you write so they never represent more than 1 percent of your stock holdings—that is, 10 calls for 1,000 shares; 20 calls for 2,000 shares. In buying puts, however, you may change the ratio. (Notice that here we are comparing "writing" calls to "buying" puts.)

In short, if you are speculating, your chances of large profits are very limited if you are simply buying on cash and only playing the stock. The goal for being

Table 11–6
Cash versus Margin and Puts
Original Investment: $10,000

	Cash			**Margin (50%)**			
Trade	**Gain (Loss)**	**Dividends**	**Total Return**	**Gain (Loss)**	**Puts**	**Dividends**	**Total Return**
#1	$ 450	$150	$ 600	$ 900	(250)	$300	$ 950
#2	500	150	650	1,000	500	300	1,800
#3	(1,000)	200	(800)	(2,000)	750	400	(850)
#4	(800)	75	(725)	(1,600)	(400)	150	(1,850)
#5	(800)	75	(725)	(1,600)	2,500	150	950
#6	4,000	250	4,250	12,000	(400)	500	12,500
		Totals:	**$3,100**				**$13,500**

Time frames are unimportant for this illustration of advantages and disadvantages of margin purchases on stock while hedging with puts. The table indicates that there are no guarantees. There is always a way to lose as well as win. But margin increases profits and puts can offer a successful hedge or even increase profits. Generally, however, as the result above may indicate, margin trading on stock and hedging with puts can often be the more practical strategy.

#1 Illustrates how margin increases profit potential even though there may be a loss on puts.

#2 Illustrates capital gains on the stock as well as on the puts. The stock dropped, puts went up and were sold at a profit. Then the stock advanced for further gains.

#3 Illustrates how the puts limited losses, for without the puts, the capital loss would have been $1,600.

#4 Illustrates that it is possible to lose on the puts as well as the stock. In this case, losses are more than double what they would be if only the stock were traded.

#5 Illustrates the additional gains that can occur if profits are realized on both the puts and the stock. In this case, as in *#2*, the stock would have had to have been held through turnaround, although the puts were sold.

#6 Illustrates the exceptional gains that can occur when using margin if a stock more than doubles in price.

directly in the market should be maximum capital gains; otherwise, let some fund do the investing for you or continue to invest in your company's 401k program.

Margin gives you the leverage you need. When leveraging with margin, hedge with puts. The cost of the puts will affect your break-even point, as already indicated, but the position will help you cut your losses or even allow you to profit.

In Table 11–6, you will find a comparison of cash and margin trades. The margin trades are hedged with puts. Note how margin increases your profit potential and gives your investment additional leverage. Note also that the more you trade, the less chance you have of coming out ahead, so when you have a good stock, stick with it. There are other important lessons in Table 11–6 which are explained in the table notes.

Notes

1. Charles J. Caes, *Selling Covered Calls: The Safest Game in the Options Market* (New York: Liberty Hall, 1990), 69–82.

2. *Tools of the Bear* (Chicago: Probus, 1993), 99–102.

12

CORRECTING COMMON MISCONCEPTIONS ABOUT STOCK INVESTING

Independent investors often harbor some very fanciful misconceptions about the stock market. Those that follow often surface in the classroom and during general discussion.

1. *Stocks would not be listed on the exchanges if they were not worthwhile investments.*

Untrue. No stock is guaranteed, whether or not they are listed on a foreign (Table 12–1) or U.S. stock exchange or over the counter. Just take a look at the stock listings and compare the current price of stocks with their yearly high/low prices; you will immediately see that many stocks are below their high for the year. Not everyone makes money in the stock market. Stock investing is a tough game, especially today when we have a global economy. Things happening as far away as China can have an impact on prices on the stock markets around the world.

There is no formula for success. But there are formulas for failure, and these include being lazy in your research, not paying attention to the news, and not understanding the basic rules of investing.

2. *The stock market is the best place for one's money.*

Untrue. It is probably one of the better places to put your money if you want to try beat inflation. But, again, there are no guarantees. To be successful in the stock market, you must learn to use all the tools that are available to you and learn to stay on top of your investments. Understanding basic economics also helps, particularly the way that interest rates and the law of supply and demand affect stock prices.

3. *Stock listings in the daily newspapers provide all the information required to select or sell a stock.*

Untrue. Stock tables are simply daily reports with a couple of special flags included to tag stocks reaching new highs or new volumes, or otherwise performing above or below average in some way. The information in stock tables represents little more than a snapshot of yesterday's trading and perhaps a glimpse of what the highs and lows for the year have been. Stock tables are good for tracking prices of your current holdings and for serving to flag stocks that might be worth further research, but they should not serve as the basis for making any buy decisions.

Table 12–1
Exchange Listings

Overseas Markets

Closing Prices — JAPAN (Japanese Yen)

Stock	Cur.	Prev.	Stock	Cur.	Prev.
Ajinomto	1310	1320	Renown	490	490
Alps	1540	1510	Ricoh	616	607
Amada	1150	1150	Sankyo	2550	2570
Anitsu	1250	1220	Sanwa Bank	2260	2250
Asahi Chem	715	714	Sanyo	510	512
Asahi Glas	1200	1200	Seikisui	1350	1370
Bank of Tokyo	1600	1640	Sharp	1750	1720
Banyu	928	930	Shionogi	1000	1010
Brigestone	1590	1580	Shiseido	1180	1180
Brother	587	599	Skylark	2790	2760
Canon Cam	1700	1700	Sony	6390	6350
Calpis	990	998	Stanley	767	767
Casio	1360	1350	Sumitomo Bnk	2190	2200
Dai Nippon	1860	1880	Sumitom Chm	494	489
Daiei	1880	1900	Sumitomo Cp	1040	1050
Dai – Ichi Kan	1960	1990	Sumitomo Elc	1600	1600
Daiwa House	1630	1650	Sumitomo Tst	1530	1560
Daiwa Sec	1700	1740	Taisei Cp	667	679
Descente	675	680	Takeda	1310	1340
Eisai	1780	1790	Tanabe Sei	935	950
Fanuc	4270	4310	TDK	4470	4450
Fuji Bank	2270	2280	Teijin	470	480
Fuji Elec	515	506	Tokio Mar	1330	1330
Fuji Photo	2430	2470	Tokyo Elec	3370	3370
Fujisawa	1200	1220	Toppan	1340	1360
Fujitsu	1080	1050	Toray	685	678
Green Cross	1130	1150	Toshiba El	808	802
Heiwa Real	897	910	Toyoda Mach	680	680
Hitachi	970	957	Toyota	2100	2110
Honda	1780	1730	Yamaha M	938	940
Indus Bank	3310	3290	Yamaichi	912	909
Isuzu	461	462	Yamanouchi	2060	2070
			Yamoto	1290	1330
			Yaskawa	460	461
			Yasuda	801	810
			Yokogowa	954	985

Stock	Cur.	Prev.
News Corp	9.59	9.59
North BH	3.57	3.57
Oakbridge	0.68	0.68
Pan Cont	1.68	1.76
Pac Dunlop	5.37	5.35
Pioneer C	3.18	3.24
Placr Pac	2.93	2.95
RGC	5.00	5.05
South Pac	0.45	0.45
Santos	4.04	4.08
TNT	2.25	2.25
Westpac	5.13	5.16
WField	8.50	8.35
WMC	7.12	7.33
Woodside	3.97	4.00

LONDON (In pence unless marked $)

Stock	Cur.	Prev.	Stock	Cur.	Prev.
AA Corp	$48.63	$49.38	Kloof Gld	$9.94	$10.13
Abbey Nat	486.00	485.00	Ladbroke	207.00	205.00
Allied Lyons	617.00	622.00	Land Sec	700.00	707.00
Argyll	251.00	251.25	Lasmo	131.50	129.50
Asc Brit Fds	556.00	556.00	Leg & Gen	508.75	501.00
BAA	1005.00	995.00	Leslie	$1.18	$1.23
Barclays	553.00	555.00	Lloyds	592.00	584.00
Bass	523.00	525.00	Lon Rho	157.00	157.00
B.A.T.	472.00	475.00	Loraine	$3.45	$3.45
BET	130.00	132.50	Lucas	215.00	208.00
BICC	438.00	442.00	Marks	423.00	423.00
Blue Circle	354.00	352.00	MEPC	490.00	497.00
Boc Group	723.00	717.00	Nat Power	475.00	464.00
Body Shop	218.00	221.00	Nt West Bk	492.00	495.00
Boots	547.00	545.00	NFC	246.00	249.00
Bowater	495.00	502.00	Ofsil	$34.88	$35.13
Bracken	$0.45	$0.45	Pearson	667.00	672.00
Brit Aero	508.00	512.50	P & O	690.50	687.00
			Pilkington	194.00	194.00
			Powergen	565.00	553.00
			Prudentl	332.00	323.00
			Racal El	220.00	222.00
			Randfont	$9.38	$9.44
			Rank	421.00	418.00
			Reckit	637.00	636.00
			Redland	574.00	573.00
			Reed Intl	875.00	903.00
			Reuters	2015.00	2005.00
			RMC	974.00	970.00
			Rolls Royce	192.50	189.00
			Rothman	416.00	420.00
			Royal Ins	276.00	272.00
			RTZ	858.00	850.00
			Rustenburg	$18.88	$19.25
			Saatchi	139.25	140.00
			Sainsbury	387.50	383.00

Stock	Cur.	Prev.
BMW	871.00	874.00
Commrzbnk	363.50	366.50
Continental	288.50	290.00
Daiml Benz	853.00	854.50
Degussa	513.00	512.50
Deutsch Bk	823.00	824.50
Douglas	565.00	558.50
DT Babcock	277.00	268.50
Dresdnr Bk	414.00	415.80
Henkel	645.70	645.70
Hochtief	1077.0	1055.0
Hoechst AG	328.00	322.10
Hoesch	212.00	206.50
Holzmann	950.00	939.00
Horten	230.00	230.00
Karstadt	570.00	567.00
Kaufhof	510.00	496.00
KHD	148.00	144.80
Kloeckner	141.00	137.00
Krupp	212.00	206.50
Linde	881.90	877.00
Lufthansa	197.00	195.00
Man	447.50	450.00
Mannesmn	425.00	429.00
Metallges	190.00	190.00
Munch Rvrs	3200.00	3100.00
PKI	515.00	515.00
Porsche	907.00	919.00
Preussag	484.00	489.00
RWE	465.00	462.50
Schering	1089.00	1074.0
Siemens	705.00	704.50
Thyssen Hu	274.50	274.50
Varta	362.00	369.00
Vew	358.00	351.50
Viag	463.30	461.50

Toronto Markets

Quotes in Canadian funds; in cents unless marked $.

Stock	Volume	High	Low	Close	Chng.
Abti Prce	29445 $	18½	18½	18½	....
Agnico E	130900 $	15¾	15¾	15¾ –	⅜
Air Canada	406460 $	7¾	7½	7⅝ –	⅛
Alt Energy	131236 $	19¾	19¼	19¾ +	¼
Alta Nat	112900 $	17	16¾	17 +	⅛
Anderson	24815 $	34⅜	34¼	34⅜ +	⅜
A Barick	147179 $	33	32½	32¾	....
Atco I f	10800 $	15¾	15½	15½ –	¼
Dylex A f	646410	0.96	0.90	0.95 +	0.04
ELAN Eng	155300 $	9¾	9½	9¾ +	¼
Euro Nev	98860 $	42¼	41½	41½ –	⅞
FCA Intl	6331	3.70	3.70	3.70 –	0.05
FPI Ltd	4704 $	5	5	5	....
Fahnstk A f	600 $	11¾	11¾	11¾ +	⅛
Fairfax f	4800 $	71	70	71	....
Fed Ind A	9600 $	8	7¾	8	....
Finning L	500 $	22¼	22¼	22¼ +	½
Nova Cor f	328766 $	10	9¾	10	....
NS Power	259621 $	12¾	12½	12½	....
Nowsco W	18000 $	21	20¾	21 +	½
Onex C f	60700 $	15¼	15¼	15¼ –	⅛
Oshawa A f	3800 $	22¾	22¾	22¾	....
PWA Corp	125794	1.14	1.12	1.12 –	0.01
Pgurin A f	46000	3.65	3.45	3.55 +	0.05
PanCan P	1660 $	39¼	38½	39¼	....
Petro Cdn	175249 $	14½	14	14½ +	½

The fact that a stock is listed on an exchange is no guarantee of performance, whether it is a U.S. or foreign exchange. That is why there are always short sellers surveying the lists for possible opportunities.

4. *Trading volume is the best indication of a stock's eventual direction because it illustrates the demand trend.*

Untrue. Prices can go up or down on high volume. (See Table 12–2.) A stock may have exceptional trading one week and relatively little trading the next. Investor interest can be real or contrived. Volume can go up on false news, misinterpreted news, or insider buying or selling. By no means can you assume that because volume has been increasing, the price of a stock is showing promise. Heavy volume is only a flag for further research. It indicates investor interest, but it does not indicate whether that interest is valid or invalid.

5. *Stocks with yearly lows are good buys.*

Untrue. The only thing you can be sure of when it comes to stocks selling at their annual lows is that a lot of people have lost a lot of capital. Stocks can always go lower. Back in the 1980s, Western Union was a very popular stock, so popular that many investors and fund managers kept holding onto it while its price continued to drop, first from $42 to $33, then to $29. When it kept hitting new lows, an overeager market kept adding shares to portfolios. But the stock continued to drop, from $29 to $22, to $18, and finally to $2¼. No one seemed willing to believe that the stock could fall even further, and they kept buying even while the news got worse and worse. Quarterly and annual revenue reports kept showing reductions in net income or outright losses, but everyone felt that the stock would rebound. Margin traders kept answering margin calls until they finally had to throw in the towel. Call buyers kept rolling over to subsequent series of options, taking loss after loss. The smart players were the short sellers of stocks and calls and the buyers of puts. They made out well.

6. *Stocks with low P/E ratios are always good buys.*

Untrue. The P/E ratio is one of the most confusing investment ratios for the new investor. It seems to come in and out of vogue every five or six years and at this writing is currently the "in" ratio. But the price-to-earnings ratio has little significance all by itself. It is basically a report on the current trading pattern of a stock. The ideal P/E ratio for some stock groups is not the ideal for other groups. And, more confusing yet, the ideal P/E ratio for one stock is not ideal for another.

7. *The stock market is the place to get rich.*

Untrue. Absolutely untrue. The stock market is the place to get *richer* but not to get rich. There are many rich people with money in common and preferred stocks, but they were rich before they invested. There are just too many things going against the stock investor, not the least of which is the time it may take for a stock to turn its potential into actuality. A second problem is the knowledge and skill to select successive winners. Most independent investors cannot pick winner after winner. As a matter of fact, most of the pros cannot, either. However, the pros know how to balance their portfolios, make selective use of margin, and employ options to their advantage. They can weight their portfolios to compensate for losses in one sector. They have the money to wait long term for turnarounds and the money to use for backup.

An investor can possibly become rich trading in puts and calls, because these types of investments show extreme percentage gains (or losses). But stocks require high capital investment and generally move rather slowly. The use of margin can multiply profits, but it can also result in quick losses, in which case there is less

Table 12–2
Volume Leaders

NYSE	Volume	Close	Change
Hanson	7,870,600	$21\frac{1}{8}$	$+\frac{1}{4}$
TelefMex	3,682,600	$61\frac{1}{2}$	$-\frac{1}{4}$
US Surg	3,634,100	20	$+1\frac{5}{8}$
MylanLabs	3,041,700	$20\frac{3}{8}$	$-2\frac{3}{8}$
AmT&T	2,714,300	$53\frac{1}{2}$	$+\frac{3}{4}$
TimeWarner	2,511,400	$43\frac{1}{8}$	$+1\frac{7}{8}$
Chrysler	2,437,800	$58\frac{7}{8}$	-1
Merck	2,357,000	$31\frac{1}{2}$	$+\frac{1}{4}$
RJR Nabisco	2,334,900	$6\frac{3}{8}$	$+\frac{1}{8}$
WalMart	2,317,700	$27\frac{1}{4}$	$-\frac{1}{4}$
EMC Cp	2,033,700	23	$+\frac{3}{4}$
Coca-Cola	2,023,500	$41\frac{1}{2}$	$+\frac{3}{8}$
YPF	2,016,500	$25\frac{1}{2}$	$+\frac{3}{8}$
Citicorp	2,000,700	41	$-\frac{1}{8}$
NASDAQ			
Intel	4,145,200	$72\frac{1}{4}$	$+\frac{3}{8}$
AcclmEntn	3,943,600	$22\frac{1}{4}$	$-\frac{3}{4}$
CentxTlmgt	3,839,500	$10\frac{1}{4}$	$-\frac{1}{4}$
SftwrTool	3,336,800	$11\frac{7}{8}$	$+1\frac{5}{8}$
Pyxis	2,938,600	27	$-1\frac{1}{4}$
LotusDvl	2,791,900	$85\frac{1}{2}$	$+5\frac{3}{4}$
QVCNetw	2,580,400	$40\frac{1}{8}$	$+1\frac{5}{8}$
TeleComm A	2,417,900	$24\frac{1}{4}$	$+1\frac{1}{4}$
Perrigo	2,407,900	$24\frac{1}{2}$	$+\frac{3}{4}$
SeagateTech	2,345,200	$28\frac{1}{8}$	$+\frac{1}{8}$
MCI Comm	2,283,900	25	$-\frac{1}{8}$
Novell	2,246,800	$24\frac{1}{4}$	$+\frac{1}{8}$
AMEX			
EnergySvc	3,389,300	$3\frac{13}{16}$	$+\frac{1}{8}$
ExplorLA	1,397,600	$1\frac{1}{4}$	$+\frac{3}{16}$
MorganStanYen pwt	1,101,300	3	. . . . .
Datametrics	827,000	$2\frac{15}{16}$	$+\frac{1}{16}$
ViacomB	743,400	$27\frac{5}{8}$	$+1\frac{3}{8}$

The Smart Money checks daily to spot volume leaders. High volume often flags a stock that may be gaining popularity. But the Smart Money would never make a purchase just because a stock makes this list. They know high volume in itself is a guarantee of nothing except current interest. The reason for that interest must be uncovered by thorough detective work.

Source: *The Wall Street Journal*

money for reinvestment. The investor can easily find himself where he started after five years of profits and one of losses. This is why it is important to hedge and to use stocks and options in varying combinations, thereby allowing the possibility for high profits if a stock moves in either direction.

8. *Dividends are guaranteed.*

Untrue. Neither common nor preferred stock dividends are guaranteed.

A corporation is under no legal obligation to pay dividends unless they are actually declared. This means that when you look at the stock tables in your favorite financial newspaper, the dividends indicated are only what has been paid in the past. There is absolutely no guarantee that they will be paid in the future.

The board of directors can at any time elect to cancel or postpone dividends on common stock or to postpone dividends on preferred stock.

9. *A 2-for-1 stock split doubles your money.*

Untrue. The stock split is a marketing ploy. If you own 100 shares of AT&T at $60 per share and a 2-for-1 split is declared, on the record date for the split you will have 200 shares worth $30 each. Before and after the split, your equity is the same: $6,000.

What the stock split gives you is the potential for making additional money. Now with each dollar the stock advances, you make $2 instead of $1. Bear in mind that if the stock goes down in price, you lose $2 instead of $1. The stock split, however, brings the stock down to a more marketable price and should increase demand. Most of the time, a stock split works to the advantage of the stockholders but not always.

10. *It is better to trade stocks than options.*

True and untrue. It depends on what your goals are. For the independent investor who is primarily a speculator and looking for rapid capital appreciation, options are often not only more attractive because of their volatility, but also because they allow a certain amount of safety because of their low price. When you buy an option, you cannot lose any more than you paid for it.

For instance, suppose you decide that AT&T has the potential for doubling in price within the next two years and want to buy 200 shares. At $60 per share, you will have to put up $12,000. On the other hand, let's say you can purchase two in-the-money calls for roughly $1,200. The calls leave you much more liquid and give you the potential for even greater profit than you might realize from owning 200 shares of AT&T.

It is true that if there is any downturn in the stock, you can quickly have time decay and intrinsic depreciation double-teaming to render your holdings worthless, but you can hedge with low-cost puts and always roll over to the next series of calls to stay in the game. Even if you lose on the first two or three calls you buy, if the stock is indeed worthwhile, when it advances your gains on the calls will quickly make up for losses.

Timing is essential, however, in the buying of calls, and this timing takes a long time to master. The people who are usually the most successful in option (as well as stock) trading are those who know when a stock is ready to head north.

Consider the trader who invests $12,000 in a stock. He can wind up tying up his cash for years. The call buyer, however, is playing with relatively less money, and expiration dates force decisions. She is not likely to tie up her capital as the stock investor does, and she can realize higher yields. (Bear in mind that the call buyer is not entitled to dividends because she does not own the stock, only the right to buy the stock under certain conditions.)

Risk/reward factors and an investor's experience and goals are necessary considerations in actually determining whether or not options or stock are better investments. In either case, the guiding principle is "be careful." This means learn the hedging techniques that are most appropriate for your investment style and your investment goals.

11. *The small investor cannot do as well as the pros in the stock market.*

Untrue. The small investor can actually do better but he must realize that he cannot play the game the same way that the Big Money does. To begin with, the small investor is an outsider; he does not know about events until they happen. The Big Money is on the scene when things are developing.

This means the small investor has to use techniques and follow advice that are best suited to the way he must necessarily play the game. He has some major disadvantages: less money for backup and leverage, outdated information, higher commissions, and a mountain of data that is usually confusing as well as late. Worst of all, the Big Money has already taken advantage of any nonrandom fluctuations in prices, and the little guy has got to be satisfied with squeezing what he can out of remaining price movements.

His best advantage is guerrilla warfare. Go in slow, get out fast, use option and stock combinations, put and call combinations. He's got to hedge and diversify mainly with options instead of stock. Otherwise, he is much better off picking any one of the more successful funds listed in *Money* magazine every month and letting a professional manage his investments.

13

GUIDELINES FOR LIMITING LOSSES AND INCREASING PROFITS

There are absolutely no guarantees in the stock market. All the important ratios can point to a strong and healthy market and fundamental and technical analyses can find a valued stock that should advance, but the shares will decline anyway. So, what can you really do? The best bet is to take a perspective and attitude that will keep you from stumbling on the basics and from making mistakes that should not be made, and to follow the guidelines below.

1. *Set your objectives and then develop a strategy that will help you meet them.*

Understand that quick or high reward only comes with exceptional risk. If you are a speculator, you will be purchasing very different stocks than if you are an investor.

The speculator wants to work her portfolio. She likes the cyclicals or stocks in which a strong market is suddenly developing. She wants to trade often because she wants to double her money as soon as she can. She's willing to take risk, hedge as necessary, but trade often. The investor generally wants to limit risk, is in no hurry for his capital gains, and will probably play for total yield. The best strategy is a mix, a portfolio that is part speculative and part long-term investment. However, it takes a long time to develop the skills to manage such a portfolio. Successful stock investing does not come easy.

2. *Be sure you understand the fundamental math of investing.*

This includes not only how to determine P/E ratios and earnings per share but also how to interpret balance sheets and profit and loss statements. Stock investing is mainly a game of arithmetic. The numbers have to be right, or you do not want to let go of your money. You do not have to be a mathematician to play the market, but if you do not like arithmetic or are weak on the subject, hone your skills.

3. *Be sure to have a basic understanding of economics.*

In particular, you should understand the effects of interest rates, inflation, unemployment, the law of diminishing returns, economies of scale, and supply and demand—all of which are discussed in this text. There is no need to be an economist, but you must have an understanding of how national and international developments can effect the market and/or your stock.

4. *Read the financial papers.*

Keep on top of developments that can affect your stock or flag stocks you may be interested in buying or selling. Subscribe to one or two financial newsletters as well as, perhaps, to publications like *Money* magazine, *Investor's Business Daily, Barron's,* or *The Wall Street Journal.* The more information you have, the more likely you will be to make the right decisions.

5. *Do not go naked in the market.*

Learn to hedge economically but sufficiently. Consider writing covered calls or covering a long position by writing puts. The market occasionally makes sudden downturns even during bull phases; and stocks, of course, often go the opposite way you expect them to go. Be prepared for the worst and you will find ways to limit losses and increase profits over the long term.

6. *Never select a stock entirely by yourself.*

When you find one that you may be interested in, tuck it in the back of your head and discuss it with your broker when you get the chance. If the two of you like it, then wait for a recommendation from one of your newsletters or from one of the experts interviewed in *Barron's* or other publications. Now, you are 10 percent closer to possibly picking the right stock. If you are going to hedge with options, your trade will have a better chance of success.

7. *Understand opportunity cost.*

The stock market is not always the best place for your money. There are always alternative investments like Treasury bonds or notes, or even certificates of deposit. There is clearly a time to be in the market and a time not to be in it. If you are always 100 percent in stocks, rethink your position.

8. *Diversify through options and warrants.*

The small investor puts himself in a precarious situation when he builds a portfolio of stocks. He ties up a lot of money he may need. This means he can wind up selling stocks before they reach break-even points or ever show a profit in order to buy a new home, get his children through college, or take a long-anticipated vacation. The money he invests with should remain untouched until his objectives are met. But this is hard to do when all of your funds are in the stock market—unless you balance your portfolio with low-priced options. In this way, you maintain a safer level of liquidity and are not forced into unnecessary transactions.

PART THREE

BUYING CALLS

CONTENTS

14

UNDERSTANDING CALL OPTIONS

As Chapter 2 defined them, calls give legal right to their owner to purchase the underlying security at a fixed price for a period specified in the option contract. Anyone can buy a call or sell short (write) a call, but as someone who is very bullish on the market, you will mainly be interested in buying calls at the lowest price possible and then selling them at the highest price possible. Understand however, that rarely will you get them at their all-time low or sell them at their all-time high.

Writers and buyers of calls have very different objectives, and so the considerations that each must make and the way they apply their trading tools are very different.

The writers of calls are basically short sellers, and they have two ways in which they may write: as covered or uncovered writers. Strategies for uncovered writers must necessarily be very different from those for covered writers, although their goal is the same: income from their options. However, because the covered call writers need to consider the impact of the price movement for the underlying stock on their total position, their effort is much more complicated, though potentially safer, than that of the naked writer.

Buyers of calls are regular-way brokers and their goal is capital gains not income. Hopefully, they may also become sellers of options, either to capture their capital gains or to reduce their losses. Table 14–1 lists the basic differences between common stock and call option trading, and Table 14–2 reviews options terminology as it applies to calls.

As investors come to learn more about the options markets, they are developing increasing interest in trading calls. The tremendous leverage that calls provide allows incredible rates of return. The low price at which they can be purchased allows portfolio diversification.

Leverage with Calls

The leverage provided by being long in options is that the movement in their price is based on the movement in the underlying stock. Consequently:

- You can play high-priced stocks for little investment.

Table 14–1
Basic Differences between Common Stock and Call Option Trading

Stock Trading	Call Option Trading
Certificates represent ownership.	Transaction statements prove trade.
Stock can be held indefinitely.	Option contracts expire.
Common stock represents part ownership.	A call is an "option to buy" common stock.
Stock ownership means voting privileges and right to share in dividends.	No voting privileges, no right to dividends.
Stocks can be purchased on margin.	Calls can only be purchased for cash.
Stocks can be purchased in odd lots (less than 100 shares).	Each call represents 100 shares of stock.

Table 14–2
Option Terminology Reviewed

At-the-Money	An option that has an exercise price equal to the market price of the underlying security.
Buyer	A trader who purchases options.
Call	An option giving right to buy underlying security under the terms of the contract.
Closing Transaction	The transaction that terminates the trader's position.
Covered Writer	A short seller of an option who is long on an offsetting option or other underlying security.
Exercise Price	Also called "strike" or "striking" price. It is the market price at which the option holder may put (sell) or call (buy) the shares of the underlying security.
In-the-Money	An option that has exercise value.
Opening Transaction	The transaction in which the trader takes his or her position.
Out-of-the-Money	An option that does not have exercise value.
Put	An option giving the right to sell the underlying security under the terms of the contract.
Seller	The trader who sells a contract to the buyer.
Underlying Security	The common stock on which puts and calls may be bought or written.
Writer	Short seller of a put or call.

- Small percentage changes in the underlying stock can mean large percentage changes in the price of the option.

Notice in Example #44 how inexpensively the following stock can be played by taking a position in the related calls, which for this example are in-the-money calls. In-the-money calls have a strike price that is less than the current market price of the underlying stock and tend to move close to point-to-point with the movement of the underlying stock. (This movement is dependent upon the time to expiration and how far in-the-money the call is.)

EXAMPLE #44. Cost of a Call in Relation to Price of a Stock

Stock	Price	Call Premium (price)	Cost to You (for 1 call)
ASA	$47½	$2¾	$275.00
Boeing	45⅜	¾	75.00
Borden	17¼	2½	250.00
Compaq	73½	6⅛	612.50
GM	50	7	700.00

There will be other calls on each of these stocks for more or less money depending upon their intrinsic and time value, but for example purposes the above listings will do. If you wonder how the cost for the call was derived in each case, it was by multiplying the call premium by 100. Remember that each call (or put) is the equivalent of 100 shares of stock, but the price listed is per representative share.

In any event, you can easily grasp that you can play 100 shares of ASA stock, which would ordinarily cost $4,750, for a mere $275. A two point advance in any of the above stocks in the next five days would mean, probably, a two-point advance in the related call. In the case of ASA, that means a more than 70 percent increase on the ASA call, and a more than 200 percent increase in the Boeing call, while the underlying stocks have only moved around 2 percent. For Compaq and GM, the rate of return on the calls will not be quite as high, but it will certainly be much more than that for the underlying stocks.

Portfolio Diversity with Calls

The low price of calls also allows quality portfolio diversity because stocks that may be too highly priced for the average investor can be played through the related calls. Example #45 gives some representative portfolios, in which each investor has $20,000 with which to trade stocks or options.

You will notice by these comparisons that just dealing in stocks not only limits diversification but also limits the leverage that can be afforded with each position. This is because the number of shares that can be purchased will be fewer and the percentage gain with each ⅛ price movement will be less.

Remember, however, that there are special risks associated with dealing with options, not the least of which is that they are decaying assets. So, if you select an underlying stock that remains in a very narrow trading range until the expiration date of your call, you will probably lose money. You need to pick an underlying stock that has market muscle over the short term.

EXAMPLE #45. Comparative Portfolios

	Position	Market Value
Investor #1	100 shares, IBM	$ 5,600
	100 shares, AT&T	6,400
	150 shares, Citicorp	8,000
		$20,000
Investor #2	10 calls, IBM	$ 2,600
	10 calls, AT&T	2,250
	150 shares, Wendy's	7,150
	300 shares, Snapple	8,000
		$20,000
Investor #3	20 calls, IBM	$ 5,200
	20 calls, AT&T	5,500
	20 calls, Wendy's	3,300
	30 calls, Snapple	6,000
		$20,000

Ideally, Investor #3 is smart enough to be dealing with only in-the-money calls, which will have intrinsic value. Otherwise, the calls can expire worthless. This does not mean, however, that out-of-the-money calls should not be considered, for indeed the possible gains from out-of-the-monies can be beyond comprehension if a stock suddenly takes off. But out-of-the-money positions should represent only a small percentage of the total portfolio value, because being out-of-the-money, they have no intrinsic value and will decay quite rapidly as expiration dates approach if the underlying stocks have not advanced significantly.

Risk

Buying calls is a big-buck strategy if you want it to be. Imagine if you could buy 10,000 shares of a stock such as GM when it is in a bull phase. But at this writing GM is at $55 per share, which means your investment must be $550,000. With 10,000 shares, every one point upward movement in the stock is $10,000 in profits for you.

But let's face it, you do not have the money to buy 10,000 shares of GM, and if you did have this kind of money, you probably would not take the chance of putting it all in one stock. However, you can possibly afford 100 calls on GM, which would be the equivalent of 10,000 shares of stock. One hundred not too far out-of-the-monies could probably be gotten for from $5,000 to $10,000 or safer in-the-monies for about $40,000. This means for as little as five grand you can achieve results that a stock picker needs a half-million dollars to achieve.

But long calls are risky positions for the following reasons:

1. Few investors understand how price movements will vary depending upon the intrinsic and time values.

2. They depend upon the short-term movement of the underlying stocks, and not many investors are good short-term stock pickers.

3. Their low price excites greed, and inexperienced investors, who have not yet been able to develop patience and discipline, often overextend themselves. Call buyers are noted for paying too much money for their options.

Basics of Winning and Losing

As the buyer of a call, you are a cash trader. Calls (or puts) cannot be purchased on margin, although you can use whatever equity is in your margin account to trade them. As the buyer of a call, you have the ability to "play" the movement of high-priced stocks for very little money, but you do this under the risk that the call you buy will decay with time. This means the clock is against you; whereas the writer of a call has the clock on his or her side. As time goes by, everything else being equal, the call will depreciate in value. As a long buyer of calls, you benefit only if the stock moves up in price, whereas the writer of the call can possibly benefit if the stock does not advance, moves down in price slightly or greatly, or moves up in price slightly. The circumstances under which you, as a long buyer of calls, can profit are thereby limited, but the extent of your profits far exceeds what they can ever be for the writer, whose proceeds are limited to the premium he or she receives.

EXAMPLE #46. Losing by Buying a Call: Stock Advances but Not Beyond Striking Price

You buy five calls on IBM selling at $48 per share, and pay $1,000 in premiums. The striking price is $50, which is the price at which you have a legal right to purchase the stock.

The stock never goes beyond the striking price by expiration, but instead closes at $49¾ per share. As your call is worthless, you lose the entire premium you paid, unless you managed to sell the call prior to expiration for whatever premium you could get.

Because you were dealing in out-of-the-money calls, the chances for you to exercise your option and buy the underlying stock was negligible.

EXAMPLE #47. Winning by Buying a Call: Stock Advances but not Beyond Striking Price

You buy five calls (at $1 each) on IBM selling at $48 per share, and pay $1,000 in premiums. The striking price is $50, which is the price at which you have a legal right to purchase the stock.

The stock never goes beyond the striking price, but does advance to $49¾ per share. The calls, meanwhile, would have advanced 1 to 1½ points, depending upon the time value as determined by market interest. That would mean a $500 to $750 profit for you, or, in other words, at least the doubling of your investment.

As you can see, the underlying stock need not advance beyond the striking price for you to profit by buying calls.

EXAMPLE #48. Losing by Buying a Call: Stock Drops

You buy five calls on IBM selling at $48 per share, and pay $1,000 in premiums. The striking price is $50, which is the price at which you have a legal right to purchase the stock.

The stock drops in price and is at $40 at expiration date. As your call is worthless, you lose the entire premium you paid, unless you managed to sell the call prior to expiration for whatever premium you could get.

As the above example indicates, buying a call is a bullish position on the underlying stock. If the stock goes down in price, the call will depreciate in value and be worthless if not unloaded before expiration date.

EXAMPLE #49. Winning by Buying a Call: Stock Advances

You buy five calls (at $1 each) on IBM selling at $48 per share, and pay $1,000 in premiums. The striking price is $50, which is the price at which you have a legal right to purchase the stock.

The stock advances well beyond the striking price to $60 per share. The calls, meanwhile, would have advanced roughly 10 to 12 points, depending on the time value as determined by market interest. That would mean a $5,000 to $7,500 profit for you, or, in other words, at least the quintupling of your investment.

Intrinsic Value

The price of a call, like the price of a put, is based mainly on its intrinsic value plus its time value. But the intrinsic value of a call is measured in just the opposite way than it is measured for a put. The call has intrinsic value when its striking price is lower than the current market price of the underlying stock. You were introduced to this idea in Part 1 of this book. The idea is further demonstrated in the following example.

EXAMPLE #50. Determining Intrinsic Value of a Call

Stock Price	Strike Price	Intrinsic Value
$22.00	$25	None
22.50	25	None
23.00	25	None
24.00	25	None
25.00	25	None
26.00	25	$1.00
28.50	25	3.50
30.00	25	5.00

When you get to Example #65, you will see that for the above given stock prices, the intrinsic value of a put is just the opposite. That is, at $30, there is no intrinsic value and at $22 there is a $3 intrinsic value when the striking price is $25.

A call is considered in-the-money when it has intrinsic value. This means that the owner of the call can profit if he exercises his option.

Besides intrinsic value, calls, like puts, have time value, and this time value is determined by time remaining until contract expiration. Many factors will determine what this time value is, including market demand for the option based on expectations for the underlying stock and interest rates, although many analysts will say these factors belong under a separate heading called volatility.

In any case, consider the calls on Citicorp given in Table 14–3. You will see here that the market value for the calls exceeds the amount by which the calls may be in the money. Thus, intrinsic value is not the only determinant for the premium which an option commands.

Disadvantages of Buying Calls

It is easy to paint a picture of the advantages of buying calls—the leverage from the low prices, the ability to determine maximum loss, their value in diversifying a portfolio. But the disadvantages should not be de-emphasized. These disadvantages have already been touched upon, but a few are better explained through specific examples.

To begin with, the bid and ask prices for options can usually entertain wide disparity. Neophytes are generally overanxious to take their positions as soon as possible, interested in the calls in the first place because of volume or positive price movement in the underlying stock. So, generally, what happens is that they wind up paying the ask price, which can be as much as ½ point higher than the current bids,

Table 14–3
Time-Decay Considerations

Stock: Citicorp   Strike Price: $35

Trading Day	Stock Price	Call Premiums
1	35	½
2	35	½
3	35	⅜
4	35	⅜
5	35	¼
6	35	¼
7	35	⅛
8	35	⅛
9	35	—

Expiration

Time decay is working against the value of the call. Despite the fact that the stock price has not changed, as the expiration date approaches the call loses value. In the above example, losses seem low—a mere ⅜ of a point. But this represents a 75 percent loss on the investment. If the calls cost $1,000, on Day 9 they would only be worth $250.

depending upon the price of the option. That is, higher-priced options usually have greater spread between bid and ask prices than do the lower priced.

Generally, the best advice is always to bid between the current bid and ask price if you absolutely must be in a hurry to take your position. So, if the bid is $2½ and the ask is $3, try and go in at $2¾. One-quarter of a point can be a lot of money in options trading. This is illustrated in Example #51.

EXAMPLE #51. Bid and Ask Spreads Mean a Lot

A. Buying at the ask
You are interested in purchasing calls on IBM. The last trade was $2 3/8, and the current bid and ask prices are $2¼ and $2¾. You buy 10 calls at $2¾, for a total of $2,750 plus $60 in commissions. The stock advances only slightly and the news changes as the expiration dates near. You manage to sell the calls for $2¾.

1. Bought 10 calls: $2,750		1a. Sold 10 calls: $2,750
Buy commissions: + 60		Sell commissions: − 60
Total cost: $2,810		Total income: $2,690

Cost:	$2,810
Income:	2,690
Loss:	$ 120

Because you bought at the bid, you wound up losing money. In the following table, you will fare better because you will have bought between the current bid and ask prices. That is, you will have purchased the calls for $2.50 each. As a result, commission costs will be slightly less on the buy transaction.

2a. Bought 10 calls: $2,500	2a. Sold 10 calls: $2,750
Buy commissions: + 60	Sell commissions: − 60
Total cost: $2,560	Total Income: $2,690

Income:	$2,690
Cost:	$2,560
Gain:	$ 130

Carefully bidding for the options, then, even if you are only talking about ¼ of a point, can mean the difference between a loss and a gain. Again, the people in-the-know tell us that call traders are usually over-eager to take their positions and wind up paying more for calls than they have to. Put traders, on the other hand, always seem to be much more careful about their bidding.

Time decay is also an important element in call buying because, while time works for the writer, it works against the buyer. As the expiration date approaches, the call faces downside pressure and only stronger movement in the underlying stock can keep its premium up. (See Options Derivatives below.)

Demand is another important element. Some underlying stocks are much more popular with options traders than others, which is clearly demonstrated by the options listings themselves. You will easily notice that a stock like IBM has many series of options traded daily, but some stocks like Wendy's or Dow Jones have few. A great deal depends upon the premiums that an option can command. If premiums are low, writers are not about to chance selling short. If they do not want to write the options, there are no contracts to buy.

Options Derivatives

The pros use some very sophisticated methods to help them determine the potential movement in options premiums. These methods evolve around four special tools called "options derivatives." These options derivatives are performance measures called delta, gamma, theta, and vega.

Delta is a term used to define a finite measure within some variable. And in options analysis, it defines the expected change in premiums due to changes in the underlying security. An in-the-money option may very well have a 100 percent delta, indicating that for every point that the underlying stock moves, the option will move one point. A 50 percent delta means that the option will move ½ point for every one point movement in the stock. Delta ratings will change depending upon the time to expiration and will also vary from one series of option to another.

Gamma ratings revise the delta valuations for future movements. Given an option with a 100 percent delta and a 5 percent gamma, it would be expected that future movements would be based on a delta of 105 percent.

Theta is a tool for trying to determine time value. As the expiration date approaches, puts or calls will deteriorate but not all at the same rate. The Big Money wants to know what to expect. The theta rating, then, tells the Big Money the percentage of decrease to expect. An option .05 theta rating may be expected to depreciate by 5 percent with each passing day, as long as the underlying stock does not do anything at all in terms of price movement.

Vega, the last of the measures, is used to analyze the underlying stock. A .05 vega rating for a stock indicates that the premium would increase the premium plus the vega rating for whatever volatility range has been defined for the underlying security.

These very sophisticated tools are fun for mathematicians, and sometimes they work well. But sometimes they do not. There are too many variables influencing the rate of price movement for premiums and these elusive little rascals are hard to predict no matter which mathematical tools are being employed to asses their volatility and direction.

LEAPS

Long-term options are available for those whose strategies entail premiums that will not be as affected by time decay. These are called LEAPS. LEAPS is an acronym for "long-term equity anticipation securities." These are puts and calls with maturities up to three years.

LEAPS provide investors with an opportunity to take advantage of the low price and high leverage aspects of puts and calls without necessarily having to put up with the fast decay that is characteristic of shorter term options. LEAPS are listed separately in the financial news, usually at the end of the short-term option listings.

15

PLAYING THE MONEY POSITIONS

Call buyers are bullish on the underlying stock, so they want high performers supporting their options positions. They want to buy calls that have striking prices that can be attained quite easily by the underlying stock during the term of the options contract. They certainly do not want a stock that will only trade in a very narrow range or, worse yet, a stock that is going to head south for the term of the contract.

Selecting Calls

Options traders always have a great selection of choices as well as numerous combinations to play. They can buy and sell more than one series of options on numerous stocks and play as many combinations as their money can cover and their inventive intelligence can keep track of.

Take, for example, the following call listings on Storage Technology. Buying any of these available calls would be of little interest to you unless you believed the stock was going to move up in price in the short term.

EXAMPLE #52. Selecting Calls to Write

Stock: Storage Technology   Price: $28

Stock Price	Strike Price	October	November	December
$28	$30	1¼	1½	1⅞
30	30	2	2½	2¾
37	30	7	7¼	7⅝
52	40	12	12⅛	12¼
62	45	17	—	—

Despite the fact that many of these options are actually in-the-money, they will only be valuable if they are going to advance in price. In other words, just because an option is in the money does not mean it is a safe investment. Basically, you have greater leverage with out-of- and at-the-monies. The higher-priced calls, which are usually the in-the-monies, offer less leverage, but they are ideal for more conservative plays and for leaving open the option of exercising rights to take a position in the underlying security.

Let's look at some of the conundrums involved in selecting and selling calls. Assume you have been drawn to Storage Technology because you feel that in the near term it will show strong advance. Buying the out-of-the-monies (Table 15–1) will offer you a great deal of leverage and, therefore, a chance to make some very big bucks very quickly; on the other hand, you can lose everything very easily. Buying the in-the-monies will offer you a lot of downside risk, but the rate of return is hardly likely to be anywhere near what it will be for the low-priced out-of-the monies (should the stock advance beyond the striking price).

You would rather be buying the calls long than buying the stock long because with the calls you need invest a lot less money, and the leverage is far beyond what would be offered by positions in the underlying stock. Because you have been tracking Storage Technology, you feel that its movement in the short-term is highly predictable and bullish. That is, you are fairly certain it will advance strongly over the short term. The best way to play the stock, you decide, is to buy the calls.

You have a number of calls to choose from, clearly evident by simply checking the daily options listings or calling your broker. But which calls will represent the smarter plays?

First of all, realize that the listed prices below are probably not the prices at which you will actually be able to buy the calls. Premiums listed are usually the price at which the option was last traded. For instance, the bid and ask prices for the October 25s are probably actually $7/8-1\frac{1}{4}$, and for the November 25s, $1\frac{1}{8}-1\frac{1}{2}$.

Second of all, understand that the higher premiums are for the in-the-money puts, with those having later contract expiration dates being the highest.

Third, remember that these are call premiums, so the higher the stock price above the striking price, the higher the premiums.

Generally, it is best for a call buyer to play in-the-monies; however, the premiums are relatively high, so it costs a lot more to take that opening position for options with intrinsic value than it does with those that have no intrinsic value. The high price also means that, whatever the delta is for the calls, the rate of return will be relatively low.

Table 15–1
Money Positions for Calls

Stock Price	Strike Price	Call
$20	$25	Out-of-the-Money
20	15	In-the-Money
20	20	At-the-Money
25	20	In-the-Money
20	20	At-the-Money
15	20	Out-of-the-Money

Beginning with Example #52, we will look at a number of closing decisions to determine the kind of considerations a call trader must weigh. Even if you employ the options derivatives discussed in the last chapter, you will quickly learn that there is a lot of luck in making money on options.

EXAMPLE #52-A. Deciding When to Sell a Call

You buy 10 October 25s at $3¼.   Cost: $3,250

Strike Price	Trading Day	Stock Price	October 25 Premium
$25	1	$28	3¼
25	3	30	5½
25	5	28	3⅛
25	7	27½	2½
25	10	28½	3½
25	15	25	2
25	17	27	2½
25	18	28	2⅞
25	20	26	1
	Day before Expiration	22	0

Notice in the above example that the call movement in relation to the stock price movement cannot be exactly predicted. This is because market forces and time decay work together to push and pull on the prices of the puts. For instance, on Day 1 the stock is at $28, and the premium is at 3¼; on Days 5 and 18, however, although the stock is at the same price, the premiums have changed. You were doing all right until the day before expiration, when the option went out of the money. Here you are at a loss, having bought the calls for $3,250 but now finding them worthless after they drop out of the money.

As it turned out, you selected the wrong calls, or else held them too long; after all, you could have profited on Day 3. True, indeed, you were playing the in-the-monies, which are generally the more conservative play; but there are absolutely no guarantees that you will profit even when you write out-of-the-money calls.

Suppose you had purchased, say, November 25s instead?

EXAMPLE #53. How Call Options Can Rebound

You buy 10 November 25 Calls at $½. Cost: $1,500

Strike Price	Trading Day	Stock Price	November 25 Premium
$25	1	$26	1½
25	3	30	5¾

Strike Price	Trading Day	Stock Price	October 25 Premium
$25	5	$28	3¼
25	7	27½	2½
25	10	28½	3½
25	15	25	1¼
25	17	27	2¼
25	18	28	3⅛
25	20	26	⅞
25	25	22	¼
25	27	23½	¾
25	30	24¾	1
25	35	25	1
25	40	27½	2½
25	45	28	3
25	Day before Expiration	28¼	3¼

In this case, you began showing a profit very early during the contract period, but if you sold on Day 25 would have realized a substantial loss ($1,750). If you were smart enough to sell on Day 3, you would have realized a $4,250 profit. However, if you sold between Days 15, 20, and 35, you would have realized a loss just as you would have in the previous example.

So, you picked the right underlying stock. You guessed that Storage Technology would remain in a relatively narrow trading range and probably had more upside potential than downside.

What you picked wrong in the first example was the expiration date. (Another analyst could easily argue that you picked the wrong striking price or just sold too early.) So, you lost money because of some unexpected downside swings in the price of the underlying stock. The November contract date, however, allowed time for the underlying stock to continue its advance.

Was there any way to prevent the mistake of writing the October 25s? No, none at all, except for the guiding principle that the more time you allow yourself to profit on an option, the better off you will probably be. Much, however, depends upon the premium you will have to pay for the later expiration. There are no guarantees; luck is still an important element in making money in stock and options trading.

Buying In-the-Money Calls

Note that in all cases the calls with intrinsic value are those that have striking prices below the stock price of the underlying stock. They are in-the-money (Table 15–2)

Table 15–2
In-the-Money Calls

Stock Price	Strike Price	Call
$20	$15	In-the-Money
25	20	In-the-Money
18	15	In-the-Money
15	10	In-the-Money

As long as the striking price is less than the market price of the stock, the call is considered in-the-money.

because the writers of the calls are in a position to profit after exercising their rights. They can buy the stock at the striking price and immediately cover their positions by selling it at the current market price.

When an in-the-money option premium equals the difference in price between the stock price and the striking price, then it is said to be trading at parity. Thus, a call with a premium of $10 when the stock is at $20 and the striking price is at $10 is trading at parity. If the premium advances $2, then it is trading at "2 + parity." As the expiration date of the contract approaches, the option will trade at or very close to parity if it is in-the-money. You will find that few options trade at or very close to parity prior to expiration unless they are far in-the-money.

In the examples that follow, you will see how you can win and lose by buying in-the-money calls. Please note that there is some repetition in the presentation of these examples and in the way subtopics overlap. This repetition is for reinforcement.

EXAMPLE #54. Losing by Buying In-the-Money Calls: Stock Is Called

Calls with a striking price of $25 are available on Cotter Industries. The stock is selling at $30 per share, placing the subject calls in-the-money by $5. The premium for each call is $5 (meaning each call costs $500). You buy six calls (each representing 100 shares of the underlying stock) for a total cost of $3,000.

The stock drops to $27 per share, and the calls decrease in value to $200 each. Shortly afterward, and quite unexpectedly, the option is exercised. You must, therefore, buy the underlying stock at $25 to cover your position. As the stock is currently at $27, your paper gain is still $2 per share (or $1,200). However, you paid $3,000 for the calls, so you have actually lost $1,800 to date. You can continue to hold the stock, hoping it will advance enough for you to cover your losses, or you can sell it right away to prevent further loss.

Transaction Summary
Bought six calls at $500 each: ($3,000)
Paper profit on underlying stock: 1,200
Loss: $1,800

Now that you know you can lose with in-the-monies, let's look at a winning situation.

EXAMPLE #55. Winning by Buying In-the-Money Calls: Stock Is Called

Again, Cotter Industries. But this time the stock advances. Striking price is $25, and the stock is selling at $30 per share, placing the calls in-the-money by $5. The premium for each call is $5 (meaning each costs $500). You buy six calls (each representing 100 shares of the underlying stock). Cost is $3,000. The stock climbs to $34 per share. The calls are now commanding premiums of $9 (or $900 each). Their total value is now $5,400.

Transaction Summary
Sold six calls at: $5,400
Bought six calls at $5 each: −3,000
Gain: $2,400

You must pay very special attention to the expiration date because as it approaches the chances of an in-the-money put option being exercised increases. Additionally, time decay works against the value of the option, and if you don't sell the call before expiration it becomes worthless.

Buying At-the-Money Calls

Calls are at-the-money when their striking price is equal to the price of the stock (as indicated in Table 15–3). Buy and sell commissions considered, at-the-monies would be out-of-the-money. Always keep in mind that broker commissions will affect the true intrinsic value of an option. That is, while theoretically they may have intrinsic value because of the relationship between the stock and the striking price, in reality, trading costs reduce the break-even point and thereby affect the intrinsic value.

In the following examples, you will see how you can gain or lose money by trading at-the-money calls. To simplify the examples, call movement in relationship to price movement of the underlying stock is arbitrary, expiration dates are not considered, and buy/sell commissions are not included.

EXAMPLE #56. Losing by Writing At-the-Money Puts

Calls with a striking price of $20 are available on Baker Products. The stock is selling at $20 per share, placing the related calls at-the-money. The premium for each call is $1 (meaning each call costs $100). You buy six calls (each call representing 100 shares of the underlying stock) at a cost of $600.

The stock drops to $18 per share, and the calls decrease in value to $¼. The stock, then, has dropped a mere 10 percent, but your calls have depreciated 75 percent. It is now decision time. Do you sell your call and take your losses or hope for a rebound before the expiration date? If you sell, you lose $475.

Transaction Summary

Bought six calls at $100 each:	$600
Sold six calls at $25 each:	−125
Loss:	$475

On the other hand, you can wait and possibly wind up with a worthless option.

Profiting on writing at-the-money calls is illustrated by the following example, which simply reverses the above scenario.

EXAMPLE #57. Winning by Buying At-the-Money Calls

Calls with striking price of $20 are available on Baker Products. The stock is selling at $20 per share, placing the related calls at-the-money. The premium for each call is $1 (meaning each call costs $100). You buy six calls (each call representing 100 shares of the underlying stock). Cost is $600.

The stock climbs to $22 per share, and the calls advance to $200 each. The stock has gained a mere 10 percent, but your calls have doubled in value. You decide to sell the calls and take your profits while you can.

Transaction Summary

Sold six calls at $200 each:	$1,200
Bought six calls at $100 each:	− 600
Gains:	$ 600

Table 15–3
At-the-Money Calls

Stock Price	Strike Price	Call
$20	$20	At-the-Money
25	25	At-the-Money
15	15	At-the-Money
10	10	In-the-Money

When the market price of the stock and the striking price for the call are the same, the call is considered at-the-money.

To reiterate, because at-the-money puts are so close to having intrinsic value, just the very slightest move in the price of the underlying stock means the difference between being in the black or the red (before trading commissions).

Buying Out-of-the-Money Calls

Out-of-the-money calls (Table 15–4) can be extremely volatile. More often than not, however, they expire worthless. However, because of their low price they can be purchased in great quantity, and should they advance in price the rewards can be outstanding.

EXAMPLE #58. Losing by Buying Out-of-the-Money Calls

Calls with a striking price of $20 are available on CTZ Industries. The stock is selling at $18 per share, placing the related calls out-of-the-money. The premium for each call is $.50 (meaning each call costs $50). You buy six calls for $300.

The stock drops to $16, and the calls decrease in value through the contract period, becoming worthless very early and eventually expiring worthless. You lose your entire investment. The stock has only declined 11 percent, but you have lost 100 percent of your investment.

Transaction Summary

Bought six calls at $50 each:	$300
Calls expired worthless:	000
Loss:	$300

In the next example, you will see that it is possible to also profit by buying out-of-the-money calls.

Table 15–4
Out-of-the-Money Calls

Stock Price	Strike Price	Call
$20	$25	Out-of-the-Money
25	30	Out-of-the-Money
15	20	Out-of-the-Money
10	15	Out-of-the-Money

When the striking price is higher than the market price of the stock, the call is out-of-the-money.

EXAMPLE #59. Winning by Buying Out-of-the-Money Calls

Calls with a striking price of $20 are available on CTZ Industries. The stock is selling at $18 per share, placing the related calls out-of-the-money. The premium for each call is $.50 (meaning each call costs $50). You buy six calls for $300.

The stock drops to $16, and the calls decrease in value. At one point in the contract period, they actually become worthless. But the stock suddenly rebounds and advances to $22. The calls, meanwhile, advance to $2 (or $200 each).

Transaction Summary

Sold six calls at $200 each:	$1,200
Bought six calls at $50 each:	– 300
Gain:	$ 900

In this last example, a mere 10 percent increase in the price of the stock has allowed you to triple your money. Given a delta of 100 percent (which is not unrealistic for an in-the-money option, which the above represents), for each point that the stock advances, the calls will advance one point or $100. Thus, each one-point movement in the stock will mean additional gains of $600 for you.

16

STRATEGIES

Sometimes traders like to employ various strategies that further limit downside risk or increase the chances of profit. These strategies are numerous and can include long puts and long calls, short puts and short calls, or any other unique combination including numerous calls and puts on one side and numerous puts and calls on the other.

For our purposes, however, we need only concentrate on straddles and combinations, and only one kind of each—the long straddle and the long combination. The Big Money and the guys intrigued with the arithmetic of options can play the heavier combinations, but as these require a lot of up-front investment and are, therefore, too cumbrous for low break-even points, they are not appropriate for most investors.

The Long Straddle

The straddle is a put and call combination that gives the trader the legal right to require the writer to purchase and/or sell the options at the contract price. Specifically, the straddle consists of an equal number of puts and calls with the same striking price and expiration date.

Straddles are extremely difficult to execute because they require almost simultaneous closing transactions covering different options. They are particularly effective, however, when a trader expects that the underlying stock will have heavy price movement in one direction or another, but cannot be certain which way that price movement will be.

The purchase of a straddle is an expensive operation. At least one put and one call is required for construction, and this means that there will be additional up-front commissions for the trader to pay. Understandably, unless the position is not closed out (because it is not profitable to do so), there will also be additional commissions on the closing transaction. This means that whatever the winning side of the straddle is (put or call), the profits must be enough to cover losses on the other side plus commissions.

The writer of the straddle is basically interested in additional premiums he can receive by writing more than one option at a time. If the stock stays in a very narrow trading range, he can earn premiums on both the put and the call. In some cases, the losses on one side of the straddle will be less than the gain on the other side, thereby providing an additional situation in which the trader can come out ahead. There are caveats here, however. One is that the writer is still faced with possession of decaying assets, and as contract expiration approaches, both sides of the straddle will begin to depreciate in value even if the stock does not advance. A second is that during the contract period, both the put and the call may be exercised as the underlying security gyrates in price, putting one option and then the other in-the-money, thereby producing "least expected" losses. The risk of this last situation, however, can be partly guarded against by buying long the underlying security that serves as the basis for the straddle.

As a trader who is bullish on the market, however, you will be interested in buying a straddle rather than writing one. Specifically, you will be interested in the long straddle. In a long straddle, you may buy one Motorola January 20 call and one Motorola January 20 put. The strike price and expiration month are the same, as is the underlying security. Your profit will be determined in the usual way, by the difference between the costs of opening and closing out the straddle. This is illustrated for you in Table 16–1.

The Long Combination

Another strategy very much like a straddle is called a "combination." Here the underlying stock is the same, but the striking price or the expiration date is different. Thus, in a "long combination," which you would primarily be interested in, you might want to choose to buy one Motorola January 100 call and one Motorola January 95 put. Or, perhaps, instead of having different striking prices, you might opt for different expiration dates.

Table 16–2 gives an example of long combinations and long straddles. Straddles and combinations are covered again from the perspective of the put writer in Chapter 21.

Table 16-1
Trading Long Straddles

	Straddle	Cost	Sale	Profit (Loss)
A.	1 January 100 call	$1,050	$ 900	($ 150)
	1 January 100 put	600	400	(200)
		$1,650	$1,300	($ 350)
B.	1 January 100 call	$1,050	$1,750	$ 700
	1 January 100 put	600	50	(550)
		$1,650	$1,800	$ 150
C.	1 January 100 call	$1,050	$1,350	($ 300)
	1 January 100 put	600	300	300
		$1,650	$1,650	$ 000
D.	1 January 100 call	$1,050	$ 000	($1,050)
	1 January 100 put	600	2,100	1,500
		$1,650	$2,100	$ 450

This table is as applicable for combinations as it is for straddles.

A. Stock fails to move significantly. Time decay depreciates both puts and calls.
B. Stock climbs. Calls advance just a bit more than puts depreciate.
C. Stock climbs, but not enough to allow profits on calls to overcome depreciation in puts.
D. Stock falls. Puts increase enough to cover losses on calls. Could just as well have been the other way around.

Table 16-2
Comparing Long Combinations and Long Straddles

Long Straddle	Long Combinations
Buy 1 Motorola January 100 Call	Buy 1 Motorola January 100 Call
Buy 1 Motorola January 100 Put	Buy 1 Motorola January 90 Put
	Buy 1 Motorola February 100 Call
	Buy 1 Motorola February 90 Put
	Buy 1 Motorola January 100 Call
	Buy 1 Motorola February 90 Put

In a combination, the strike price and/or the expiration date may be different.

17

CORRECTING COMMON
MISCONCEPTIONS ABOUT BUYING CALLS

There are a number of misconceptions that are easily harbored by investors new to options trading. Those relating to calls are listed and replied to below. Those that relate to puts are in Chapter 22.

1. *Buying calls is a sure way to increase income from portfolios in bull markets.*

Untrue. There are no guarantees associated with buying calls long, as there are no guarantees associated with any investment tool or methodology. There are inherent problems in call buying not the least of which is the fact that any option is an asset that decays with time. This means that once the expiration date arrives, an option is rendered worthless. Buyers of options, then, whether these options are puts or calls, have to find those investments that will bring them into the black in a short time. This is no easy task.

2. *It is only worthwhile to buy in-the-money puts, because as they are in the money, you are assured a profit.*

Untrue. "In-the-money" is simply a term that describes the relationship between the striking price for an option and the price of the underlying stock. In the case of a call, this relationship is such that "in-the-money" means that the stock price is higher than the strike price (Table 17–1). It does not mean you have a profit. You only profit as a call buyer if you can sell the call at a higher price than that which you paid for it.

3. *Buying calls is a smarter strategy than writing calls.*

Untrue. It all depends upon what your goals are and what happens to be the fundamental and technical status of the underlying stock. Writing calls is for those who are somewhat bearish on the underlying stock, and buying calls is for those who are somewhat bullish. Table 17–2 gives further clarification.

Additionally, writing calls is an income play, and buying calls long is a capital gains play. The potential gains from buying calls (or buying puts) is somewhat exceptional because of the tremendous leverage. After all, each put or call is the equivalent of 100 shares of stock, and each put and call is usually selling for a fraction of the price of the shares in the underlying stock.

Table 17–1
In-the-Money Calls

Stock Price	Strike Price	Call
$17	$15	In-the-Money
16	15	In-the-Money
15¾	15	In-the-Money
15⅛	15	In-the-Money

As long as the striking price is less than the market price of the stock, the call is considered in-the-money.

Table 17–2
The Long and Short of It

Stock Expectations	Tool and Strategy
Small retreat, minimal upside potential	Short call
Strong retreat	Long put
Strong advance	Long call
Small advance, little downside danger	Short put

4. *A call is an equity security.*

Untrue. Calls are contracts that allow their owners to purchase or sell the underlying common stock at the contract price for the contract period. They are not equities and should not be mistaken for such.

5. *Calls can be exercised any time before they expire.*

True only in the case of American-style options. Both calls and puts may be American-style or European-style options. In the case of the former, options may be exercised by the holder any time after purchase but before the expiration date. European-style options may only be exercised during a specific period prior to expiration. Most options traded on the U.S. exchanges are American-style options, but to be certain you should check with your broker before making any trades.

6. *Margin means the same thing for call buyers that it does for stock traders.*

Untrue. Buying calls long can only be done through cash transactions. However, if you have a margin account, any equity in that account may be used toward the purchase of your calls.

7. *An investor must be either a buyer or a seller of a call.*

Untrue. He may be both, consecutively or concurrently. In playing certain advanced strategies, an option trader may be both long and short in calls.

8. *The call buyer is entitled to dividends declared on the underlying stock.*

Untrue. Only stockholders of record are entitled to a dividend declared. An option holder is not a stockholder. She is simply the owner of a contract, which gives her the right to buy X number of shares of the underlying stock at whatever the strike price is.

9. *As puts and calls are opposite contracts, buying a call is the same as selling a put.*

Untrue, although both the put short seller (writer) and the call buyer are bullish on the underlying stock. The big difference is that the put writer's gain is limited to the premium he receives when he short sells the put. The call buyer, however, has unlimited profit potential. For example if she buys one in-the-money call on IBM for $200 when the stock is at $60 per share, she stands a good chance of quadrupling her money if IBM advances a mere $5 to $65 per share. A put writer who may have written a put on IBM for $200 during the same period would be limited to a maximum profit of $200.

10. *Everything you need to know to buy a call is included in the options tables found in the financial news.*

Untrue. Like any stock, commodity, or option listing, options listings only give the previous or current day's trading activities. The listing is simply a snapshot of what recently happened, and little more.

11. *The best approach for call buying is to find a stock that has just reached new lows, then buy the calls. The stock is sure to go up.*

Untrue. Stocks can always go lower. But, additionally, remember that even if this is so, the stock may not go up within the time period of the call you have purchased. The "new lows" is just a way to identify stocks in technical or fundamental trouble. It is not a tool for forecasting what will happen to those stocks. Only further research will give you any hint. (This misconception is also treated in Chapter 22.)

12. *Your broker will call you prior to expiration to remind you that your option is soon to expire.*

Untrue. Keeping track of expiration dates is your responsibility. As options expire on the Saturday after the third Friday of the month, be sure you have marked your calendar appropriately. In the case where the first day of the month is a Saturday, the expiration date is the fourth Saturday of the month.

18

GUIDELINES FOR LIMITING RISK AND INCREASING PROFIT

Many aspects of trading calls can present hazards to those unfamiliar with their characteristics. Now that you know some of the misconceptions you must avoid, you are ready to consider some of the guidelines that will help you limit your risk and possibly increase your profit from trading calls. Some of these will be repeated, but tailored to puts in Chapter 23.

There are also special risks that are applicable to both put and call trading, and a discussion of these risks may be found in Chapter 24.

1. *Understand the goals of call writers as well as call buyers.*

Knowing what the other side is after will help you further understand the nature of the game as well as the risks at hand. The goal of the writer, you well understand by now, is the premiums that calls can possibly command. However, the long buyer of calls wants to benefit from increasing stock values. He would like nothing better than to find an out-of-the-money call he can buy for ⅛ of a point and then watch it climb to $3 or $4 as the underlying stock climbs beyond the strike price and far into the money. The writer of a call, on the other hand, would be pleased to see the underlying stock stay in a very narrow trading range or else decrease in value.

2. *Understand also that many factors determine the future value of an option, put or call, including the following:*

- The price of the option and the price of the underlying stock.

- The price of the option and the value of the underlying stock's dividends.

- The time remaining until expiration of the contract.

- The difference between the striking price and the current price of the underlying stock.

- The current interest rates and the volatility of the underlying stock.

Thus, it is important that you do not expect that all calls will move in the same ratio to the movement in the underlying stock. That is, do not expect in-the-money calls or out-of-the-money calls in different stocks to be equally volatile. If you treat each option you are expecting to buy or write as though it is an entirely distinct opportunity, you will avoid taking any situation for granted.

3. *Know the underlying stock.*

If you are going to be successful at trading calls, you will need to develop the knowledge, skill, and timing for selecting stocks that can advance significantly over a short period of time. An option player is also a stock player, for any increase in the price of an option depends upon the movement in price of the underlying stock. (Writers of options, however, stand to gain if the stock does not move at all *or* if it decreases in value.)

4. *Be sure the anticipated return on your long position is worth the risk.*

Options are a gamble, and you must realize that if you want to risk your money, the rewards must be worth the gamble. If you can do half as well in fixed-income opportunities as you might expect to do with your options trading, why not take advantage of those opportunities? With options, you can easily lose your entire investment. A dollar lost is very hard to make up, and when you do make it up, have you really? That is, if you lose $1 on one trade and then make $2 on the next, you are still behind, because you would be further ahead if you never lost anything in the first place.

5. *Be sure you understand how the stock options game is played.*

This requires understanding the following:

- Contract terminology.

- Types of orders.

- Differences between puts and calls.

- Intrinsic value.

- Time value.

- Bear and bull positions.

- Expiration dates.

6. *Be sure you have a good understanding of options arithmetic.*

Without a good grasp of the fundamentals of arithmetic, it is extremely difficult to understand break-even points, to evaluate risk/reward factors, to determine money positions, and to evaluate leverage factors. (See Table 18–1.)

7. *Be willing to pay the extra money to hedge your positions when possible.*

Long positions in calls can be hedged to varying degrees, for instance, by creating straddles and combinations.

8. *Spread your risk.*

One of the additional advantages of dealing in calls is that they allow economical portfolio diversifications. For just a small percentage of what it would take to position yourself in a number of high-quality stocks, you can purchase calls on these same stocks—out-of-the-monies when you are highly aggressive and in-the-monies when you are relatively conservative. But when you decide on the calls instead of

Table 18–1
Risks/Rewards for Call Option Traders

Position	Maximum Gain	Maximum Loss
Long Call	Can be in the thousands of percent.	Premium paid.
Short Call (Uncovered)	Premium received.	Can be in the thousands of percent.
Short Call (Covered)	Premium received plus small percentage gain on stock.	Long stock position will cover loss on call but premium on call may not cover losses on stock, which can be substantial.

the stock, do not let greed drive you to putting all your money in the same class of stocks.

Spread your investment over a number of classes, such as IBM, Citicorp, and Merck. Just do not spread yourself too thin, and make sure you know well that underlying stock.

9. *Understand the difference between stock quotes and option quotes.*
Option quotes are multiplied by 100 to determine the true cost or income from an option.

10. *Understand that it is the premium that really drives the market for a particular put.*
This premium will be determined by the factors listed in #2.

11. *Be sure your goals are practical.*
This means, again, understanding the potential volatility of the underlying stock.
For instance, buying far out-of-the-money calls on AT&T is not quite as smart an investment decision as buying out-of-the-monies on more volatile issues such as GM or Medical Care of America.

12. *Keep abreast of options recommendations listed in various newsletters or financial newspapers.*
But bear in mind that by the time you get the information, the Smart Money will already have learned it, and the options may have already advanced. Keep abreast also of the news on listed stocks; takeover, buy-back, or other pertinent news can help you determine whether or not you should be a long or short stock player or a long or short option player.

PART FOUR

WRITING PUT CONTRACTS

CONTENTS

19

UNDERSTANDING PUT OPTIONS

In previous chapters, you were introduced to puts on a need-to-know basis. That is, you were given only what you needed to know to understand how they compared to, or could be used with, calls and stocks. Now, it is time to go into the subject in detail, with special emphasis on applications.

Those of you who have studied *Tools of the Bear* may find some of the topics which follow familiar sounding, but that is all. In *Bear* these topics were covered from the perspective of the buyer. But here they will be covered from the perspective of the writer (or seller). The game changes considerably for the writer. For instance, in *Bear*, in-the-money puts were suggested as the most practical play, but here, out-of-the-money puts are suggested as the better play. As in all options trading, the underlying stock is even more important than the money position of the puts.

The put writer wants the underlying stock to go up in value or stay at just about the same price as it was when he wrote the put. He's basically bullish on the underlying stock.

He also realizes that writing puts is not a strategy for making big bucks, but what it does do is provide him with additional opportunities for income from his portfolio, additional opportunities to limit risk, and additional opportunities to diversify his entire portfolio. In short, it helps him to make his portfolio as dynamic as possible, with many sources of income as well as techniques for hedging.

Risk

Have no doubt about it! Writing puts is a risky business and not to be tried by the inexperienced investor. They are covered in this text for four reasons:

1. Few investors are aware of them or understand them.

2. They can bring additional income to a portfolio during times of relatively stagnant prices.

3. They put you in the black immediately because you are selling not buying on the opening transaction.

4. They are, after all, a tool of the bull.

The arithmetic of puts, however, necessitates that the writer take some special precautions. Puts may be the opposite of calls by definition and application, but this does not mean if something works for writing calls, the opposite will work for writing puts. *Never make this mistake.*

For instance, covering calls by being long in the underlying stock is a recommended income strategy. However, in the case of puts, the recommended way to cover entails being short in the underlying stock. This is mainly because of the additional unlimited risk for being short on the underlying stock.

The put writer makes best sense when realizing that shorted puts:

- Need constant vigilance.

- Should not be written in quantity but sprinkled through a portfolio.

- Should not be written in bear markets.

- Are best utilized when they are out-of-the-money, expiration dates are near term, and the underlying stock has strong downside resistance.

- Are most appropriate in portfolios that are diversified enough to diffuse risk either through long and short positions in stocks in various industries or through well-weighted long and short positions in stocks and options combinations.

- Are the same as having a long position in stock and a short position in a call, except that shorted puts are immediate income and, therefore, put the writer immediately in the BLACK.

- Are not securities but contracts.

- Can only be fully covered by long puts on the same stock that will not expire any earlier than the puts written, and that have striking prices equal to or higher than the shorted puts.

The Writer's Perspective

The put writer is a short seller of puts. The put gives legal right to its owner to sell the underlying stock at the striking price until the expiration date of the contract. Anyone can be either a writer or buyer of puts. In fact, you can be both at the same time.

What is the advantage of being a put writer rather than a stock trader? As the buyer of stock, you must generally invest a great deal of money to take a position in order to benefit in bull markets. Additionally, the stock must advance in price for you to profit.

As the writer of a put, however, you do not have to put up any money when you sell short, although you must maintain enough money in your account to cover the margin requirements, which are very different from those required for stock traders. (See Table 19–1.)

Table 19–1
Types of Margin

Strategy	Requirement
Trading Stock	There must be a minimum deposit of $2,000 in cash or equivalent securities. (Usually only 75 percent of the market value of the securities applies.) If trade is $4,000 or more, investor must put up 50 percent or more of all money over $4,000.
Buying Puts	Full payment must be made on all trades, but securities in a cash or margin account may serve as collateral.
Naked Puts	Payment cannot be less than the premium of the option plus 5–20 percent of the value of the underlying security.

You also have time on your side because a put is a wasting asset, just as the call is. As time goes by, everything else being equal, the put will lose value. As a writer (short seller), this means you are profiting as the put drops in price.

Additionally, as a put writer, you benefit if the stock does not advance, advances slightly or greatly, or moves down in price slightly. You are immediately in the profit zone as soon as your trade is executed. Your account is immediately credited for the price of the put less the broker's commission. Writing puts is quick income, as long as the stock does not take a nose dive.

EXAMPLE #60. Profiting by Writing a Put: Stock Holds

You write five puts on IBM selling at $48 and receive $1,000 in premiums. The striking price is $45, which is the price at which the buyer of the put has the right to sell the stock.

The stock remains at $48 per share by expiration date. The contract, therefore, expires worthless. You have made $1,000.

So, if the stock holds or does not drop blow the striking price, you gain. If you purchased the stock, however, under these same conditions you would have been a loser.

EXAMPLE #61. Profiting by Writing a Put: Stock Drops but Stays above Strike Price

You write five puts on IBM selling at $48 and receive $1,000 in premiums. The striking price is $45, which is the price at which the buyer of the put has the right to sell the stock.

The stock remains at $45 per share by the expiration date of the put. The contract, therefore, expires worthless. You have made $1,000.

Here the stock actually dropped in price, but you still profited because you were smart enough to pick the right underlying stock—a stock that would not fall below the striking price by expiration date.

EXAMPLE #62. Profiting by Writing a Put: Stock Gains

You write five puts on IBM at $48 and receive $1,000 in premiums. The striking price is $45, which is the price at which the buyer of the put has the right to sell the stock.

The stock climbs to $60 per share by expiration date. The contract, therefore, expires worthless. You have made $1,000.

If you had purchased 500 shares of the stock, you would have made about $6,000. But remember this, you would have had to put up at least $12,000 to buy the stock (given 50 percent margin) but in writing the puts, you did not have to put up a cent. Rather, your account was immediately credited for $1,000.

EXAMPLE #63. Losing by Writing a Put: Stock Falls

You write five puts on IBM at $48 and receive $1,000 in premiums. The striking price is $45, which is the price at which the buyer of the put has the right to sell the stock.

The stock falls to $40 per share by expiration date. The owner of the contract exercises his option. This means he has the right to sell the shares at $45. He exercises his option to do so, then immediately covers his short position by buying the shares at the current market price of $40 per share. His gain on the trade is $5 per share on 500 shares, or $2,500.

You, however, have lost some money. True, you made $1,000 from writing the put, but you lost $2,500 from meeting your contractual obligations. You were required to buy the stock at $45 per share to cover your position. (The buyer of the put, remember, had the right to sell it to you.) But the stock is only worth $40.

You do have the alternative of holding onto the stock, which may advance far enough for you to cover your losses. Sometimes this is the very smart thing to do. But, then again, the stock may fall even further in price, and your losses will multiply.

EXAMPLE #64. "Buying Back" a Put

You write five puts on IBM selling at $48 and receive $1,000 in premiums. The striking price is $45, which is the price at which the buyer of the put has the right to sell the stock.

The stock falls to $44 per share before expiration date. As you are afraid that the stock will fall further, you decide to enter a closing transaction by buying back the put.

> Because the stock has fallen in price, the puts have increased in price. They are now worth a total of $1,250. So, when you buy them back, you will have a loss of $250.

You can now see the flexibility you have when dealing with options. You can close out your positions whenever you feel it is to your advantage. In Example #47, you decided to "buy back" your option to cut your losses. You could also have held on to your short position, hoping the stock would do a turnaround and advance in price, leaving the contract worthless.

Puts are occasionally written by investors who plan to acquire the underlying stock at a price that is less than the current market value. In this case, the put writer exercises her option and acquires the underlying stock at the exercise price less the premium. If she never gets the chance to exercise her option, she will at least have benefitted from the put premium.

Intrinsic Value

The price of a put, like the price of a call, is based mainly on its intrinsic value plus its time value. But the intrinsic value of a put is measured in just the opposite way it is for a call. The put has intrinsic value when its striking price is higher than the market price of the underlying stock. You were introduced to this idea in Part 1 of this book.

EXAMPLE #65. Determining Intrinsic Value of a Put

Stock Price	Strike Price	Intrinsic Value
$30.00	$25	None
28.50	25	None
26.00	25	None
25.00	25	None
24.00	25	$1.00
23.00	25	2.00
22.50	25	2.50
22.00	25	3.00

When a put is in the money, it has intrinsic value. This means that the owner of the puts can profit if he exercises his option. If an in-the-money position is advantageous to the buyer, it stands to reason that it is disadvantageous to the writer (buyer, short seller).

Besides intrinsic value, puts, like calls, have a time value which is derived mainly from the time remaining until expiration of the contract, but which is also affected by other factors, including such things as supply and demand and interest rates.

Consider the case for puts on Citicorp given in Table 19–2. You will notice that if the intrinsic value of an option were the only determining factor for its market price,

Table 19–2
Time-Decay Considerations
Stock: Citicorp   Strike Price: $35

Trading Day	Stock Price	Put Premiums
1	$35	1⅜
2	35	1¼
3	35	1⅛
4	34½	1
5	34½	⅞
6	34½	¾
7	34	1
8	34	⅞
9	34	¾

Expiration

Time decay is working against the value of the puts. Theoretically, they should be worth more on Day 9 when they are in-the-money than on Day 1 when they are at-the-money. But as the expiration date approaches, time decay works against any intrinsic value. This means time is on the side of the option writer. The lesson: The closer the expiration date, the better the opportunity for writing a profit. Note that even if you wrote an in-the-money on Day 4, you would have had a small profit by Day 9 if you "bought back" the put.

then the premiums for the Citicorp puts would be significantly less for in-the-money positions and actually zero for out-of-the-money positions.

Disadvantages of Writing Puts

There are clearly strong disadvantages to shorting puts, despite the fact that the strategy provides quick income. And it is best to be aware of them right up front.

When you short (write, sell) a put, you can never make more than the premium you receive, yet you can lose much more than you could by trading stock. This is due to of the tremendous leverage puts offer because of their low price.

Consider the following, wherein a stock is selling for $30 per share and someone buys 1,000 shares of the stock at market price. At the same time, you sell 10 puts (each put represents 100 shares). "Cost" for the stock before commissions is $30,000. Income from the sale of the puts is $625 ($⅝ × 1,000). (Expiration dates are not necessary for this example.)

EXAMPLE #66. Put Price Movement

Trading Day	Stock Price	Put Strike Price	Put Premium	Money Position
1	$30	$25	5/8	Out-of-the-Money
5	28	25	7/8	Out-of-the-Money
10	24	25	1 3/8	In-the-Money
20	20	25	5 5/8	In-the-Money

Notice how the put premium changes as the stock price begins to fall. The closer it gets to being in-the-money, the higher the premium. Also, the greater the intrinsic value, the higher the premium, which is another way of saying the same thing.

In Example #66, if the stock trader held the stock until the 20th day of trading, then sold, she would have realized a $10 per share loss, or $10,000. You, on the other hand, would have realized a loss of at least $5,000, depending upon whether or not you "bought back" (entered a closing transaction) the put or were called and had to cover your position by trading in the underlying stock. (Note that the trader does not actually buy back his put on the closing transaction. What he actually does is liquidate his position by purchasing a put of the same series as the put he shorted.)

Considering such possibility of heavy losses, why would anyone want to write a put? First, in a bull market for a given stock they offer the chance to boost income from a portfolio. Second, they offer the chance to gain even if the stock falls slightly, does not move at all, or goes up in price. In other words, you have three ways to win.

But success in writing puts is very dependent on the money positions of the puts in which you are dealing. Out-of-the money puts are relatively low-priced, which means if they move the wrong way, there is potential for extreme losses. In-the-money puts put the stock in danger of being called at any time; thus, the writer is immediately at risk when her order is executed. At-the-money puts need only move slightly to place the option in-the-money and at risk of being exercised. (See Tables 19–3, 19–4, and 19–5.)

Most authors and teachers generally sum up put trading by declaring that writers of puts come out losers when the price of the underlying shares decline and come out winners when the price of the underlying shares climb. But this is not entirely true, for the put writer can also win when the stock drops in price, as long as it does not fall below the striking price, and as long as he is writing out-of-the-money puts.

Covered Puts

Those of you familiar with covered calls, which can be covered by long positions in the underlying stock, might assume that puts, which are the opposite of calls, may be covered by being short in the underlying stock. However, the arithmetic of investment will not allow this to be true.

Table 19–3
Advantages and Disadvantages
of Writing Naked In-the-Money Puts

Advantages	Disadvantages
Premiums tend to move in a fairly determinable relationship to the underlying stock.	The stock can be called at any time. Thus, the writer must assure that the premium assures a profit as soon as the order is executed.
If the stock is highly volatile, it is possible to realize impressive capital gains by writing, closing out, and later rewriting—providing the price swings are impressive and predictable.	Losses can be heavy if the stock goes up in price.
	The usual risks of writing options are detailed in Chapter 24.

Limited coverage of a put may be done by taking a short position in the underlying security or securities. But such a position still leaves the put writer uncovered in the long run.

True covered puts can only be realized by taking a long position in another put covering the same underlying security or securities. But there is a caveat here. The

Table 19–4
Advantages and Disadvantages of Writing Naked
At-the-Money Puts

Advantages	Disadvantages
The chances of the underlying stock being called are less than those for in-the-monies, though more than those for out-of-the-monies.	Only a small downward movement in price will put the call in-the-money. Remember that as a put writer, you want the stock to go up in price, however slightly.
The value of the put will depreciate rather quickly as the expiration date nears, as long as the underlying stock does not depreciate much below the strike price.	Bull market in the underlying stock can result in high losses because of inherent leverage associated with the low price of puts.
If the stock is highly volatile, it is possible to realize impressive capital gain by writing, closing out, and later rewriting—provided the price swings are impressive and predictable.	Usual risks of writing options are detailed in Chapter 24.

Table 19–5
Advantages and Disadvantages of Writing Naked Out-of-the-Money Puts

Advantages	Disadvantages
The chance of the underlying stock being called only exists if the option goes in-the-money.	The relatively low price of these calls means there is potential for losses in the thousands of percent should the option go in-the-money.
Time decay of the call is relatively rapid in the last weeks of the contract.	Income is relatively low.
If the stock does not advance beyond the strike price, you stand to profit regardless of how much the option may have increased in price.	Usual risks of writing options are detailed in Chapter 24.

long position must be in a put that expires at the same time or after the shorted put—and the strike price cannot be less than the exercise price of the shorted put.

This may be illustrated by a writer who sells one AT&T December 60 put. He can only cover his position fully in one way, and that is by buying one AT&T December or later, 65 or higher put. This assures that if AT&T declined and the writer was put (required to buy the stock at $60), he could exercise his long put and sell at $65, for a $5 (or $500) gain.

When a put writer tries to cover her position by shorting the underlying stock, she also bears the risk of her shorted position. If the price of the underlying stock starts to increase instead of decline, the losses can be extensive. This is illustrated in Example #67.

EXAMPLE #67. The Challenge of Covered Puts

Short 1,000 shares and write 10 puts

Trading Day	Stock Price	Put Strike Price	Put Premium	Money Position
1	$30	25	5/8	Out-of-the-money
Last	70	25	—	Out-of-the-money

The put expires out-of-the-money, so you get to keep your premium. However, losses on the underlying stock can be disastrous. There is no limit to losses on short positions in stock.

If you are not covering your shorted puts through a long position in another put as explained above, then you will be required to maintain margin with your broker, which may either be in the form of cash or securities. But in a truly technical sense, you must maintain a margin account under any circumstances. All brokers require that options be traded in margin accounts having a $2,000 minimum balance in cash or equivalent securities.

Margin Math

Table 19–1 compares margin requirements for buying and shorting stock and buying and shorting puts. Table 19–6 gives the specific math for naked writers of puts.

For each trade, the writer of an option must have on deposit the total value of the premium plus 20 percent of the stock price less the amount the option is out-of-the-money. Thus, there is an added incentive to writing out-of-the-money options: Margin requirements are less. However, the margin can never be less than the premium plus 10 percent of the price of the underlying security.

If the short positions are covered by long positions in an equal number of puts that do not expire earlier and are at higher striking prices, no margin is required.

Table 19–6
Margin Math for Put Writers

Premium	Stock Price	Strike Price	Amount Out-of-the-Money	Margin Requirement
$2	$30	$35	$500	$300
3	40	42.50	250	850

For each trade, the writer must put up the total value of the premium plus 20 percent of the stock price less any amount the option may be out-of-the-money. Thus, as each put represents 100 shares of stock, the premium is multiplied by 100. The margin requirement is, therefore, calculated in either of the following ways:

$$\$200 + (.20 \times \$3000) - \$500$$
or
$$\$200 + \$600 - \$500$$

For OTC naked options, the formula differs. In this case, the margin requirement is the full amount of the premium plus 45 percent of the underlying stock's market price, less the amount the put is out-of-the-money.

20

PLAYING THE MONEY POSITIONS

Put writers generally operate under the philosophy that the future market value for a stock will probably be its current price, plus or minus 15 percent by the time of expiration. So they try to write puts with striking prices that assure the underlying stock will not make it past the striking price during the term of the contract.

They certainly do not want a stock that has the potential for falling below the striking price, because if this happens the puts they have sold short (written) will increase in value. If the stock does increase in value, they may be forced to buy the puts back at a higher price or meet their contract obligations by acquiring the underlying security at a higher price than the current market price.

Selecting Puts

As in the case with calls, so it is in dealing with puts. It's a shopper's paradise. There are so many selections, so many combinations to play, and so many options on just one stock. Take, for example, the following put listings on Storage Technology, which have been contrived for purposes of example. Writing any of the available puts would be of little interest to you unless you believed the stock was going to stay in a very narrow trading range for the next few months.

EXAMPLE #68. Selecting Puts to Write

Stock: Storage Technology   Price: $28

Stock Price	Strike	October	November	December
$28	$25	$1\frac{1}{4}$	$1\frac{1}{2}$	$1\frac{7}{8}$
28	30	2	$2\frac{1}{2}$	$2\frac{3}{4}$
28	35	7	$7\frac{1}{4}$	$7\frac{5}{8}$
28	40	12	$12\frac{1}{8}$	$12\frac{1}{4}$
28	45	17	—	—

The first expiration date is one month away.

You have been drawn to Storage Technology because you feel on the near term it probably will not fall very much in price. In fact, if anything, you expect that it will increase in value. You would rather be selling calls or buying stock long, but you do not see any worthwhile candidates for big bucks. You have been tracking Storage Technology, and you have its price movement down pat. The best way to play the stock, you decide, is to short (write) the puts. It is better to short a stock you know well than to take a chance of going long on puts or stock you are unfamiliar with.

You have a number of choices in the case of Storage Technology. Which is the best?

First of all, realize that the listed prices in Example #68 are probably not the prices at which you will actually be able to write the puts. These listings are usually the ask prices. For instance, the bid and ask prices for the October 25s are probably $7/8–1\frac{1}{4}$, and for the November 25s, $1\frac{1}{8}$–$1\frac{1}{2}$.

Second, understand that the higher premiums are for the in-the-money puts, with those having later contract expiration dates being the highest.

Third, remember that these are put premiums, so the higher the striking price above the stock price, the higher the premiums.

Again, you are faced with the question: Which puts are the most attractive?

Generally, it is best to play the out-of-the-monies; however, the premiums are so low that very often they are entirely unattractive. It is also best to play the options that have very close expiration dates, because in this case, time decay is rapid, and as the puts decay, your profits (because you are a writer) will increase.

For illustration, let's select three and play them out. Hopefully, these will give some insight into considerations that put writers must make and how luck remains an important element in all trades.

EXAMPLE #69. Deciding When to Close out a Position

You write the 10 October 25s at $1\frac{1}{4}$.
  Income: $1,250

Trading Day	Stock Price	October 25 Premium
1	$28	$1\frac{1}{4}$
3	30	$\frac{1}{2}$
5	28	$1\frac{1}{8}$
7	$27\frac{1}{2}$	$1\frac{1}{4}$
10	$28\frac{1}{2}$	$\frac{7}{8}$
15	25	2
17	27	1
18	28	$\frac{7}{8}$
20	26	$\frac{5}{8}$
Day before Expiration	22	$2\frac{3}{4}$

Notice in the above example that the put movement in relation to the stock price movement cannot be exactly predicted. This is because market forces and time decay work together to push and pull on the prices of the puts. For instance, on Day 1 the stock is at $28 and the premium at 1¼; on Days 5 and 18, however, although the stock is at the same price, the premiums have changed.

You were doing all right until the day before expiration, when the option went into the money. Here you are at a loss, having written the calls for $1,250 but now being forced to enter a closing transactions at $2,750. Your losses: $1,500.

As it turned out, you selected the wrong puts. True, indeed, you were playing the out-of-the-monies, which are generally the safer play, but there are absolutely no guarantees that you will profit even when you write out-of-the-money puts.

Suppose that you had written the November 25s instead?

EXAMPLE #70. How an Investment in Put Option Writing Can Rebound

You write the 10 November 25s at $1½.
  Income: $1,500

Trading Day	Stock Price	October 25 Premium
1	$28	1½
3	30	¾
5	28	1¼
7	27½	1½
10	28½	1¼
15	25	2¼
17	27	1¼
18	28	1⅛
20	26	⅞
25	22	3
27	23½	1¼
30	24¾	1¼
35	25	⅞
40	27½	¾
45	28	½
Day before expiration	28¼	⅛

Bear in mind that this turns out to be profitable because you are a writer of these puts. If you were the seller, your losses on Day 45 would be over 66 percent.

After Day 35, the puts were again out-of-the-money, so your position was safe. The puts remained out-of-the-money through expiration. Your profit: the initial premium of $1,500. So, you picked the right underlying stock. You guessed that Storage Technology would remain in a relatively narrow trading range and probably had more upside potential than downside.

What you picked wrong in the first example was the expiration date. (Another analyst might easily argue that you picked the wrong striking price.) So you lost money because of some unexpected downside swings in the price of the underlying stock. The November contract date, however, allowed time for the price to adjust to the expected price level.

Was there any way to prevent the mistake of writing the October 25s? No, none at all. And herein is the lesson once again: There are no guarantees; luck is still an important element in making money in stock and options markets. You can do everything you are supposed to and still lose money.

Now, what about in-the-money puts? Can you ever make money writing these? Yes, of course, as the following example indicates.

EXAMPLE #71. Deciding When to Cover Short Positions

You write 10 October 35s at $7
   Income: $7,000

Trading Day	Stock Price	October 35 Premium
1	$28	7
3	30	5
5	28	7
7	27½	7½
10	28½	6½
12	30½	4¾
13	31½	3½
14	27	7¾
15	25	10
17	27	7½
18	28	6½
20	26	8⅝
Day before expiration	22	12

As the writer of these puts, you have heavy losses on Day 20, whereas the buyer would have profits.

In this example, as the writer, you would have been able to profit by purchasing 10 puts of the same series on Days 3, 10, 12, 13, and 18. But would you have? You may have gotten greedy and decided to hold on for greater profits than would be available on any of those days. And remember that throughout the contract period the buyer could have exercised his rights at any time. If he did so on any days in which put prices were higher than what you received in premiums, you would have sustained losses, as much as $5,750 on the day before expiration. (Remember, the expiration date is usually 11:59 on the Saturday after the third Friday during the month of expiration. The exception is if the first day of the month is a Saturday, then the fourth Saturday is expiration day.)

Covering with Long Puts

Anytime you write puts, be sure to cover your short positions by also buying an equal number of low-priced puts. In this way, you hedge against any sharply depreciating prices in the underlying stock that will put your short position in harm's way, and you will effect the hedge at little cost. The puts in which you go long, remember, will cover your short positions only if the strike prices are higher and the expiration dates are the same or better.

Let's repeat an earlier illustration to emphasize this important point: A writer who sells one AT&T December 60 put can only cover his position fully in one way, and that is by buying one AT&T December 65 (or later) or higher striking put. This assures that if AT&T declined and the writer was "put" (required to buy the stock at $60), he could exercise his long put and sell at $65, for a $5 (or $500) gain.

Writing In-the-Money Puts

Note that in all cases the puts with intrinsic value are those that have prices below the striking price. They are in-the-money because the buyers of the puts are in a position to profit after exercising their rights. They can short the stock at the striking price and immediately cover their positions by buying the underlying security at the current market price.

While in-the-money puts can represent a worthwhile opportunity for writers, they can more often than not be highly disadvantageous. The in-the-money puts, however, are often very tempting to put writers because they command higher premiums. However, in-the-monies can be subject to exercise immediately, in which case the writer will be forced to cover her position, probably at a loss. It is true that rights are rarely exercised as soon as puts are in-the-money, but the danger always exists for the writer.

Writing in-the-money puts, however, can be profitable, as Table 20–1 indicates. This profit can be obtained by finding puts that have premiums that exceed the intrinsic value of the option by enough points to assure gain if the stock is called. In other words, the premiums on in-the-money puts must always exceed the difference between the striking price and the underlying stock by enough to cover all transaction fees and ensure a substantial profit. Otherwise, in most cases, dealing in the put is just not an attractive proposition for a potential writer. When the premium is at such a profitable range, it may be said that the in-the-money put is at a write advantage.

In the examples that follow, you will see how you can win and lose by writing in-the-money puts. There is some repetition in the presentation of these examples and in the way subtopics overlap. This repetition is for reinforcement.

Table 20–1
Write Advantages (In-the-Money Puts)

Example	Current Stock Price	Put Premium	Strike Price	Write Advantage
#1	24	1	25	0
#2	24	1¼	25	+ ¼
#3	22	3	25	0
#4	22	3½	25	+ ½
#5	22	4	25	+ 1
#6	20	5	25	0

If the premium plus the current price of the stock is more than the strike price, you are immediately in a profitable position even when you write an in-the-money put. But do not let the size of the premium fool you as in #6. Do your arithmetic to determine the immediate advantage of writing an in-the-money put. The puts that have later expiration dates, though the same striking prices, will command higher premiums—usually. Remember to consider commissions when calculating your actual break-even point.

EXAMPLE #72. Losing by Writing In-the-Money Puts

Puts with a striking price of $25 are available on Cotter Industries. The stock is selling at $20 per share, placing the related puts in-the-money by $5. The premium for each put is $5 (meaning each put costs $500). You write six puts (each put representing 100 shares of the underlying stock) and receive $3,000 in premiums. The money is yours to keep. The option is in danger of exercise at any time.

The stock drops to $15 per share, and the puts increase in value to $10 per share. Shortly afterward, and quite unexpectedly, the option is exercised. You must, therefore, purchase the underlying stock at $25 to cover your position. As the stock is currently at $15, your losses are $10 per share.

Transaction Summary

Loss on covering short position on underlying stock:	$6,000
Wrote (sold) six puts at $500 each:	–3,000
Loss:	$3,000

Now that you know you can lose with in-the-monies, let's look at a winning situation.

EXAMPLE #73. Winning by Writing In-the-Money Puts

Again, Cotter Industries. But this time the stock advances and time also decays the value of the puts.

Striking price is $25, and the stock is selling at $20 per share, placing the puts in-the-money by $5. The premium for each put is $5 (meaning each put costs $500). You write six puts (each put representing 100 shares of the underlying stock) and receive $3,000 in premiums. The money is yours to keep. The stock climbs to $24 per share, but very slowly and not until a couple of days before expiration. The puts are now worth only $1, at which price you buy them back. Cost to cover your short position: $600

Transaction Summary

Wrote (sold) six puts at $5 each:	$3,000
Covered short position at $600 per put:	− 600
Gains:	$2,400

In each of the above examples, the writer must pay very special attention to the expiration date. This is because as the date approaches the chances of an in-the-money put option being exercised increases greatly. In this case, there will be increased losses or reduced profits because the writer must also trade in the underlying stock.

Is it really worth writing in-the-money puts? Occasionally, and as long as you are aware of the disadvantages.

In many cases, they can be extremely profitable. Suppose that you write an in-the-money put on IBM and receive $800 in premiums.

And suppose the stock climbs and the options go out of the money; you will have made $800. If the stock advances, you still have an opportunity to benefit by buying back the puts at a lower price. And if the stock does not move at all or just slightly, time decay on the puts will allow you to profit also, though not as much.

It is impractical to try and cover all the arithmetical advantages that occur as puts move further away from the money and/or closer to expiration dates. Perhaps the previous examples help to at least show that there are many possibilities.

Additionally, as in-the-money puts usually move close to point-to-point with the movement in price of the underlying stock, the percentage of gain or loss is less volatile. At-the-money and out-of-the-money puts, however, can be "wild and crazy guys." You may write three out-of-the-money puts on Dow Jones for $1.50 each (or, $450) only to lose five times that if the stock suddenly declines and goes in the money, driving put premiums to $7.50.

On the other hand, though they often are not, any in-the-money option is in danger of being exercised at any time.

Writing At-the-Money Puts

Puts are at-the-money when their striking price is equal to the price of the stock. Actually, if broker commissions are taken into account, at-the-monies would be out-of-the-money. Always keep in mind that broker commissions will affect the true intrinsic value of an option.

At-the-money puts can be very volatile because slight changes in the price of the underlying stock can place them in- or out-of-the-money, thereby changing their premiums markedly.

Before writing at-the-money puts—as with as any option—always consider the prospects for the underlying issue and the size of the premium. If the stock is showing fundamental and technical weakness, buy puts or sell short the underlying stock. On the other hand, if the stock is showing very strong fundamentals and technical strength, forget about writing puts and, instead, buy calls or the underlying stock.

In the following examples, you will see how you can gain or lose money by writing at-the-money puts.

EXAMPLE #74. Losing by Writing At-the-Money Puts

Puts with a striking price of $20 are available on Baker Products. The stock is selling at $20 per share, placing the related puts at-the-money. The premium for each put is $1 (meaning each put costs $100). You write six puts (each put representing 100 shares of the underlying stock) and receive $600 in premiums. The money is yours to keep.

The stock drops to $15 per share, and the puts increase in value to $5 per share. Shortly afterward, and quite unexpectedly, the option is exercised. You must, therefore, purchase the underlying stock at $20 to cover your position. As the stock is currently at $15, your losses are $5 per share ($3,000).

Transaction Summary

Covered short position:	$3,000
Wrote (sold) six puts at $1 each:	− 600
Loss:	$2,400

At-the-money puts usually have relatively small premiums in consideration of the risk involved. This author generally only likes at-the-money options for covered call strategies; they are not usually worth the gamble for put writers.

In the next example, you will see it is possible also to profit by writing at-the-money puts.

EXAMPLE #75. Winning by Writing At-the-Money Puts

Puts with a striking price of $20 are available on Baker Products. The stock is selling at $20 per share, placing the related puts at-the-money. The premium for each put is $1 (meaning each put costs $100). You write six puts (each put representing 100 shares of the underlying stock) and receive $600 in premiums. The money is yours to keep.

The stock climbs to $25 per share, and the puts fall out-of-the-money and to $⅛ ($12.50 each). Rather than wait until expiration date, you decide to buy them back and assure your profit.

Transaction Summary

Wrote (sold) six puts at $1 each:	$ 600
Covered short position at:	– 75
Gains:	$ 525

Because at-the-money puts are so close to having intrinsic value, the very slightest move in the price of the underlying stock means the difference, often, of being in the black or the red. Whether or not it is worth writing at-the-money puts depends a great deal upon how well you can predict the short-term behavior of the underlying stock and whether or not the write advantage (Table 20–2) is favorable.

Writing Out-of-the-Money Puts

This is the type of put that offers you some level of safety, although the premiums you will be earning will be relatively small.

Out-of-the-money options just do not demand as high a premium as the other money positions. However, do not take it for granted that out-of-the-money puts are always the smartest selection. You will need to evaluate a number of variables including the size of the premium. These include the actual amount the put is out of the money, the time remaining until expiration date, the volatility of the underlying stock, current interest rates, and other opportunities presenting more attractive risk/reward ratios. (See Table 20–3.)

Table 20–2
Write Advantages (At-the-Money Puts)

Example	Current Stock Price	Put Premium	Strike Price	Write Advantage
#1	$25	⅛	$25	+ ⅛
#2	25	1	25	+1
#3	25	3	25	+3
#4	25	3½	25	+3½

Do not let the size of the premium fool you, as in #4. Do your arithmetic to determine the immediate advantage of writing an in-the-money put. The puts that have later expiration dates, though the same striking prices, will command higher premiums—usually. Do not forget to allow for commissions in determining your break-even points.

Table 20–3
Write Advantages (Out-of-the-Money Puts)

Example	Current Stock Price	Put Premium	Strike Price	Write Advantage
#1	$26	2⅛	25	3⅛
#2	26	1¾	25	2¾
#3	28	¾	25	3¾
#4	28	1¼	25	4¼
#5	30	½	25	5½
#6	30	¼	25	5¼

Because these are out-of-the-money, you are immediately in a profitable position and will remain so until the puts go in-the-money. The puts that have later expiration dates, though the same striking prices, will command higher premiums—usually.

In the following examples, you will see how you can gain or lose money by writing out-of-the-money puts.

EXAMPLE #76. Losing by Writing Out-of-the-Money Puts

Puts with a striking price of $20 are available on CTZ Industries. The stock is selling at $22 per share, placing the related puts out-of-the-money. The premium for each put is $1 (meaning each put costs $100). You write six puts (each put representing 100 shares of the underlying stock) and receive $600 in premiums. The money is yours to keep.

The stock drops to $12 per share, and the puts increase in value to $8 per share. The puts are now in-the-money. Shortly afterward, and quite unexpectedly, the option is exercised. You must, therefore, purchase the underlying stock at $20 to cover your position. As the stock is currently at $12, your losses are $8 per share ($4,800).

Transaction Summary

Covered short position on underlying stock:	$4,800
Wrote (sold) six puts at $1 each:	– 600
Loss:	$4,200

Out-of-the-money puts usually have relatively small premiums in consideration of the risk involved, but as the chances of the options being exercised are slim, the positions are worth consideration.

In the next example, you will see that it is also possible to profit by writing at-the-money puts.

EXAMPLE #77. Winning by Writing Out-of-the-Money Puts

Puts with a striking price of $20 are available on CTZ Industries. The stock is selling at $22 per share, placing the related puts out-of-the-money. The premium for each put is $1 (meaning each put costs $500). You write six puts (each put representing 100 shares of the underlying stock) and receive $600 in premiums. The money is yours to keep.

The stock climbs to $25 per share, and the puts fall further out-of-the-money and to $⅛ ($12.50 each). Rather than wait until expiration date, you decide to close out your position to assure your profit.

Transaction Summary

Wrote (sold) six puts at $1 each:	$ 600
Covered short positions at:	– 75
Gains:	$ 525

In any case, it is always wise to try to cover your put positions, though it is usually not arithmetically advantageous. You cannot fully cover your positions by shorting stock, because there is only a narrow price range in which the shorted stock affords coverage. Shorting or buying calls at the same time is of no advantage, either, in covering your puts. The only true method of covering a shorted put is to buy another put with a more advantageous striking price and expiration date than the one shorted.

21

WRITING STRATEGIES

Just as with calls, there are many ways to employ puts in various combinations to help you meet your goals as safely or aggressively as possible. In the previous chapter, we looked at some of the considerations related to buying and selling puts, but just learning how to trade them does not constitute a strategy.

There are actually many strategies for put writing, some entailing the use of short or long calls, some employing long positions in puts. In some cases, the strategies are highly complex and require great knowledge and skill to master. But there are some basic strategies that are easy to understand and employ and that bring a new dimension to your investment knowledge and applications. These are described in following sections.

But first, understand that you cannot look at writing puts as being comparable to fixed-income investments, as some investors have a tendency to do. This is for the following reasons:

- Many factors affect the premiums of puts, including the volatility of the underlying stock, interest rates, and expiration dates. So, there really is nothing "fixed" about the premiums.

- Put writing programs need constant management because income can actually be reduced or canceled because the writer has had to cover his or her position. Additionally, if the wrong type of put is written, the writer can actually lose money.

- With fixed-income investments, there is no commission each time income is distributed, but with puts there is a commission associated with, and based on, the size of premiums. This commission can mean the difference between profit and loss.

Basic Income Plays

The main reason for writing puts is to produce income, something that happens as soon as your order is executed.

You have already been introduced to the two most basic strategies, those of covered and uncovered writing. Now we will bring them together and build upon

217

them, using them as steps for learning additional strategies also designed mainly to produce income. (These are also summarized in Table 21–1.)

Writing uncovered puts entails shorting a put on an underlying stock that you hope will not decline in price enough to place your option in the money. The idea, then, is to write puts on stocks not only with strong fundamentals but also with strong technical positions. For instance, you would not want to write puts on stocks that, despite the apparent strength of their balance sheets, are suddenly hitting new lows. Unlimited losses are always the risk, whether you are selling short options or stock. In the following example, you will find an accounting of successful writes.

EXAMPLE #78. Income from an Uncovered Put

A. 1. Sold short 1 Tandy Dec 45 put: $275
   2. Option expired out-of-the-money: 000
            Profit: $275

B. 1. Sold short 1 Tandy April 50 put: $350
   2. Bought 1 Tandy April 50 put: 75
            Profit: $275

If Tandy stock were to drop significantly, perhaps to $20 per share, losses on the put would be considerable. The option would go in-the-money at the same time that it has moved up significantly in price. This means the writer of the option would have to take losses on either the stock or the option.

Table 21–1
Basic Strategies Employing Shorted Puts

Strategy	Short Puts	Long Puts	Short Calls	Long Calls	Different Strike Price	Different Expiration
Uncovered Write	X					
Covered Write	X	X			Short put same or lower	Short put same or earlier
Short Combination	X		X		Strike price and/or expiration different	
Short Straddle	X		X			
Price Put Spread	X	X			Shorted put has higher strike price for bullish position	
Diagonal	X				Yes	Yes

A covered put prevents such risk. In a covered put, there are simultaneous long and short positions in puts on the same underlying stock. As stressed many times, this position only works if the short put does not have a greater striking price or an earlier expiration date. The purpose is to provide income and insurance in case the underlying stock falls in price.

The following example illustrates an opening position for a covered put.

EXAMPLE #79. Covering a Put

Opening position:
     Sold short 1 Tandy Dec. 45 put
     Bought 1 Tandy Dec. 50 put

Remember that a writer of a put is also known as a short seller, and that this position would not work if the long position expires earlier or if its striking price is lower.

In this case, if Tandy stock were to drop significantly, or even to zero dollars per share (very unlikely), what would be lost on the shorted put, which would necessarily have to be bought back at a higher price ($45), would be made up for by the long put, which can be sold at an even higher price ($50).

To increase income, a trader will try something called a short combination. In this case, he sells one or more calls and puts on the very same underlying stock. The puts and calls will have different striking prices and/or different expiration dates.

EXAMPLE #80. A Short Combination

Opening position:

Sell 1 Placer Dec. 20 Call:	$ 600
Sell 1 Placer Jan. 20 Put:	500
Value of Position:	$1,100

The position brings in a great deal of immediate income, but whether or not the writer will eventually get to keep any part of it depends upon the movement of the underlying stock. The spread is 11 points, so the full amount of the premium will be kept only if the stock does not advance and hold above or below the striking price.

At face value, this position seems to be a golden opportunity. Imagine the income if you were shorting 10 puts and 10 calls. It would be $11,000. Just remember that here you have two short positions. One does not cover the other, but rather adds to the risk position at the same time that it adds to possible income. Losses here can be unlimited.

There is another position quite similar to the short combination, except in this case the calls and the puts not only have the very same underlying stock, but also the very same expiration date and the very same striking price. This is called the short straddle.

EXAMPLE #80-A. A Short Straddle

Opening position:

Sell 1 Placer Dec. 20 Call:	$ 600
Sell 1 Placer Dec. 20 Put:	400
Value of Position:	$1,000

In this case, the spread is 109 points. If Placer does not advance beyond 30 or drop below 10, some or all of the premium will remain intact. You can apply some easy arithmetic to learn what would happen if the stock went one way or another, thereby affecting either the shorted put or the shorted call. If the stock remains close to $20 until the expiration date, the maximum profit will be realized. The chances of that happening, however, are extremely slim.

A Buy Play

The other objective for writing puts we might call a "buy play." Here the primary objective is not income from premiums, but rather a favorable position in the underlying stock. Generally, a call might be used for this purpose; and for all practical purposes, going long on in-the-money puts is the most direct way to take an option to purchase an underlying stock at the selected striking price.

A second way, of course, is simply to place a limit order to get the stock at the required price. But this can represent a holding pattern that active traders cannot tolerate. The more dynamic traders generally like to be producing income or opportunity every moment they can. Thus, they may prefer shorting puts for their purpose.

The advantage in taking the round-about approach through shorted puts is that here no money has to be put up front, other than what might be required for margin purposes. But in a well-formulated and effective portfolio, the margin requirements are probably already satisfied by cash or equivalent securities.

So, by shorting the required number of puts, the trader is making money while stalking the underlying stock.

For example, suppose that Ford Motor Company is currently at $52 per share, but you want to purchase it at $50 per share. However, you are not interested in placing a bid and putting your money on hold. You are a producer, and you want your portfolio producing all the time. Therefore, you consider a situation wherein:

- You are earning income while you are waiting for your opportunity, and

- You are able to get a discount if and when you purchase the underlying stock.

To do this, you write 10 Ford June 50 puts for $3 (for a total of $3,000). If the stock never declines to the striking price, you get to keep the $3,000 you received in premiums. If, on the other hand, the stock drops below $50 and the options are exercised, you get the stock at a discount. That is, you pay $50 a share less the $3 you received in premiums. Either way you come out okay.

But, of course, there is always the negative side. Where there is opportunity, there is risk. There are no free lunches in the stock and options markets. You pay for opportunities by accepting risk. And here the risk is that you put yourself in danger of unlimited losses, for, after all, you are playing with an uncovered short position. (There is also the separate risk of having the stock fall even further after you buy it.)

Advanced Strategies

The New York Institute of Finance has a course they call Exotic Options. It is very aptly titled because it brings students into put and call strategies that are extremely complicated but effective. They remain in the realm of the highly sophisticated professional trader. They are mentioned below only to emphasize that put and call strategies are numerous, compound, and complex. There are very few independent investors, however, who employ them in their quest for income or capital gains. Those strategies that entail put writing are price put spreads, which utilize puts and calls with the same striking prices but different expiration dates; put time spreads, which utilize puts with the same expiration date but different striking prices; and diagonal spreads, which use different striking prices and different expiration dates.

Beyond these strategies are the more exotic strategies, which entail positions in one or more underlying stocks, and more than one type of put and/or call.

Assessing Risk

Writing puts can mean unlimited losses. This is because short positions theoretically have no ceiling, but they do have a floor. The short seller makes money when the position he has taken declines in price and loses money when that position advances in value. Any security or contract can only decline to zero but can advance ad infinitum.

Puts are mainly for squeezing additional income out of portfolios in bull markets. Thus all investors need to assess the risk/reward factors involved in their decision to write puts. That is, they must decide how much risk they are willing to take to get the premiums they are after.

The primary types of risks to be weighed may be grouped under the following categories:

- Stock selection risk
- Market influence risk
- Option selection risk
- Financial risk

The stock-specific risk relates to the quality of the underlying stock for your writing program. Any investors trying options writing for the first time easily get tied up in semantics or arithmetic. Often the neophyte's first instinct is wrong when it comes to making comparisons about options writing. He may easily confuse, for instance, bear spreads with bull spreads.

The put writer wants a strong underlying stock, make no doubt about this. This is because when a stock increases in price, a put decreases in price. And it is the goal of the writer to have his put move lower after he writes, so if he has to buy it back, he can do so at less cost. The nightmare is when an out-of-the-money put moves in-the-money because the underlying stock has dropped too many points. In this case, losses can be very heavy.

Market-influence risk refers to general market performance, which often influences the price movement of most stocks. This is where the beta rating of a stock serves a very useful purpose. Beta ratings indicate the volatility of a stock in relation to the performance of Standard & Poor's 500 Index. Stocks with a beta of one tend to move in a direct relationship with the S&P Index. Ratings of more than one indicate higher volatility, and ratings below one indicate lesser volatility. Writing a put on a highly volatile stock is a very risky play. Writers of puts should consider as the underlying security relatively stable stocks with good earnings forecasts as well as steady volume and upward price movements.

Option selection risk refers to the type of put being written. It stands to reason that in-the-money puts can place the writer immediately in harm's way, because these are subject to exercise at any time. And at-the-money puts can be very volatile, because a slight movement of price in the underlying stock, one way or another, can cause the put to triple or quadruple in price or lose high percentages of their value. On the other hand, far out-of-the-money puts will not command much of a premium, so they offer little opportunity when weighed against the inherent risks of shorting puts. The recommended objective is to find near-the-money puts with close expiration dates on strong underlying stocks.

Financial risk for our purposes refers to the impact that your writing program may have on your portfolio. As losses on writing puts can be extensive, backup money will have to come from what margin you have on account. Most investors have securities in their margin accounts, which are pledged as collateral for other trades. It is important to remember that your broker usually only counts 75 percent of these securities toward margin requirements. So, if you incur heavy losses from writing, you may be forced to sell your other securities at a loss to cover your positions, then dig into whatever other money you may have to pay back your broker.

22

CORRECTING COMMON MISCONCEPTIONS ABOUT PUT WRITING

The way in which the options markets work plus the confusing terminology and arithmetic associated with options often causes investors to harbor some serious misconceptions. Those which follow seem to be the most common.

1. *Writing puts is a sure way to increase income from portfolios in bull markets.*

Untrue. There are no guarantees associated with put writing. It is true that you have more chances to profit from put writing because you can earn premiums if a stock advances, if it remains in a very narrow trading range, and even sometimes if the stock depreciates, though this last is dependent upon the money position of the put you write, as well as the performance of the underlying stock.

2. *As puts and calls are opposites, writing a put would be the same as buying a call.*

Untrue. This very common misconception is highly understandable, because call writers make money when a stock goes up, as do put writers. However, put writers can also make money when a stock goes down (but not below the strike price). Call buyers cannot turn a profit if the underlying stock goes down, and then only if the decline is very slight.

Puts and calls are not easy to understand, and it has always been this author's suggestion that the best way to enter the options market is to first deal in covered calls, then progress to uncovered calls, then to puts. The uncovered writing should only come after exceptional study and experience with the covered calls.

One important difference between puts and calls from a writer's perspective is that the put writer is bullish on the underlying stock and the call writer is bearish.

A second important difference between puts and calls is that the put gives its owner the right to sell 100 shares of stock, whereas the call gives him the right to buy 100 shares of stock. In other words, if you feel that Boeing is about to increase in price and there are attractive out-of-the-money puts available on the stock, you might want to write a put. On the other hand, if you feel Digital is going to fall in price, you might want to write a call.

3. *In-the-money, at-the-money, and out-of-the-money positions are the same for both puts and calls.*

Untrue, as Table 22–1 indicates. Puts and calls are on opposite sides of the options seesaw, so do not confuse the money positions for puts with those for calls. Other-

Table 22–1
Money Positions for Puts and Calls

Stock Price	Strike Price	Put	Call
$20	$25	In-the-Money	Out-of-the-Money
20	15	Out-of-the-Money	In-the-Money
20	20	At-the-Money	At-the-Money
25	20	Out-of-the-Money	In-the-Money
20	20	At-the-Money	At-the-Money
15	20	In-the-Money	Out-of-the-Money

wise, you may find yourself writing in-the-money puts when you had absolutely no intention of doing so.

4. *Writing puts is a smarter strategy than buying them.*
Untrue. It all depends upon what your goals are and what the fundamental and technical status of the underlying stock happens to be. Writing puts is for those who are somewhat bullish on the underlying stock, and writing calls is for those who are somewhat bearish. Table 22–2 gives further clarification.

5. *A put is an equity security.*
Untrue. Just as with calls, puts are contracts that allow their owners to purchase or sell the underlying common stock at the contract price for the contract period. Stock options are not equities and should not be mistaken for such.

6. *Puts can be exercised anytime before they expire.*
True only in the case of American-style options. Both puts and calls fall under the categories of American-style or European-style option. In the case of the former, options may be exercised by the holder anytime after purchase but before the expi-

Table 22–2
The Long and Short of It

Stock Expectations	Tool and Strategy
Small advance, minimal downside risk	Short put
Strong retreat	Long put
Strong advance	Long call
Small retreat, little upside potential	Short call

ration date. European-style options may only be exercised during a specific period prior to expiration. The category that the options you trade may fall under is not defined in the options tables; this information must be obtained from your broker. Most options traded on the U.S. exchanges are American-style options.

7. *Puts are called in-the-money when they are profitable.*

Untrue. In the case of American-style options, in-the-money just means that the option has intrinsic value and can be exercised for a position in the underlying stock under favorable circumstances. Whether or not the option is profitable depends upon how much you paid for it or for how much you sold it short.

8. *Transaction costs for trading in puts or calls are limited to the commissions paid for opening or closing transactions.*

Untrue for short positions. For short positions (those of the writer), there will be the inherent costs of margin, and on top of that the opportunity costs that might be incurred.

9. *Margin means the same thing for options traders that it does for stock traders.*

Untrue. In stock trading, margin refers to the credit available from your broker for buying shares of a stock. In options trading, margin refers to the money in addition to the value of the option that may be required before you can trade.

Margin requirements for options trading vary from brokerage to brokerage, but minimum margin is set by the Federal Reserve Board and the various stock exchanges. This means that first the Fed sets margin, then the exchanges match or increase the requirements, then brokerages match or increase the requirements imposed by the exchanges.

Uncovered writers are usually in potentially precarious situations, so their margin requirements are usually very strict and very steep, as you learned in this text. When the market heads in the opposite direction to what is beneficial to the option writer, the broker will call for additional margin as may be required to keep the broker out of harm's way. Because of their low price, options are extremely volatile. In the case of writing puts, a 10 percent decrease in the underlying stock can mean a 300 percent or more loss to the writer, particularly when the underlying option moves from an in-the-money position to an out-of-the-money position or from an out- to an in-the-money position.

At this writing, most brokerages require a writer of uncovered puts to have a minimum of $25,000 in his margin account. This is a rather steep and outrageous requirement, for not all positions share the same amount of risk. Still, the broker is the one who can be left out of the money, so to speak, and he wants to make sure that the put writer is always in a position to meet his contract requirements or close out his position.

10. *Put options are exercised as soon as they go into-the-money.*

Untrue. It is relatively rare for a put to be exercised as soon as it goes into-the-money or even while it is in-the-money, but the danger always exists. Some analysts write that the chance is about 1 in 10. That's still too high from a writer's perspective. Once a put is in the money, it is always in danger of being exercised

11. *An investor must be either a buyer or a seller of a put.*

Untrue. She may be both, consecutively or all at once. Any option may be purchased long or sold short, just as the underlying stock may be bought long or sold short. With a put, however, it gets a bit tricky because its movement is very different from a stock's. When you buy a put long, you are bearish on the underlying stock; but when you buy a stock long, you are bullish. When you sell a put short, you are bullish on the underlying stock; but when you sell a stock short, you are bearish on the underlying stock.

12. *If a put is written out-of-the-money, the writer is assured a profit because the option will not be exercised.*

Untrue. A put can easily move into-the-money within the expiration date, no matter how low it is in price, as Example #81 indicates.

EXAMPLE #81. Losing by Writing an Out-of-the-Money Put

Striking Price: $20   Expiration Date: August 22

Date	Stock Price	Put Price
June 18	$24	$1
June 20	23.50	1
June 25	23	1¼
July 2	22	1½
July 9	21.50	1⅝
July 16	20	2⅛
July 23	19	2⅛
August 6	18	2⅜
August 13	17	3⅛
August 22	16	3¾

The writer of this put will find himself having to cover his position by buying the stock at $20 and selling in at $16—a loss of $4 per share.

13. *Everything you need to know to buy a put is included in the options tables found in the financial news.*

Untrue. Like any stock, commodity, or option listing, put listings only give the previous or current day's trading activities. The information contained in these fact sheets is certainly beneficial in helping you find options that might be worth writing or selling because of their last recorded trades, but there is certainly not enough data to allow a trader to make a decision.

First of all, the information is history, even if it is very recent history. Second, there is usually a bid and ask price for premiums and the premiums listed in options represent only the price of the last trade. Third, before deciding on any option, you have to research the underlying stock. Successful option trading requires not only the ability to locate premiums, strike prices, and expiration dates that are advantageous, but also the ability to find the underlying stock that can provide the near-term price movement you need to benefit from writing your puts.

14. *The best approach for put writing is to find a stock that has just reached new lows; it is sure to go up in price.*

Untrue. Stocks can always go lower. Many stocks repeatedly make the new lows list on their way to bottoming out. Actually, the only thing you can be sure of about stocks making the new low list is that:

- A lot of people have lost a great deal of the capital by holding the stock.

- A lot of short-sellers have made a great deal of money.

- Put buyers, naked call writers, and short sellers have been making money, while put writers have been losing money.

When stocks go into a bear spin, they tend to drop in price very quickly and very deeply. As a put writer, you just cannot take a chance on stocks showing weakness.

15. *Over-the-counter options are handled in the same way that major exchange options are handled.*

Untrue. Over-the-counter (OTC) options, which are generally referred to as "conventional options," are handled very differently from exchange options. The OTC options market is extremely informal, and trades are not guaranteed by the Options Clearing Corporation. Thus, before trading here, you will want to make certain that some third party is guaranteeing the options and that this third party is financially secure enough to meet its commitments. In many instances, you will be pleased to learn that the third-party guarantee is from a major brokerage house listed on any of the exchanges. Just make sure, for you will want to be sure that the third party is still in business when you try to exercise your option.

16. *Your broker will call you to remind you that your option is soon to expire.*

Untrue. Keeping track of expiration dates is your responsibility. As options expire on the Saturday after the third Friday of the month, be sure that you have marked your calendar appropriately. In the case where the first day of the month is a Saturday, the expiration date is the fourth Saturday of the month.

23

GUIDELINES FOR LIMITING RISK AND INCREASING PROFIT

There are basic rules for put writers to follow to minimize risk and increase rewards. Making money with put options is hard enough without taking the position of the short seller, who always stands to lose much more than he or she can gain. This is because profits are limited to the size of the premium, but losses are not. Thus, as in selling short stock or buying long calls, the put writer must tread very carefully.

1. *Be sure you understand how the stock options game is played.*
   This requires understanding:

   - Contract terminology.

   - Types of orders.

   - Differences between puts and calls.

   - Intrinsic value.

   - Time value.

   - Bear and bull positions.

   - Expiration dates.

2. *Be sure you have a good understanding of options arithmetic.*
   Also includes the following: how income is figured, how brokerage commissions affect your break-even point, the effects of stock splits and dividends on underlying options, and the cost of hedging. Knowing this basic arithmetic will not only allow you to keep score of your profits and losses, but it will help you understand risks and rewards for each position you take.

3. *Do not believe that options listings present all the data you will need to make a trade.*
   Options listings, like stock listings, are no more than a scoreboard showing past trading results. The listings will help you spot options with attractive premiums, but you will also need to learn as much as you can about the underlying stock. The options trader must also be a good stock picker, whether she is writing or buying long. Selecting that underlying stock necessitates researching its fundamentals and

technical performance, then eagerly getting some professional opinions. When the professionals match your enthusiasm, it might be time to take a position.

4. Understand the goals of put buyers as well as put writers.

Knowing what the other side is after will help you further understand the risk at hand. The goal of the writer, you well understand by now, is the premiums that puts command. However, the long buyer of puts wants to benefit from declining prices for the underlying stock. He would like nothing better than to find an out-of-the-money put that he can buy for ⅛ of a point and then watch it climb to $3 or $4 as the underlying stock falls into-the-money. Writers of such a put would realize extreme losses.

5. Be sure the anticipated return on your investment is worth the risk.

Don't play options or stock for returns that are not much better than you can get from a bank or other fixed-income opportunities. Investing necessitates risk. Do not chance risk for returns that you can get elsewhere without taking risk. (See Table 23–1.)

6. Be willing to pay the extra money to hedge your positions when possible.

Puts can be covered, as you have learned, in a couple of ways, although the only way to totally cover a short position in a put is to buy long another put on the same underlying stock. But the long put cannot expire earlier or have a lower striking price. Granted, this is a more costly position, but hedging in this way can mean the difference between profit and loss.

7. Spread your risk.

Do not write puts in any great quantity, no matter how certain you may feel about the underlying stock. It is easy to let greed guide you into collecting as many premiums as you can with one short sale. Remember that the greater the possible income, the greater the possible risk. Pepper your portfolio with shorted puts; do not smother it with shorted puts.

8. Understand the difference between stock quotes and option quotes.

If a stock is quoted at $2½, this means the stock can be sold short for $2.50 per share. If an option is quoted at $2½, this means the option can be written for $250.

Table 23–1
Risks/Rewards for Options Traders

Position	Maximum Gain	Maximum Loss
Long Put	Can be in the thousands of percent.	Premium paid.
Short Put	Premium received.	Can be in the thousands of percent.
Long Call	Can be in the thousands of percent.	Premium paid.
Short Call	Premium received.	Can be in the thousands of percent.

This is because each put represents 100 shares of stock. Example #82 illustrates this point.

EXAMPLE #82. Income from One Put

Premium Listing	Income Before Commissions
1/8	$ 12.50
1/4	25.00
3/8	37.50
1/2	50.00
5/8	62.50
3/4	75.00
7/8	87.50
1	100.00
1 1/4	125.00
1 1/2	150.00
2	200.00
2 3/8	237.50
2 5/8	262.50
3 3/4	375.00
3 7/8	387.50

---

9. *Understand that it is the premium that really drives the market for a particular put.*

When the premiums are too low for a specific striking price and expiration date, no one is going to be interested in gambling on writing puts. However, if the premiums are high and there is money to be made, then writers will be willing to take the gamble associated with shorting puts.

10. *Be sure your goals are practical.*

There are often a large number of options available on a particular stock, and that means you have a lot of choices, a lot of games to play. And you can sell short or buy long. Be sure to study striking prices and expiration dates as well as the size of the premiums to make sure the option is worth further research. Further research will entail learning as much as you can about the potential of the underlying stock during the term of the contract.

11. *Keep abreast of options recommendations.*

Some of the financial papers have columns dedicated to option writing and buying. There are also newsletters and services that specialize in puts and calls or that at least include options recommendations along with stock recommendations. Read and study as much as you can.

24

SPECIAL RISKS

There are additional risks associated with trading stock options that are above and beyond the selection of appropriate underlying stocks and puts or calls. These have to do with the special characteristics of options markets, which function very differently from the stock markets with which you may be familiar, yet at the same time are highly dependent upon the performance or situations of the underlying stocks on which options are traded.

These risks are as follows:

- Market disruptions.

- Secondary market cancellations.

- Exercise restrictions.

- Broker insolvency.

Market Disruptions

Premiums for puts and calls are affected by a number of market and trading considerations, and especially by whether the options are in-the-money or out-of-the-money. If you were to check options listings, you would find that options, whether they are puts or calls, will be higher for the in-the-money positions, and so it is possible for someone to be short tens of thousands of dollars worth of puts or long the same amount in calls. Look at Table 24–1 and you will see, by checking the volume column, just how many puts or calls at each striking price have been written.

Bearing this in mind, it is easy to realize the amount of money or risk that some investors may possibly have tied up in their short or long positions, particularly if they are dealing in multiple puts or calls, or both. Now, if anything were to halt the trading in the underlying stock, there would be no basis for trading in related options, and a lot of investors would literally have their money robbed.

Trading in optionable stocks may be halted for a number of reasons, including the following:

- Order processing, in which unusually heavy short or long interest in the underlying stock causes excessive backlog.

Table 24–1
Daily Volume and Performance of Puts and Calls

			Call		Put	
Option/Strike		Exp.	Vol.	Last	Vol.	Last
IBM	45	Jul	60	12¾	. . .	. . .
57¼	50	Jul	55	7¾	109	⅜
57¼	50	Oct	—	—	303	1⅛
57¼	55	May	386	2½	458	3/16
57¼	55	Jun	102	3⅜	296	⅞
57¼	55	Jul	372	4⅛	625	1⅜
57¼	55	Oct	43	5⅝	393	2¹¹/16
57¼	60	May	689	3/16	213	2⅞
57¼	60	Jun	1,048	13/16	266	3⅜
57¼	60	Jul	531	1½	47	3⅞
57¼	60	Oct	414	3¼	382	5⅛
57¼	65	Jun	23	⅛	. . .	. . .
57¼	65	Jul	52	7/16	. . .	. . .
57¼	65	Oct	81	7/16	. . .	. . .

Checking the volume columns in this listing (from *The Wall Street Journal*) will give you some idea of the amount of damage that would be done if IBM puts and calls were ever to be prohibited from being exercised. Fortunately, while it is within the realm of possibility that the OCC might intervene with normal clearing house operations to prohibit the exercise of certain options on any underlying security, such action is highly unlikely.

Source: *The Wall Street Journal,*

- Bankruptcy filings, in which a stock goes into Chapter 11 and trading is temporarily halted or moved to another exchange; or goes into Chapter 13, in which trading is discontinued.

- Major market upheavals, such as the occasional extraordinary retreats in prices that occur sporadically, or occur as the result of crashes, such as that which occurred in October 1987.

When market activity for a stock is suddenly halted, anything can happen. The stock may open at any later time at a price far above or below what its last trade was. If the price is far above the last trade because of, perhaps, something like a takeover or merger, then those shorting stock, shorting calls, or buying long puts will come out heavy losers. If the price is far below the last trade because of, perhaps, news of a Chapter 11 filing, then those shorting puts or buying long calls or stock will be heavy losers.

Secondary Market Cancellation

Integrity is an important quality for any trading market, whether it be in equities or stock options. Without the ability to secure investor confidence, markets will decay. Thus, like any marketplace, the options markets (meaning the various exchanges and the way they respond to and relate with the Options Clearing Corporation and adhere to S.E.C. regulations) do everything in their power to assure investor confidence.

One example of this is the order limitations that are placed on contracts. This limitation applies to individual as well as investment group orders and is based on the trading volume for an underlying stock over a six-month period. A heavily traded stock like IBM would have the maximum position limit of 8,000 contracts, but a less heavily traded stock might have a position limit as low as 1,000.

Another example of protecting market integrity is the way the Options Clearing Corporation (OCC) assures that writers and buyers of options can be brought together. And a third example is the way in which the OCC assures the efficient management of money and information. Flow of funds is assured through an extensive network of over 200 clearing banks in the United States and foreign markets. Through this financial network, the OCC assures that foreign funds can be transferred quickly and efficiently. The options markets are cash markets, and this gives further impetus for a sophisticated network to facilitate cash flow.

Nevertheless, as important as liquidity and speed are to the integrity of any securities market, they cannot be absolutely guaranteed. As a result, under very special situations, options may have to be canceled, either because they are too volatile in price or volume, or because the market for them has dried up. However, when cancellation is to occur, the options markets do their very best to delay the event until the selected series expires. Still, cancellation of a series of options presents a particularly negative situation for a trader currently in the red, for he cannot continually reposition himself until he is finally in the black or has resolved that he is stalking the wrong class or series of options.

Exercise Restrictions

As you have learned, there are basically two styles of options: American-style and European-style. The names have nothing to do with the geographical location where the options are listed and traded. You will find that both European- and American-style options are traded on the U.S. stock exchanges dealing in options. What distinguishes the styles is when the options are exercisable. The American-style may be exercised any time after it is purchased until it expires. The European-style may be exercised only during a specified period prior to expiration; this period is not the same for all European-style options.

Nonetheless, both the OCC and the options markets can intervene to prevent put and call traders from exercising their rights. When this happens, both the short sellers and long buyers of options are caught with unmarketable positions until the restriction has been lifted. You are advised to consult your broker for current details of the impact of exercise restrictions on options traders. Information is also available from the Options Clearing Corporation.

Broker Insolvency

Brokerage accounts are protected by the SIPC and also by additional insurance taken out by the brokerage. The SIPC (Securities Investor Protection Corporation) is federally chartered and modeled after the Federal Deposit Insurance Corporation. All registered broker-dealers and members of national securities exchanges are required to be members unless they qualify for exemption. The SIPC is specifically designed to protect investors against losses in case the brokerage they have been dealing with becomes insolvent.

Generally, then, stock investors have very little to worry about. Not only is it relatively rare for brokerages to go out of business, but if they do, their accounts are afforded some protection by the SIPC. Options traders, however, are not in as safe a position as stock traders. If a brokerage goes under, options traders may find that each and every one of their positions has been closed out without their knowledge. This could mean very serious losses for them.

To prevent such a catastrophe, the OCC has put into place certain safeguards. These include financial requirements that specify minimum net capital standards, minimum margin requirements, and minimum collateral. The OCC also requires members to make periodic contributions to its clearing fund. Contributions to the clearing fund must be either in cash or in U.S.-backed securities that meet the OCC maturity requirements.

PART FIVE

WARRANTS AND RIGHTS

CONTENTS

25

WARRANTS

Warrants are also a type of option. More specifically, they are instruments that give the owner the right to buy or sell fixed-income securities or equity stock to the issuer of the warrant. There are time limitations to which the owner must respond as well other contractual obligations, just as there are for the calls and puts discussed in previous chapters. There are some basic differences, however, between warrants and puts and calls. Puts and calls are basically stock derivatives and have short-term expiration dates; a warrant, however, is a stock derivative that may not expire for 10 years or more and may also be perpetual.

A second very important difference is that equity options can be exercised immediately if they are American-style or during a relatively short-term time frame if they are European-style, but with warrants, the owner usually has to wait a year before even considering exercise.

Holders of warrants do not have any position in the underlying stock. All they have is a legal right to purchase that stock under certain conditions. If dividends are declared on the stock, warrant holders are not entitled to any distributions. Nor do they have any voting privileges because they own the warrants.

Types of Warrants

Warrants are worth consideration for any investor who is neither interested in tying up a lot of cash in his investment program, nor concerned with income from dividends or covered options. This is because warrants offer substantial rates of return; they are low-priced yet tend to move in coincidence with the underlying stock.

There are two types of warrants available to equity stockholders:

- Subscription warrants.

- Stock purchase warrants.

Subscription warrants are instruments that give stockholders of record special "rights." These special rights are also known as subscription privileges. The subscription warrant comes in the form of a certificate that is issued by whatever corporation is offering the rights. The certificate will specify the amount of stock that may be purchased and the conditions under which the purchase may take place. These warrants, which represent the "legal right" of their owners to participate in stock subscription programs, are assignable. (See Chapter 26 for a discussion of "rights.")

Stock-purchase warrants, on the other hand, are often made available only to holders of specific corporate securities, such as bonds or preferred stock. They are, therefore, often referred to as equity privileges. However, they may also be issued as stand-alone securities. Each stock-purchase warrant entitles the owner to purchase a certain number of shares in the underlying stock for whatever period is specified. Some warrants, however, have no expiration date.

Listings and Terminology

Warrants are listed in the stock tables under the appropriate exchange. They do not have separate listings as do puts and calls. You can easily identify them by the initials "wt" under the "stock" column.

There are some terms associated with warrants with which every trader must be familiar. These are listed and defined below.

- Unit of trade. The fraction of a dollar at which warrants are usually traded. In most instances, warrants are listed in $\frac{1}{8}$ increments. Very low-priced warrants, however, may trade at $\frac{1}{16}$ or sometimes as low as $\frac{1}{64}$.

- Out-of-the-money. When the market price of the underlying stock is less than the purchase price specified by the warrant.

- In-the-money. When the market price of the underlying stock is higher than the purchase price specified by the warrant.

- Intrinsic value. A warrant that is in-the-money.

- Expiration date. The date at which a warrant expires, after which time its holder is left with a worthless certificate.

- Exercise. Using the legal right given you by the warrant or warrants you own, to take a position in the underlying stock at a price that is less than the current market price.

- Shares per warrant. The number of shares that each warrant entitles the holder to buy.

- Exercise price. This is the price that the owner of the warrant must pay in order to take a position in the underlying stock. In most circumstances, the exercise price of a newly issued warrant will be in excess of the current market price for the underlying security. (See Example #83.)

Role of Warrants

From a financial standpoint, warrants offer an economical alternative to other means of more costly credit. To stockholders, they mean a chance for greater participation in the success of the issuing corporation, with little investment. This is further illustrated in the following example.

EXAMPLE #83. Use of Warrants

Pipton Publishing is selling at $25 per share. The corporation would like to raise money but feels that if it issued bonds or preferred stock, it might not be able to pay its obligations if for any reason new business plans did not pay off.

To solve the problem, Pipton decides to issue warrants to purchase the shares of stock at $25. You, as one of the stockholders who feel the corporation has strong profit potential and want to be in a position to benefit, purchase the warrants. The issuing corporation benefits from the increased income, and you benefit from the chance to eventually sell the warrants at a higher price or to eventually exercise your legal right to buy the underlying stock if and when it is advantageous to do so.

If, in two years, the stock is at $30, you can exercise your rights to purchase the underlying stock at $25, then sell it immediately at the current market price for a gain of $5 per share. Or you can just sell your warrants as you would stock, for they would be worth much more than you paid for them when they were out-of-the-money.

While corporations will usually issue warrants as a separate means of financing, they are usually tied to bonds, preferred stock, or debentures.

Determining Value

When a warrant is first issued, it generally has no intrinsic value, for it is out of the money. But this does not mean it is worthless. Remember that in the investment arena, people will pay for a security or an option whatever they believe it will be worth in the future.

In terms of determining the intrinsic value of an option, we may use the following formula:

Value of Warrant = Stock Price − Exercise Price × Shares per Warrant

We may apply the formula under two different circumstances to show how intrinsic value is determined and can be changed, the first being when a warrant is first issued and the second after the stock has decreased in value.

EXAMPLE # 84. Determining Intrinsic Value

Pipton Publishing issues warrants that entitle holders to purchase two shares of common stock for each warrant at $15 (the exercise price) per share. The common stock is selling for $10 per share. The intrinsic value of each warrant would be:

Stock Price – Exercise Price × Shares per Warrant = Warrant Value

   $10   – $15   ×   2   =   0

Now, let's suppose that the underlying stock increases over the next two years to $18. The intrinsic value of each warrant would be:

Stock Price – Exercise Price × Shares per Warrant = Warrant Value

   $18   – $15   ×   2   =   6

The market value for the warrant, however, might be much more than $6. A great deal depends upon how much time remains before the warrant expires and what the market anticipates the underlying stock will do until that expiration date.

If we are to assume that you paid $1 for the warrants when they were out-of-the-money, and that you purchased 200 of them, then after two years you will have seen your original $200 investment increase to $1,200. That is a rather fantastic return under any circumstances, let alone in just two years.

Table 25–1 further illustrates the remarkable rate of return available from stock-purchase warrants provided the underlying stock brings the warrant into-the-money.

Table 25–1
Determining the Intrinsic Value of a Warrant

A. 1 Share per Warrant

Stock Price	–	Exercise Price	×	Shares per Warrant	=	Intrinsic Value
$20	–	$25	×	1	=	$0
22	–	25	×	1	=	0
24	–	25	×	1	=	0
26	–	25	×	1	=	1
28	–	25	×	1	=	3
30	–	25	×	1	=	5

B. 2 Shares per Warrant

Stock Price	–	Exercise Price	×	Shares per Warrant	=	Intrinsic Value
$20	–	$25	×	2	=	$0
22	–	25	×	2	=	0
24	–	25	×	2	=	0
26	–	25	×	2	=	2
28	–	25	×	2	=	6
30	–	25	×	2	=	10

26

STOCK RIGHTS

Like warrants, stock rights are privileges to purchase additional shares of stock. They are called "preemptive rights" because owners are given the opportunity to purchase additional common shares before any other individual or group may do so.

There are other differences between rights and warrants:

- Rights are never perpetual and usually expire in 30 to 60 days.

- Rights usually carry an exercise price that is below the current market value of the related stock.

The main purpose of these rights is to give current stockholders the ability to subscribe to additional stock and thereby maintain their proportionate ownership in their corporation. If they do not take advantage of these preemptive rights, then stockholders chance losing voting stock to investors who may have an agenda that competes against their own interests.

The issuance of rights requires special action by the board of directors of a corporation. Sometimes such issuance can only be effected by an amendment of the certificate of incorporation. Because the stock to which the rights will entitle holders represents a public offering, the issuing corporation must file for permission from the Securities and Exchange Commission.

Advantages to Stockholders

A corporation may decide to raise additional money by issuing an additional one million shares of stock. Like any corporation, it has a number of ways in which it can market this new stock. It has the option of selling the shares on the open market as well as the option of negotiating with investment banking concerns to buy the shares at some discount to the market value. But it can also raise whatever money it needs by offering special rights to current stockholders, allowing a discount to shareholders as an incentive to get them to participate. If the stock is selling at $100 per share, the rights may give the shareholder the opportunity to buy at $90 per share.

An eligibility requirement is imposed on shareholders, however. They must own the underlying stock as of a specified date, which is technically known as the "record date." After that record date, any stock purchased is "ex-rights," or without rights. Stock traded before the record date is "cum rights." *Cum* is Latin for *with*.

On the face of it, it appears that this is an offer too good to be true. But whether or not stockholders will be able to profit from the rights depends upon what happens to the market price of the stock during the subscription offer. It can very well happen that the price of the shares falls below $90 and just remains there; the stockholders, if they want to buy additional shares, may be wiser to bid for them on the open market.

Theoretical Value

There are formulas for determining the cum-rights (Table 26–1) and ex-rights (Table 26–2) value of preemptive rights, but it is important to realize that these establish a theoretical rather than a market value.

The cum-rights value is determined by subtracting the subscription price of the new stock from the market price of the old stock and dividing this by one plus rights required for one share.

EXAMPLE #85. Formula for Cum-Rights Value

Old market value – New stock subscription price
──
    1 + Rights required for 1 new share

Using the above formula, we may determine the value of the rights in the following case. Assume that British Telecom has announced it will issue 10 million new shares of stock. The old stock market price is $50, and the new stock subscription price is $40. The number of rights needed to buy one new share is two.

EXAMPLE #86. Applying the Formula for Cum-Rights Value

$$\frac{\text{Old stock market value } (\$50) - \text{New stock subscription price } (\$41)}{1 + \text{Rights required for 1 new share (2)}} = \$3$$

Once the expiration date has occurred, the stock goes ex-rights and its price must be adjusted to compensate for the fact that new owners will not be able to benefit by the rights offering. This means that British Telecom stock must now have a depreciated market value $47 per share, which is derived by taking the original value ($50) and subtracting the $3 that we have determined the rights to have been worth.

Once a stock is ex-rights, the rights themselves are traded on the open market just as the stock is traded. The rights can be bought and sold just like stock. But what are the rights, trading independently of the stock, actually worth? This may be determined by the following formula.

Table 26–1
Determining the Cum-Rights Value

Old Stock Market Value	–	New Stock Subscription	+	(Rights Required for 1 New Share	+ 1)	=	Cum-Rights Value
$50	–	$41	+	(2	+ 1)	=	$3
50	–	40	+	(2	+ 1)	=	2
40	–	35	+	(4	+ 1)	=	1
40	–	34	+	(2	+ 1)	=	3
30	–	24	+	(5	+ 1)	=	1

Table 26–2
Determining the Ex-Rights Value

Ex-Rights Strike Value	–	New Stock Subscription	+	Rights Required for 1 New Share	=	Cum-Rights Value
$50	–	$41	+	2	=	$4.50
50	–	40	+	2	=	5
40	–	35	+	4	=	1.25
40	–	34	+	2	=	3
30	–	24	+	5	=	1.2

EXAMPLE #87. Formula for Ex-Rights Value

$$\frac{\text{Ex–rights value of stock} - \text{New stocks subscription price}}{\text{Rights required for one new share}}$$

We know what the ex-rights value of the stock is. We arrived at the number ($47) by subtracting $3 from the original market price. We also know what the new stock subscription price is because this has been defined ($40). The rights required for one new share is also known ($3). We need only plug these numbers into the above formula to determine the ex-rights value.

EXAMPLE #88. Applying the Formula for Ex-Rights Value

$$\frac{\underset{(\$47)}{\text{Ex–right value of stock}} - \underset{(\$40)}{\text{New stocks subscription price}}}{\text{Rights required for one new share (2)}} = \$3.50$$

We see the value of the rights change in this instance, but it does not necessarily have to. Nevertheless, the theoretical ex-rights value is important to traders trying to determine what they are really getting for their money. But notice the word theoretical. The market value of the rights will always be determined on the basis of supply and demand, these seats on the economic seesaw being influenced by the changing market value of the underlying stock and investor expectations for the rights. On top of these influencing factors is the decay factor. Like puts and calls and most warrants, rights decay with time. In the early part of the subscription period, they usually have a higher market value, given an unchanging price for the underlying stock. However, as the subscription period comes closer to expiration, the rights will have downward sloping demand.

The offering of preemptive rights to raise money was once highly popular with a few select U.S. corporations, AT&T among them. However, they are a rarely used financial instrument today, except, perhaps, in some foreign markets.

27

CORRECTING COMMON
MISCONCEPTIONS ABOUT WARRANTS
AND PREEMPTIVE RIGHTS

Some common misconceptions related to warrants and rights are listed below.

Warrants

1. *Warrants always expire within 10 years.*

Untrue. Typically, warrants will expire around 10 years from issue date; however, some have expiration dates as long as 20 years or may be perpetual.

2. *Warrants are publicly issued stand-alone securities.*

Untrue. It is rare for a warrant to be issued as a stand-alone security to the public. The majority of the time, they are part of a package that includes a new bond or preferred stock.

3. *Warrants usually have intrinsic value when issued.*

Untrue. Warrants usually have no intrinsic value when they are first issued. They attain intrinsic value only when the market price for the underlying stock is higher than the striking price for the warrant. But this does not mean that at issue a warrant is worthless. They usually have a market value that reflects investor expectations for the underlying stock.

4. *There is no waiting period to exercise warrants.*

Untrue. Generally, there is a waiting period of one year before a warrant can be exercised.

Rights

1. *Rights are long-term securities, usually expiring after 10 or 20 years.*

Untrue. Rights are short-term privileges that usually expire in one to two months. These privileges are granted by corporate charter and allow stockholders to maintain their proportionate amount of ownership in the issuing corporation.

2. *One right is the equivalent of 100 shares of stock.*

Untrue. In the case of preemptive rights, it is generally traditional to issue one new right for each share of corporate. There is, however, no reason why the ratio cannot be changed.

3. *When preemptive rights are issued, all stockholders are entitled to participate.*

Untrue. Stockholders must have ownership of the stock on a record date set by the board of directors of the issuing corporation. After the record date is set, another date is set by NASD (National Association of Securities Dealers); this is the ex-rights date. This ex-rights date is the dividing line for those shareholders who may and may not participate in the offering. Those who buy the stock prior to the ex-rights date are entitled to the rights; those who purchase it after the ex-rights date are not.

4. *The ex-rights date has no effect on the stock of the issuing corporation.*

Untrue. Once a stock goes ex-rights, its market price is adjusted downward by the value of each right. This adjustment is necessary because someone buying the stock after the ex-rights date is acquiring less, that is, just the stock instead of the stock plus one preemptive right.

28

GUIDELINES FOR LIMITING RISKS AND INCREASING PROFITS

Warrants

In the case of warrants, it is important to realize that at issue they have no intrinsic value. Intrinsic value occurs when the market price of the attached stock climbs above the fixed price at which the investor can exercise his or her right to buy shares. But like any option, warrants are faced with time decay and will depreciate as they age. Though this is of no particular concern during the early years after issue, every investor has to be aware of expiration dates before buying them on the open market.

You have two ways to utilize a warrant:

- Exercise the warrant at a profit, which means buying the attached shares at the allowable price and selling it at a higher price.

- Trade the warrant as you would stock, selling the warrant at a higher price than you paid for it.

Rights

In the case of rights, expect that they will be a rarity among companies incorporated in the United States. If and when they are issued, it is generally as part of a recapitalization plan. (Not to be confused with reorganization under court jurisdiction, "recapitalization" is a voluntary change in capital structure with the consent of holders of the types of securities to be affected.)

Just as with warrants, there are two ways to profit with preemptive rights: through exercise or trading them on the exchanges. The big drawback with trading rights, however, is that commissions can be highly prohibitive, and for this reason break-even points are higher than they are for other types of investments. Most advisors recommend that, unless an investor is highly knowledgeable and skilled, he should stick with using rights to acquire new shares rather than trying to trade them as he would other options.

GLOSSARY

Advance-decline indicator. Technical indicator usually used in conjunction with the Dow Jones Industrial Average (DJIA) to predict market direction. The guiding philosophy is that when the indicator and the DJIA move in the same direction, the trend will continue. If the indicator peaks but the DJIA does not, the market is approaching its high. If the indicator bottoms but the averages continue to fall, the market is approaching its low.

All or none. Order to a broker specifying that the entire order must be filled or not executed. Order helps the trader take advantage of economies of scale and keep his break-even point low.

At-the-money. Option with a striking price equal to the price at which the underlying stock is selling. See also in-the-money and out-of-the-money.

Authorized shares. Amount of common and preferred shares a corporation is authorized by its charter to issue.

Bear. Term referring to an investor who expects a declining general market or a declining market for a specific stock. Someone may be bullish on the market but bearish on certain common and vice versa.

Bear market. A market in which prices are declining. This is a market in which short sellers, call writers, and put buyers make their money.

Beta. Measure of the relative volatility of a stock relative to the performance of the Standard & Poor's 500 Index. A beta of more than "1" indicates more volatility than the index; of less than "1," less volatility than the index; of "1," the same volatility.

Bull. Term referring to an investor who expects the general market or a given stock to advance. Someone may be bearish on the market but bullish on certain common and vice versa.

Buying long. The usual way of trading stocks or options, in which a position is taken with the hope of later unloading it at a higher price.

Call money rate. The special interest rates given to brokers.

Capital gains. Profit made from trading stocks, options, bonds, or other financial instruments. Should not be confused with dividends or total return.

9/26 - Sold 100 shares, Dover:	$6,200
2/12 - Bought 100 shares, Dover:	5,900
Capital gain:	$ 300
Dividends:	36
Total return:	$ 336

Class. Puts and calls covering the same underlying security.

Closing purchase. Transaction that covers a short position.

Combination. Option strategy in which positions are taken in both puts and calls having a different striking price and/or expiration date.

Commercial paper rate. Interest rate available on dealer placed high-grade corporate promissory discount notes.

Constant dollar plan. Method of investing in which the total value of a portfolio remains as close to being fixed as possible. Investors generally use this approach when they are interested in squeezing as much income from their portfolio as possible.

Covered writer. Most frequently, the short seller of a call who also owns the underlying stock, enabling him to meet his contract obligations if the contract is exercised. The definition also applies to covered put writers or anyone who has an offsetting position providing the equity needed to cover contract obligations when called on to do so.

Current ratio. Ratio revealing the liquidity of a corporation and determined by dividing current assets by current liabilities.

Contingency order. Conditional order specifying prerequisites before it can be executed. An example would be an order to sell 10 calls on Medical Care of America but only after 1,000 shares are purchased.

Current ratio. The ratio of a corporation's assets to its liabilities.

Day orders. Order that must be executed on the same day or canceled. All orders are considered day orders unless otherwise specified.

Decaying asset. Any asset, such as an option, with a time value that diminishes as its expiration date approaches.

Delta. Option derivative measuring changes in premiums and comparing them to changes in the underlying security.

Discount rate. The interest rate charged to depository institutions by the Federal Reserve.

Dollar cost averaging. Investment technique that requires investing the same amount of money at specific intervals over extended periods of time.

Exercise price. Also known as the strike price. This is the dollar price at which options holders may put or call the underlying stock.

Ex-dividend date. Date that determines which stockholders are entitled to forthcoming dividends.

Ex-rights. Term describing a situation in which common stock is no longer available with preemptive rights.

Expiration date. Date on which puts, calls, or other options or privileges expire.

Fill-or-kill. Order that must be executed as soon as the floor broker receives it, or else must be canceled. "All or none" instructions are inherent in fill-or-kill orders.

Fundamental analysis. Analyzing a stock in terms of its current and future financial, managerial, and marketing strength.

Immediate-or-cancel. Similar to a fill-or-kill order but without the "all-or-none" contingency.

Inflation. Continuous advances in the general price level, which eventually result in reducing the purchasing power of money.

In-the-money. A term specifying the money position of an option. A call is in-the-money when the price of the underlying stock is above the strike price; a put is in-the-money when the price of the underlying stock is below the strike price. Examples are given in the explanation of "Out-of-the-money."

Leverage. A strategy for making a little money do the work of a lot of money. Puts, calls, warrants, and trading on margin are some ways of achieving leverage in the financial markets.

Limit orders. Orders establishing a specific price at which they can be placed.

Market orders. Orders that are to be executed as soon as they reach the trading floor. Strategy is not recommended for put and call buyers except under some very special conditions, mainly those relating to hedging strategies.

Margin account. Account that allows a trader to borrow money from her broker to complete trades.

Margin call. Notice from a broker requiring an investor to deposit cash or securities to meet his debt obligations to the broker.

Out-of-the-money. Term specifying the relationship of an option's striking price to the market price of the underlying stock. If the stock price is higher than the strike price, then a put is in-the-money but a call is out-of-the-money. If the stock price is lower than the strike price, then the put is out-of-the-money and the call is in-the-money. If the stock price and the strike price are the same, then both the put and the call are at-the-money.

Stock Price	Strike Price	Put	Call
$20	$30	In-the-Money	Out-of-the-Money
35	30	Out-of-the-Money	In-the-Money
30	30	At-the-Money	At-the-Money

Over-the-Counter (OTC) market. Market for stocks that lack the financial and marketing muscle to qualify for listing on the major exchanges.

P/E Ratio. The price-to-earnings ratio of a stock, determined by dividing the price of one share of the stock by the earnings per share.

Share Price	Earnings Per Share	P/E Ratio
$60	$10	6
45	10	4.5
40	10	4
32	10	3.2

Premium. The price of an option.

Prime rate. Rate banks charge customers with excellent credit ratings.

Put. Option that gives the owner the right to sell an underlying security at a fixed price during a specific time period. The put buyer is bearish on the underlying stock, and the put writer is bullish on the underlying stock.

Random walk theory. Theory holding that stock prices are unpredictable and an investor selecting stocks at random is likely to do just as well as those depending upon fundamental and/or technical analysis.

Regulation T. The Federal Reserve regulation setting initial margin requirements for those who want to trade on credit.

Selling short. Method of investing designed to profit when stock or option prices fall. The stock or option is sold first then purchased at a later date, hopefully at a lower price.

Series. Options of the same class (all on the same underlying stock) that have the same strike price and same expiration date.

Short interest. Total number of shares sold short for given stocks. This listing can be found in the financial sections of major daily newspapers or in the daily and weekly financial papers.

Shorting against the box. Selling short the same security in which one already has a long position. Most often, this is done for tax purposes.

Spread. Options strategy that requires being long in one series and short in a different series in the same class of options.

Stock rights. Privileges to buy additional shares of stock. They usually carry an exercise price below the current market price of the stock, thus giving them immediate value.

Straddle. Options strategy that includes one or more positions in both puts and calls with the same striking price and expiration date.

Street name. Stocks held on account with your broker.

Strap. Options strategy that includes positions in one put and two calls on the same underlying security having the same strike price and same expiration month.

Strike price. Price at which the buyer of an option has the legal right to buy or sell the underlying stock serving as the basis for the option contract.

Strip. Options strategy that includes two puts and one call on the same underlying security; puts and calls have the same strike price and same expiration month.

Theta. Options derivative measuring time erosion of an option premium.

Tick. The minimum price movement of a stock. This can be as low a $1/32$ of a point but more often is $1/8$ of a point.

Ticker symbol. Abbreviation by which a stock or option is defined for trading purposes. Some examples:

Stock	Ticker Symbol	Exchange
Advest	ADV	New York
Barclays	BCL	New York
Cohu	CH	American
Echo Bay	ECO	American
Lojack	LOJN	NASDAQ
MCI Comm	MCIC	NASDAQ

Treasury bill rate. Interest rate available to holders of discounted short-term government securities.

Uncovered writer. Option short sellers who are not hedging with offsetting positions, thereby not covering themselves in case contracts are exercised.

Warrant. Certificate entitling owners to purchase securities at a discount. There are two types of warrants: subscription and stock purchase. Subscription warrants are tied to new stock issues and offer first subscription privileges; stock-purchase warrants are equity privileges and generally are only offered to holders of specific corporate securities. Shareholders' equity is reduced when warrants are exercised.

Yield. The rate of return from an investment.

INDEX